Gold Med...
Awaken the Olymp...

In *Awaken the Olympian Within*, John Naber has gathered an impressive array of Olympic athletes who share their moments of challenge, perseverance and achievement. All of the individuals in this collection have found a way to harness their winning spirit and tenacity and carry it beyond the world of sport.

Digby Diehl
Literary Correspondent, "Good Morning America"

The stories of these U.S. Olympians of the modern era are truly inspiring. The ability of these men and women to triumph over adversity is a testament to the strength of the human spirit, and something from which athletes and nonathletes alike can learn.

Steven M. Bornstein
President and Chief Executive Officer, ESPN
President, ABC Sports

The reflections recorded by the great Olympic heroes in this book can be applied to the everyday lives of all. Their stories of focus, confidence, persistence and, ultimately, success, serve as a great inspiration to anyone striving to be their best.

Harvey W. Schiller
President, Turner Sports

Winning in life, as in sports is not luck but preparing every day to be the best you can be. *Awaken the Olympian Within* reinforces this thought process. A 'gold medal' read.

Peter Ueberroth

Today, more than two decades later, John Naber is still winning gold medals. For years John has thrilled audiences with his inspirational insights on not only winning in the arena, but winning in the game of life. His brilliant collection of first person accounts in *Awaken the Olympian Within* once again places John on the top step of the victory podium.

Bud Greenspan
Olympic Filmmaker

Reading the stories of these Olympians helps us understand the many and varied roads to excellence, and will challenge each reader to his or her best performance in life.

Anita L. DeFrantz
President, Amateur Athletic Foundation
Vice President, International Olympic Committee

There is a lesson on every page that makes us realize that life is more like an Olympic experience than we ever expected. You will laugh, cry, burst with pride, ache with pain and feel inspired—an emotional roller coaster awaits you.

Jim Easton
Member, International Olympic Committee
President, International Archery Federation

I am struck by the similarities in business and the trek of the Olympian. The passion of the Olympian to succeed is an inspiration to all of us. I want my grandchildren as well as my company managers to read this wonderful book.

David G. Elmore
Chairman, Elmore Sports Group, Ltd.

John Naber has done a masterful job in his compilation of the stories of some of our country's greatest athletes. Their messages of commitment and dedication are as challenging to the business community as they are inspiring to future Olympians.

James H. Blanchard
Chairman of the Board/CEO, Synovus Financial Corp.

Awaken the Olympian Within is a uniquely inspiring view of the athlete's mindset. Each story speaks to the reader in compelling terms about the enduring values of Olympic achievement.

Elizabeth Primrose-Smith
Vice President, Worldwide Olympic and Sports Sponsorships, IBM

This is a book to give to your friends, read to your kids and enjoy on your own—over and over. It is a gem! Just when we all so badly need heroes, this book gives us twenty-nine! Great stuff! Any organization, group, team or individual will find inspiration in these stories.

Michael L. Quinn
Vice Chairman, Merrill Lynch Mercury Asset Management

Take your marks, get set and launch yourself into the world of what can be described as a gold mine of highly inspirational stories. These chronicles transcend sport in a way that delivers impactful, motivational messages to virtually any audience.

Scot Smythe
Vice President, Event Marketing and Sponsorship, VISA International

I laughed and cried as I read the stories of these remarkable athletes and found myself motivated to work on fulfilling my dreams—personally and professionally. Anyone who reads this book will know that the Olympic dream is within their reach.

Sylvia A. Walker
Director, Advertising & Corporate Relations
Blue Cross & Blue Shield Association

Each Olympian's struggle and/or triumph goes far beyond the playing field and touches all manner of people, from leaders of countries to corporate audiences to children of all ages, in much the same way. It's not the boasting about the swifter and higher aspects, but the dedication to and the sharing of the inspirational side of those accomplishments that makes their stories not only appealing, but so identifiable for everyone.

Fred H. Arnold
Manager, Olympic Games Coordination, The Minute Maid Company

Awaken the Olympian Within transcends the traditional sports analogies that are typically used today in business. The 'trade secrets' revealed in these chapters provide managers with the tools necessary to achieve success. Applying the lessons in this book is like winning a gold medal of your very own.

Sara Delgado
National Sponsorship Director, AT&T

In *Awaken the Olympian Within*, John Naber has put together a fabulous collection of instructive, inspirational and entertaining stories that have relevance far beyond the athletic arena. It's also a fun read.

John C. Argue
President, Southern California Committee for the Olympic Games
Past President, Los Angeles Area Chamber of Commerce

An awesome book! It's about mental toughness, conquering the insurmountable, learning to change, making adjustments and loving the feeling of pressure. It's about awakening the Olympian, not only in yourself but in others, too.

Terry Dillman
Manager, Olympic Marketing, Xerox Corporation

These stories of personal and professional achievement will stir your heart and stimulate your mind. These stellar role models are positive, living proof that their motivational techniques have an impact. Choose one and apply it to your life at home, at work and at play.

Jackie Woodward
Director, Worldwide Sports Alliances, McDonald's Corp.

Everyone dreams about winning an Olympic gold medal, but few do. When an Olympian speaks, I listen. That's why *Awaken the Olympian Within* is such a special book. It's a 'must read' for anyone with aspirations.

Ken Blanchard
Co-author, *The One Minute Manager*

Full of gripping stories of courage and determination, *Awaken the Olympian Within* shows that achieving our dreams is very much a choice born of a disciplined and focused life, and well within the reach of each of us. Whatever your goal may be, you will put this book down with a renewed sense of optimism and confidence in your ability to succeed.

William E. Simon
former Secretary of the Treasury
former President of the United States Olympic Committee

These stories are golden. *Awaken the Olympian Within* has the power of purpose to shake awake the Olympian dreams hiding deep in the soul of each and every one of us. Compelling, intimate, thunderous. Enough exhilarating grit, grace and goosebumps for all!

Harvey Mackay
Author, *Swim With the Sharks* and *Pushing the Envelope*

A wonderful collection of the behind-the-scenes stories of some of the most electrifying moments in Olympic history and what inspired Olympic glory...This is about more than just sports, this is about how to be triumphant in life.

Tom Curley
President and Publisher, *USA Today*

Everyone is an Olympian in their own way and can achieve extraordinary heights by applying the universal principles common to Olympic champions. An inspiring read.

Dr. Stephen R. Covey
Author, *The Seven Habits of Highly Effective People*

AWAKEN THE
OLYMPIAN WITHIN

Stories from America's
Greatest Olympic Motivators

Compiled by
John Naber

The United States Olympic Committee

Griffin Publishing Group
Torrance, California

© 1999 by Naber & Associates, Inc. / Griffin Publishing Group

Second edition 2000

Published by Griffin Publishing Group under license from the United States Olympic Committee.

Use of Olympic marks and terminology is authorized by the United States Olympic Committee pursuant to 36 *U.S. Code*, Section 380.

Use of the thirty-leaf olive wreath commencing each section of the book is authorized by Naber & Associates, Inc., and is protected by copyright. © Photos on pages 12, 200, 203, 241 and 250 courtesy of ALLSPORT USA/All Rights Reserved.

This publication is a creative work fully protected by all applicable rights. All rights reserved. No portion of this book may be reproduced or transmitted in any form or by any means, electronic or mechanical, including fax, photocopy, recording or any information storage or retrieval system by anyone except the purchaser for his or her own personal use.

The material used in this publication is the sole responsibility of Naber & Associates, Inc. and Griffin Publishing Group.

10 9 8 7 6 5 4 3 2

ISBN 1-882180-98-4

PUBLISHER	Griffin Publishing Group
CHAIRMAN	Daniel R. Wilson
PRESIDENT	Robert Howland
DIR./OPERATIONS	Robin Howland
EDITOR	John Naber
MANAGING EDITOR	Marjorie L. Marks
BOOK DESIGN	Mark Dodge
COVER DESIGN	M^2 Graphics
PROJECT COORDINATOR	Bryan Howland

Griffin Publishing Group and Naber & Associates, Inc. wish to thank the many other talented and devoted supporters of the Olympic Games who made this publication possible.

The sale of this book helps support the United States Olympic Team and the U.S. Olympic Alumni Association.

Additional Olympic materials are available from Griffin Publishing.

Griffin Publishing Group	Naber & Associates, Inc.
2908 Oregon Court, #I-5	Post Office Box 50107
Torrance, CA 90503	Pasadena, CA 91115
Phone: (310) 381-0485	Phone: (626) 795-7675
Fax: (310) 381-0499	Fax: (626) 568-0446

Manufactured in the United States of America

Contents

Foreword

There is a fundamental difference between the affection America has for its professional sporting events and its deep-seated respect and love for the Olympic movement. When we watch the country's top sports performers, such as Joe Montana at the Super Bowl, Michael Jordan in the NBA finals or Tiger Woods at Augusta, we wish we were better ballplayers. But when we watch Dan Jansen get up off the ice or Kerri Strug attempt a vault with tape on her ankle, we all are moved to become better *people*.

Perhaps it's the holdover from the days of Avery Brundage, the former USOC and IOC president, who insisted that all Olympic athletes should love their sports enough to be willing to perform for free. In fact, the word *amateur* takes its root from the Latin "to love" (*amo, amas, amat*: I love, you love, he loves). The amateur athlete loves his or her sport as much as the amateur stamp collector loves his stamps.

While the word "amateur" no longer appears in the Olympic charter (and some athletes do receive substantial financial incentives to participate in their chosen fields), for many Olympic champions it is the title, not the "payday," that keeps them involved.

The motto of the Olympic movement doesn't idolize the excellent; it encourages the devoted. *Citius, altius, fortius* means *swifter, higher, stronger*, not swiftest, highest, strongest. It is the desire for improvement—the pursuit of greatness that makes better *people* of the athletes who compete for their countries.

No less than the founder of the modern Olympic movement himself, Baron Pierre de Coubertin, is often quoted as having said: "The important thing in the Olympic Games is not to win but to take part, just as the important thing in life is not the triumph but the struggle. The essential thing is not to have conquered, but to have fought well."

Perhaps that's one of the reasons that the leadership of America's corporations frequently call upon the authors of this book to inspire and motivate their employees to attempt excellence.

Without exception, the athletes who contributed these chapters have addressed groups, large and small, in their collective mission to share the power and relevance of their Olympic experiences. By such sharing of the Olympic spirit, they have contributed to the revitalization of management teams and sales organizations and, ultimately, to the improvement of organizational bottom-lines. In addition, these Olympians also speak to youth groups and civic organizations on the subjects of personal performance and the esoteric feelings of seeing your dreams come true. Their wonderful and enlightening stories bring to life the timeless truths inherent in the pursuit of excellence through hard work, discipline and strong character.

The message hidden just beneath the surface of each chapter is that Olympic champions are not extraordinary people, rather, they are ordinary people who merely have been able to accomplish extraordinary things in the area of life that matters most to each of them. If each of these athletes began simply enough, then there is hope for each of us—that we, too, can dream and reach far beyond our perceived abilities to attain untold treasures of personal satisfaction and productive value for those around us. Within each of us lies a dormant form of an Olympian, waiting to be awakened.

While many of these great athletes are medal winners (with *sixty-six* Olympic medals among them, including *forty-four* gold medals!) they also are outstanding communicators, personalities and leaders in the Olympic movement. Twenty of the chapters have been written by athletes who serve as experts in their fields, for television coverage of their sport. Almost all have been inducted into their particular sport's Hall of Fame, and five were elected by their peers to carry the Stars and Stripes in the Opening or Closing Ceremony of the Olympic Games. More than great athletes, these authors represent the cream of "Olympic ambassadors," able to instill both knowledge and inspiration through the spoken and the written word.

Naturally, these Olympians do not constitute an exhaustive list, but rather a wonderful cross-section of winter and summer, male and female, old and young, veterans and first-timers, those who stood on the top platform and those whose personal triumphs allowed them to feel like champions. They speak on diverse topics that you will find both entertaining and inspirational.

These great Olympic motivators teach us how to overcome obstacles, how to focus our attention on matters of importance, how to eliminate negative thinking, how innovations and creative thought *do* make a difference, how to attend to details and how to work hard. An added bonus is the first person singular perspective of "Life at the Olympic Games," as seen by the athlete who was actually in the competitive arena.

It is my hope that as you read the stories in this book, your favorite Olympic memories will come to mind and the timeless nature of the athletes' inspiration will once again rekindle some spark of youthful fantasy. With such knowledgable guides, you may find yourself transported to the Olympic Games themselves, imagining yourself crossing the finish line, sticking your landing, stroking to the wall, scoring the winning goal, hitting the bull's-eye or battling a difficult opponent.

Once you see yourself in the picture, it doesn't take long to begin thinking of yourself in the same terms: powerful, disciplined, visionary, resolute. You'll be delighted to realize that you've awakened the Olympian within yourself.

John Naber
Pasadena, California

Acknowledgments

The idea for this book occurred rather by accident, during a visit to one of the many fine speakers bureaus with which I am associated. On the shelf among the various titles written by the bureau's varied speakers was a paperback book with the Olympic rings visible on its spine. That book, *The Winning Spirit*, by Best of the Masters (Griffin Publishing, 1996) featured motivational essays from some of the country's finest professional speakers, each chapter written with an Olympic theme. During my more than twenty years of television coverage and corporate motivational speaking appearances, I have been networking with a variety of Olympians, each of whom brings an endearing speaking style to their audiences, in addition to inspirational stories of their athletic journeys, so I assembled my own "Olympic Team" of authors who had both the sporting perspective and the ability to communicate relevant stories from their personal experiences. Robert Sommer, the editor of *The Winning Spirit*, was quick to pass along his experiences, allowing me to sidestep many of the same potholes that he had encountered, thereby sparing me no end of frustration, I'm sure.

Perhaps the best possible mentor I could ask for when editing the following chapters was the fabulous filmmaker, Bud Greenspan, who is the Olympic movement's most distinguished storyteller. His Olympic chronicles consistently capture the essence of the athletes while conveying the inspirational truths that their performances reveal. Bud's pictures and writing are (and always will be) my gold medal standard. Thanks, Bud, for giving me something to shoot for.

The folks at Griffin Publishing Group encouraged, advised, edited and inspired me with their enthusiasm on many occasions. Bob, Dan, Robin, Marjie, Mark, Bryan and the rest...thank you for your faith in me and in this project.

As we approached the finishing stage of the editing process prior to submitting the book to our publisher, I called upon my dear friends, Digby and Kay Diehl, each one an accomplished professional wordsmith, with writing credentials far superior to my own. Their comments illuminated what worked well and revealed the sections of each chapter that needed "another pass." Each suggestion was lovingly supplied and gratefully incorporated. Cudos to both of you. Applause also to fellow Olympian, Dwight Stones, whose keen eye for detail caught many errors that escaped my red pen.

To the photographers who donated the use of their images, I pass along the athletes' genuine gratitude. Your name is proudly listed below each photo. Thanks for sharing what you do so well with our readers.

The hours spent editing the manuscripts cannot be measured by time alone. Many revisions were necessary and though each of the sentences embodied wonderful insights, if they didn't fit that particular chapter, I had to cut them loose. I now know what a devoted coach must feel like when his talented athletes never actually make it on to the team. Helping me see through each sentence, each dream, each inspirational nugget, was my wife, Carolyn. Her patient and unwavering eye for clarity and inspiration helped me many times when I honestly couldn't see the forest for the trees.

Thanks also to our daughter, Christina, who ran the copy machine for each rough draft and had to fix the meals and clean up the house during the frequent times when both her parents were working late to meet deadlines.

I am grateful to each of the Olympian authors for the time and thought that went into these stories and for their patience while waiting for the project to be completed. Despite their busy schedules, they were always quick to respond to our harried requests sent via an overworked fax machine.

I am delighted to call your attention to the Olympic rings so prominently placed on the cover alongside the "USA" insignia. The U.S. Olympic Committee is very enthusiastic about the opportunity for so many outstanding Olympians to recount their stories, and has taken a keen interest in the success of our project. Their encouragement means a great deal.

I am pleased to note that the sale of this book helps to support the training and preparation of U. S. athletes for future Olympic competitions.

John Naber

Dedication

The Olympian authors join in dedicating this book to Florence Griffith Joyner, whose excellence, enthusiasm and ability to inspire personify all of the finest qualities of the Olympic movement. Her tragic death on the eve of our book's publication makes her contribution so much more treasured. Our thoughts and our prayers remain with Al and their daughter, Mary Ruth.

DAN JANSEN

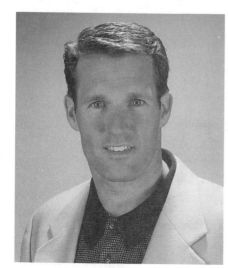

Photo provided by Dan Jansen

Dan Jansen is an eight-time world record-holder in speed skating. He was the first man to break thirty-six seconds in the 500-meters, winner of more than thirty World Cup races, fifty World Cup medals and twenty World Championship medals. He won the overall World Cup title seven times.

But the name Dan Jansen is familiar to all Olympic fans, not by the number of his successes, but rather by the tenacity of his resolve. Dan qualified onto his first Olympic Team in 1984, where he finished fourth in Sarajevo. Four years later in Calgary, he was favored to win gold. The sad news of his sister's death from leukemia reached him on the morning of his race. Falls in both of his events proved the terrible impact of the shock. Four years later, at the Games in Albertville, he finished fourth place in the 500-meter and once again failed in his quest for that elusive Olympic medal.

By the time he attended his fourth Olympic Games in Lillehammer, even his competition seemed to be rooting for his success. His book, *Full Circle,* recounts the story of his journey from the depths of his disappointment to the top-award stand—and his solitary Olympic gold medal.

Since retiring from the sport, Dan addresses audiences with his heartfelt motivational message. He covers his sport on CBS television.

There's More to Life Than Skating Around in a Circle

Dan Jansen

During a press conference prior to the 1994 Olympic Winter Games in Lillehammer, Norway, a reporter yelled out, "You realize that if you come out of these Olympics without a medal again, you'll probably go down in history as the greatest speed skater *never* to have won an Olympic medal." Well, after thanking him for pointing that out, and pointing out to him that this wasn't even a question, I had an answer for him anyway: "That's one way to look at it, but I choose to look at it another way. With this being my fourth Olympic Games, I have also had the opportunity to become one of the most *successful* Olympians of all time." Sometimes our attitude toward a situation can determine its outcome.

On February 18, 1994, as I prepared to step to the starting line for the 1,000-meter race, my eighth, and final, Olympic event, a flood of thoughts raced through my mind while I was trying to remain focused on the task at hand.

You probably already know the outcome of my final Olympic race, which I'll get back to later. First, I want to share with you some of the reasons *why* every thought in my head was positive, and filled with some of the lessons I learned along the way that enabled me to reach that state of mind.

As I get further and further into my post-athletic life, I realize more each day how these lessons can translate into success, both in business and in life.

First of all, you should understand *my* definition of success. Success *never* should be measured exclusively by results, medals, championships, quotas or profits. For me, success is very private and very personal. It means being able to look back after a big race, season, presentation, quarter, etc. and know that you did everything you could to prepare yourself and that you gave it your best effort. Winning is terrific and it's what any competitive person strives for, but it should not be the *only* measure of success.

In 1984, my only goal was to make the Olympic team; to represent the United States at the Olympic Games. I hit that mark when I made the team that was heading to Sarajevo, Yugoslavia. Once I made the team, I hoped that with a great race, a top ten finish might be possible in the 500-meters. I finished fourth, just $16/100$ ths of a second from winning a bronze medal, and was overjoyed. When I returned home from Sarajevo, one of the most common reactions I received was, "That's too bad, no medal." That's when I first realized the disparity in how various people define success.

Along with asking yourself whether you were completely prepared and if you gave it your best effort, you should also ask whether you learned anything. For an achievement to be considered a true success, you must have learned something from the experience. As Garth Brooks sings in one of his songs, "Failure isn't failure if a lesson from it is learned." I love that line because so often I read and heard the word "failure" when others discussed my Olympic experiences.

Sometimes, our greatest triumphs come from what, at the time, seem like our greatest failures or setbacks. In business, we all have setbacks. If you are in sales, you will be turned down more than you are accepted—at least initially.

PERSPECTIVE

It's not always easy to learn from our experiences. Going into the 1988 Olympics in Calgary, I was favored to win one or possibly two medals. On the morning of my first race, the 500 meters, I learned that my sister Jane, just 27 years old, was losing her year-long battle with leukemia, and probably wouldn't make it through the day. By telephone, I spoke to Jane for the last time that morning. She died just hours before I was to compete.

Needless to say, my mind was in one place and my body in another that evening. One hundred meters into the race, I fell. Four days later, in the 1,000-meter event, leading and on a world-record pace at 600 meters, I came to the 800-meter mark with just a half lap to go, and I fell again.

———❖———

Could any good come from losing a beautiful, vibrant sister?

———❖———

We all fall down or get knocked down in our arenas of life or business. We go through difficult times that we may not fully understand. These are the times when we have to decide whether we're really knocked *out* or if we are just knocked *down*. Can we get back up again?

What could I possibly learn from a situation like this? Could any good come from losing a beautiful, vibrant sister who was a mother of three?

Unfortunately, our lessons in life don't come with rules or time lines or directions. They are there for us to decipher and learn from as individuals. Sometimes this is a very difficult process to go through and it can take years.

I did a lot of thinking after those Olympics about what to take from that experience. I remembered back when I was twelve-years-old and competing for my first National Championship. I was *certain* I was going to win. My parents drove my brother Mike and me up to St. Paul, Minnesota for the weekend competition, a trip of about a five-and-a-half-hours from our home in West Allis, Wisconsin. Mike won his age group but I finished runner-up in mine. After the meet came the five-and-a-half-hour return trip, and I think I cried nearly the entire way home. I was devastated. This event seemed like my whole life at that age and I couldn't believe that I hadn't won.

My father, Harry, and my mother, Gerry, were the parents of nine children, and I was the youngest. They never pushed any of us in sports, but they were always there to support us in whatever we chose to do. My dad is a big, quiet, soft-spoken man, and yet when he had something to say it usually was important. Whenever we were down, he always had a special way of making us feel better with just an encouraging word or two.

I was expecting and hoping to hear these magical words as we returned home that day, but he just let me cry in the back seat. When we finally arrived home, he sat me down in the living room and I knew, finally, that he was going to take this pain away, that somehow, this second-place finish might even be transformed into a better experience than finishing first. The time had come for his "magic" words. He looked me straight in the eye and said, "Dan, you know there's more to life than skating around in a circle." I didn't understand what he meant. I was even a little mad at him for demeaning this huge tragedy that had just happened to me.

Well, after Jane's death and my two falls in Calgary, I finally, and completely, understood what my father had meant. Now, although I still believed in myself and still loved to compete and to win, I was able to look at winning and losing, success and failure, with a different *perspective*.

GOALS

Okay, trivia time. What is the most famous quote ever to come from Dr. Martin Luther King Jr.? Easy, right? Almost everyone would agree that it was "I have a dream…" I think he could have substituted one word in that quote and still have said the same thing. It may not have been as eloquent and probably would not have been as frequently quoted, yet, what if he had said: "I have a *goal*"? Doesn't sound right, I know, but my point is that dreams and goals essentially are the same thing. No one just wakes up one day and achieves success without *first* dreaming about it and striving to achieve it.

The problem with goals is that sometimes they can seem so distant and unattainable. If you want to improve your overall sales in the coming year by twenty-five percent, you may get into your office, think about the amount of work it would take and say, "How in the world am I going to do that?"

As Olympic athletes, if we don't achieve our goals in a particular Olympic Games event, we have to wait four years just to get another chance, knowing that there are no guarantees. Both of these scenarios can be overwhelming, *if we allow them to be*.

I learned my lesson about goals early in my career, in a summer training session. Speed skaters do a lot of cross-training during the summer months, when there is limited, if any, available ice. One of the things we do for speed, power and endurance is a drill called "hill tempos." Essentially, it means running and jumping up the largest and steepest hills we can find, which usually are ski hills. We had finished maybe eight or ten hills when my coach, Peter Mueller (a 1976 Olympic champion), looked at his watch and said, "Okay, thirty seconds rest and we're going again." By this point, I was in considerable pain and almost nauseous.

I said "Pete, I'm really hurting, I don't think I can make it up there again."

"Yes, you can," he said. "You're looking at the top of the hill the whole time you're running. I want you to look up there before you start, because I want you to know where you want to end up, but once you start running, just keep looking ten feet in front of you and pretty soon you'll find yourself at the top of the hill."

I don't even think Pete knew what he taught me that day. There is no such thing as setting your goals too high, but I learned that to achieve the ultimate goal, I must take it one race at a time, ten feet at a time or one sale at a time, no matter how distant the eventual destination may seem.

COMPETITION

You are not the only person out there striving for success and wanting to be the best. There are many others with the same goals in mind. Some of these people are part of your company or your team, and you must work together, each person with his or her own responsibilities, working to achieve a common goal.

But there are also others out there with the same goals in mind, who are *not* part of your company or team. They want to be at the top, not with you, but *instead* of you. We might call them "the enemy" or our "adversaries," but we all know that this is our *competition*.

To be successful in any sport or business, competition is a necessity. How much of an achievement would it be to win a gold medal if you were the only one in the race? Or how successful would you consider yourself if you were the number one salesperson in the country but no one else was selling your product? Come to think of it, how much *fun* would it be?

————❖————

By wanting to be like me, they could never see themselves as better than me

————❖————

The single most helpful lesson I learned about competition is very simply to *be aware* of it. Know who your competition is, including knowledge of their strengths and weaknesses. But don't *dwell* on your competition. Don't worry about them, don't try to copy them, don't even think about beating them. Worrying too much about your competition takes the focus away from making *yourself* the best *you* can be.

When I was skating at my best, I would notice certain competitors watching everything I did—every lap, every start, every stroke. By that alone, I always knew which skaters never even had a chance of beating me. By wanting to be *like* me, they could never see themselves as *better than* me.

COURAGE

Being successful can require taking chances and risks. It requires a willingness to put yourself on the line, to risk embarrassment, to have no fear of failure. I've heard people say, "My fear of failure is what keeps me motivated." Well, that may be true, but if you are really afraid to fail, then you will never be willing to try new and inventive ways to be your best or to improve. You may work hard, but you'll always stay with what got you where you are and, eventually, you'll be overtaken by someone who is not afraid to fail.

To quote the old saying: "You cannot discover new oceans unless you have the courage to lose sight of the shore."

Think of all the successful people you admire. Have any of them gone through life without *ever* taking a chance or making a big decision? I doubt it.

They thought that if I trained for both races, it might take something away from each race

Until 1992, I would have considered myself a 500-meter specialist with a better-than-average 1,000 meter. Sometimes, I would skate a great 1,000 meter, sometimes a terrible one, but rarely a consistent one. Just two years before the 1994 Olympics in Lillehammer, Norway (my fourth and final Olympics), many people in my sport told me to forget about the 1,000 meter, to train for my specialty, the 500 meter. They thought that if I trained for both races, it might take something away from each race, and my medal chances would decrease.

My coach and I never took those suggestions seriously, and it was a good thing we didn't. Over the next two years, I broke my 500-meter world record four times and became the first person ever to skate the distance in fewer than thirty-six seconds. Sometimes our weaknesses can add to our strengths. Don't ignore your weaknesses just because they may not be as easy or as much fun as your strengths.

PREPARATION

I've talked about perspective, goals, competition and courage. There is another very important ingredient of success: Preparation. Like the Boy Scouts say, "Be Prepared!" Preparation takes effort and education over long periods of time. Achieving your goals requires being both mentally and physically prepared. It requires a balance in your life—a balance between hard work and *recovery time.*

Sometimes we get so consumed with our work and our training that we forget to make time for recovery. Sooner or later, it catches up with us and our bodies and minds let us know this by not being able to perform at optimum levels. The many terms for this include fatigue, exhaustion, burnout, etc. In order for our bodies and minds to perform at maximum levels, we need time away from the physical and mental stress of working and training. Schedule your calendar to include this *recovery time.* Get away, exercise, relax, get plenty of sleep. I like to play golf to get my mind clear and rested for upcoming road trips. But remember, the key word here is *balance*—not too much of one or the other.

Being totally prepared doesn't mean that you will never have to deal with any surprises, but it does assure a calmer, more confident response when faced with the unexpected.

Many people aren't worried when they're about to make a presentation to a friend or long-time client. But what happens when it's a new face behind the desk? If you are prepared, you will not be overly affected by this. You will walk into that office with the same amount of confidence because you know your stuff!

How do you know when you've finished preparing? The answer to that question finally leads me back to February 18, 1994 and my 1,000-meter race at the Olympics in Lillehammer. Remember the race that, two years earlier, people told me to forget about?

Four days prior to that race, I had slipped once again in the final turn of the 500 meters, my best event. I finished in a heartbreaking eighth place. Well, had I listened to the naysayers, I would not have had this last chance at an Olympic medal.

I knew I was prepared for the 1,000 meters. I had always thought that if you've been through all the physical and mental preparation, you just go out there, put yourself on auto-pilot and do it. But when I warmed up on the ice that day, something felt a bit off. Physically and mentally, I felt good, but my timing wasn't quite right.

In almost every speed skating competition, we race the 1,000 meter having already raced a 500 meter earlier *that same day.* But in the Olympics there is just one event daily—no 500 meter before the 1,000 meter. I wanted my legs and body to feel as if I had already raced a 500 meter, so I found a stationary bike in the locker room and did a workout to get my legs to hurt a little bit. I needed that familiar burning feeling if I was to skate my best race. Well, that may have been the best bit of preparation I could have done because when I got on the ice for my race, my legs felt exactly as I wanted them to feel.

So when are we finished preparing? Not until we've crossed the finish line or made the sale or persuaded the customer to sign on the dotted line.

MY FINAL OLYMPIC RACE

The 1,000-meter event is two-and-one-half laps around a 400-meter oval track (100 meters per turn, 100 meters per straightaway), two skaters at a time. The race begins halfway down the far straight and finishes at the fifty-meter mark on the side nearest the television cameras. Since the inside lane is shorter than the outer, the two skaters "cross over" on the back straight, once at 400 meters and again at 800 meters.

Prior to my skating event, I watched the two favorites, Igor Zhelesovski, a dominating 1,000-meter champion from Belarus, and the Russian, Sergei Klevshenya (the silver medalist in the 500) share the ice and turn in the two fastest times up to that point: 1:12.72 and 1:12.85, both of which exceeded the existing Olympic record. The world mark was 1:12.51, set in Calgary on very fast ice, and my personal best was 1:13.01. So these were excellent results from worthy opponents—my *competition*. My *goal* had been to skate a 1:12.5, and now I realized that goal could be golden.

As I made my way to the start area, my coach, Peter, kept his comments short. "Last 200" was all he said, reminding me to continue to emphasize my technique, especially in the last half-lap of my race. It was a reminder of our *preparation* for this event.

As I stepped to the starting line for my final Olympic race, I knew I had a lot riding on the line. I did not, however, feel that this *one race* would define my entire career. Although I felt I deserved to do well, I also knew that I could live my life without an Olympic medal, if that's the way it turned out. That *perspective* allowed me to concentrate on my job without allowing the expectations of others to add pressure that might be detrimental. In fact, my last thought before the gun was one of peaceful resolution, because I knew this race would be my last Olympic appearance. Even though I loved the competition, I knew it was time to move on.

I had been hoping to start on the inner lane because the sharp inside turn is easier to handle off the start when you're not going so fast, and then you end on the inner lane, usually having someone to chase when you get tired. But I drew the outside lane. The man I was paired with, Junichi Inoue from Japan, was a better 500-meter skater. He went out quickly and by the time we "crossed over" after the first 400 meters, I was able to draft in his wake and gain valuable time before I passed him on the inner lane.

With one lap to go, the scoreboard flashed my split time. The crowd let out a roar. I couldn't see the time, but I knew it must be fast and I didn't yet feel tired.

———❖———

People say the noise was deafening, but I couldn't hear a thing

———❖———

Heading into my second-to-last turn, I was still on the inner lane. Not unlike riding in a car that turns a sharp corner, I could feel the G-force making me feel heavier, almost doubling my weight. I could feel the fatigue creeping into my legs and when I placed my left foot on the ice, my speed and the centrifugal force made the skate slip just a bit, causing me to lose balance. Here's where *courage* kicked in. Without panicking, without trying to make up for lost time, I had to control my fear, regain my balance and keep skating my line.

On the back straight, Peter held up a sign that appeared as an oasis to a thirsty man. It showed a six and a five—26.5 seconds! A fabulous lap time and, combined with my quick opener, I knew I was ahead of Igor's time at that point, but I didn't know just *how* far ahead. He was known for his blistering finishes, so I still had to hold my race together, but now I was turning on the outer lane and I felt pretty secure. I thought: "Stay on your feet!"

Coming off the last curve, I began pumping with both arms, trying to keep going, even though all my energy was gone. People say the noise was deafening, but I couldn't hear a thing. I felt as if I were moving in slow motion toward the finish line. I knew it was a good race, but I had no idea whether it would be a record.

Within moments of crossing the line, I looked toward the scoreboard, but there were so many times displayed: the existing world and Olympic records; the current leaders; the most recent skaters; the split times…it was all so blurred, I wasn't sure what my time had been…and then I saw my name and the letters "WR, 1:12.43"—a new world record! Faster than any human in history! The Norwegian spectators couldn't have been more enthusiastic in their applause.

I almost ran into my coach. Peter was skating backward when I plowed into him. We hugged for so long that I thought we might tangle blades and go down on the ice. He had been my first coach, a role model in the sport and a mentor during my difficult times. It was fitting that my career would come to a close in his presence.

———❖———

The memory of my sister and the love of my daughter came together in the happiest moment of my life

———❖———

It wasn't until after the awards ceremony that I got to skate a victory lap. I'd never won an Olympic medal before, and wasn't aware that this was part of the protocol. When I passed my family, I saw that they had placed my daughter, Jane (named after my late sister), in the arms of a security guard, in the hopes that I might see her more easily. Without a thought, I scooped her into my arms and began a long slow circuit of the

©1994 Allsport USA / Chris Cole

track. Some theatrically minded Norwegian turned off the lights in the Viking Ship arena and hit me with a spotlight. As good as it looked on television, I was blinded by the light and couldn't see a thing. I knew that people were throwing flowers, dolls and other dangerous obstacles onto the ice, and if I weren't careful, I'd trip over a flower stem and drop my baby girl on live TV. Yet in that instant, the memory of my sister and the love of my daughter came together in the happiest moment of my life.

Although my world records are gone now, I'll have that gold medal and that treasured memory forever. But success in life is not always such a tangible object as a golden medallion. It is not a certificate you hang on your office wall or a trophy you display on your desk. Success is an ongoing process. Establish your own goals and standards but *never* set limits. You, and you alone, are the person who should take the measure of your own success.

I have shared many of my favorite quotes with you, most of them from other people. This final thought is mine and sums up what I'm trying to say: I do not try to be better than anyone else. I only try to be better than myself.

Paul Gonzales

Photo provided by Paul Gonzales

Raised by a single parent as one of eight children in one of the roughest East Los Angeles neighborhoods, Paul Gonzales quickly learned the skills needed to survive on the streets where drugs, gangs and murders are commonplace.

Paul is the first ever Mexican-American Olympic champion and, in spite of being a part of an outstanding 1984 Olympic boxing team that included Tyrell Biggs, Mark Breland, Evander Holyfield, Pernell Whitaker and Henry Tillman, it was Gonzales, the light flyweight champion, who earned the tournament's highest honor: the Val Barker Cup, which signifies the most outstanding boxer of the Olympic Games.

Paul has addressed crowds in excess of 10,000, serving as a Master of Ceremonies, motivational, keynote or dinner speaker, and continues to devote his time to helping inner-city youth. He has appeared on behalf of the United Way, Boy Scouts of America, D.A.R.E. America and the Inner City Games. He was appointed Commissioner of Children, Youth and Families by Los Angeles Mayor Richard Riordan.

After his gold medal victory, he gave his medal to his mother, Anita. Paul Gonzales lives just fifteen miles from the housing project where he was raised.

2

Step Into the Ring

Paul Gonzales

Every morning I would get up, focused and looking forward to my morning run through the "hood," Boyle Heights in East Los Angeles, which early in the century had been an upper-class Jewish neighborhood. By 1978, however, it had become a disenfranchised, inner-city Latino barrio—definitely not a friendly place for a kid. I was 14 years old and a skinny little homeboy from the Aliso Village Housing Projects. The Projects were the spawning ground for gangs, drugs, violence and persuasive peer pressure. When I ran, I had to block all of that from my thoughts as well as block out the pain of training and my adolescent desire to meet girls. Nothing was more pressing to me than boxing at the Olympic Games.

My running took me through every corner of Boyle Heights. I had to cross a dozen boundaries drawn by gangs that did not welcome me. Grouchy *mamacitas* swept the walks in front of their Projects' apartments, ignoring me. Drivers would angrily honk their horns and there were the whispers: "No Mexican kid from Boyle Heights, from Aliso Village, would *ever* win an Olympic gold medal." Sometimes it was not a whisper. Sometimes it was spit from their mouths in distrust and disgust.

Never had a Mexican-American won an Olympic gold medal and no wonder: Boyle Heights boasted five of the toughest housing projects in Los Angeles, which were home to more than twenty active gangs. There were very few brown faces in our city government or any other positions of influence in the city. I would think about this as I crossed the streets and bridges and saw the early morning lights burning in City Hall when I approached downtown Los Angeles. At one time, Los Angeles City Hall was the tallest building in the city, dominating the skyline. As I ran, I would dream about the day when people like me, of Mexican descent, would be elected to top positions at City Hall. That dream would come true. In 1978, I knew that I had to focus on the 1984 Olympics, but every now and then I could not keep out of my mind what my gold medal would do for my family, my friends and my people.

———❖———

I had to cross a dozen boundaries drawn by gangs that did not welcome me

———❖———

My early morning runs in the darkness were confusing, not only because of the gang boundaries, but because there were physical barriers, too. City planners had crisscrossed East Los Angeles with freeways, bus lanes, railroad tracks and detours. My run was an obstacle course. I would have to hop over new ditches, old trolley tracks and unlighted sawhorses while avoiding gravel, recently laid asphalt and curbs. I memorized my way, only to have it frequently changed without warning.

Yet, at dawn my senses filled with the wonderful sights and sounds of my community as people began to wake and move to their morning Latino rhythms. The *tortillarias* and the bakeries would send me the smell of freshly baked *tortillas* and *pan dulce*. I had to be careful because the food was very fattening and not to be indulged in while training. I smelled the diesel of trains coming from the train yards at Los Angeles Union Station. I watched passenger airliners taking off from the Los Angeles International Airport, their lights blinking on their way to far-off places. I heard the sirens of police cars and fire engines on their way to a crime scene or a fire. This made me aware of the loneliness of athletic training, but I also had a sense of "bigness" and uniqueness that was totally mine. Every once in a while, I became almost giddy with my sense of purpose. Being a part of something bigger than myself was what my training was all about.

In 1972, East L.A. got lucky when Captain Rudy De Leon became the Commander of the Hollenbeck Division of the Los Angeles Police Department. To my knowledge, he was the first Mexican-American to command an LAPD Division. He was tough, concerned with fairness for the Latino community *and* he loved boxing. Captain De Leon put a boxing ring in the basement of the Hollenbeck Police Station and organized the local business owners into the Hollenbeck Police Business Council, with the goal of constructing a youth center in the neighborhood.

When I met Al Stankie, he was a police officer assigned to the Hollenbeck Division. He did a lot of community outreach for the Captain's Police Business Council. I use the term "outreach" in the most literal sense. Sometimes, he would reach out, grab a kid and bring him to the police station to learn to box in the ring, instead of fighting on the streets.

When I was 8 years old, all of the *vatos* from the neighborhood would gather at the park for our boxing matches. These matches were not quite gang fights, but we didn't use gloves or any kind of protection. One day, this crazy *gringo* cop pushed his way into the middle of the homeboys at the match and grabbed me. He knocked me down. In those days, the Hollenbeck police did not play around. If you wanted to fight them with bare fists, you could go for it. They were always ready and more than willing, especially crazy Officer Al Stankie. Al challenged me to come to the station and learn to fight for trophies. I faced a tough decision. I loved boxing, but a kid from the neighborhood could not just walk into the police station in broad daylight without looking like a "rat" or a snitch.

———❖———

These matches were not quite gang fights, but we didn't use gloves or any kind of protection

———❖———

One day, I sneaked in through the back door of the police station where the cops brought their prisoners of the day. At first, I was scared because I didn't want to be seen by my homeboys and, for that matter, caught sneaking into the station by the cops. I thought I heard my heart pounding, but then I realized it was noise coming from the basement, which turned out to be some guys I knew, the Arreola brothers, Andre Smith, Raphael Reyes and other kids who were working out. Officer Stankie and his partner, Officer Mail, began training us to become boxers. Some guys dropped out and others didn't show up after a couple of times. Not me. I knew this is where I belonged, in a boxing ring. As I got older, Al and I became friends. I called him "Pop" and I didn't care who saw me coming or going to the police station. I began going in the front door. Sometimes we'd enter Captain De Leon's office just to bother him. If busy, he'd yell and tell us to get out, but if he had time to spare, we'd talk and enjoy our time together.

I was changing.

I wanted to succeed, not only in my boxing, but in every way. I con-tinued my training with "Pop" Stankie and it was this training that would become the most important part of my life. I didn't know it then, but Al's relationship soon would save my life.

In Aliso Village, "the circle" is a roundabout for cars and a gathering place for gangs. One night, shots rang out and a gang member was killed. Someone mentioned my name and the cops stormed my house at six o'clock the next morning, ready to charge me with murder. Luckily, my alibi was unshakable. I had been training in the gym at the Hollenbeck Police Station with Officer Stankie.

"Pop" was always talking crazy and rhyming words and silly phrases like Muhammad Ali. He had a training philosophy he called the "ABCs backward: CBA—anything a person can Conceive and Believe, then he or she can Achieve."

———❖———

The cops stormed my house at six o'clock the next morning, ready to charge me with murder

———❖———

To this ghetto kid, stuff like that made all the sense in the world. No matter how crazy Al would get, I understood and loved what he told me. I trusted him completely. He got the phrase from his idol, author Napoleon Hill, but I didn't think it mattered who wrote the crazy stuff; it only mattered that Al said it to me and that I said it back to him.

His formula for success is simple: First step: *Conceive*. Whatever your goal in life, it must be thought-out and attainable. You must get the picture, grasp it and be able to hang on to it, all the time.

In 1976, I had watched the Montreal Olympics on television. I saw the great boxing team that America sent to those Games: Sugar Ray Leonard, Michael and Leon Spinks, Leo Randolph and Howard Davis; gold medalists one and all. I thought, "If they can do it, I can do it." Two years later, I was a seventh grader at Hollenbeck Middle School, and had just won the Junior Olympics in the eighty-five-pound category. I was small but tough.

When I became the Junior Olympic champion, I could *Conceive* the possibility of becoming an Olympic champion. It became my dream. When I thought about winning a gold medal it was not some abstract wish. I could actually feel the weight of the medal around my neck. I would be the first Mexican-American *ever* to win a gold medal for the U.S. in the Olympic Games.

Second step: *Believe*. Believing is easy to do at the beginning but harder later on. My concept of winning was so strong and so fully pictured that it was easy to believe in my dream, but I soon discovered that my dream was not nearly so important to other people. They doubted and questioned or mistook my commitment for arrogance. *How dare a kid from Boyle Heights for even one minute have the gall to think he could make it to the Olympics—to box in front of the whole world, where only the privileged few had a chance!* My closest friends and even some family members scoffed at my decision to try for greatness.

———❖———

My community was becoming a driving force, making my dream real. We were all going to the Olympics together

———❖———

Yet, as I continued to train, I also attended the luncheons that were held to raise money for me. Gradually, I found support. For the most part, people wanted to believe I could do it. Eventually, the community joined me in the first two steps of my backward alphabet philosophy. Every part of Boyle Heights, whether good or bad, would change for me as we became partners in a great adventure. The gangster-homeboys would cheer me on as I passed by on my early morning runs, the *mamacitas* stopped their sweeping and wished me well, the cars blared their musical horns *for* me. My goal, their goal, was the gold.

More and more community leaders became familiar friends. I believed in myself and they believed in me. The negative whispers of discouragement began to fade as the cheers of hope grew louder. My community was becoming a driving force, making my dream real. We were all going to the Olympics *together*.

IT TAKES A VILLAGE

Through Captain De Leon and the Business Council, I would meet many of the local merchants who helped me achieve my Olympic dream. Not corporate America, but individuals such as Ray Wolsie and his brothers who owned the hardware store; Mike and Sally Rojas, owners of a local Mexican restaurant; and Dick James from the best hotel in East Los Angeles. They organized fund-raising luncheons to help with my escalating training costs. These people, and many others, worked hard to earn a living with their businesses, and yet they sponsored and nurtured my efforts to become an Olympian.

The idea of winning a gold medal was *Conceived* and we *Believed* that I could do it. Now came step three: *Achieving* the gold.

If a boxer wants a berth on the U.S. Olympic Team, he must carefully pick the right tournaments. The trainer has to be able to "peak" the athlete at exactly the right time. It takes political know-how and every imaginable talent to make all the decisions exactly right. You also need all the luck and good fortune in God's universe to get to the Olympics. When you're a Mexican-American from East Los Angeles, the recipe calls for double the ingredients.

Only a dozen American boxers make it into the ring to compete for the gold every four years. My good friend, Adriane Areolla, was set to go to Moscow in 1980 and surely would have won an Olympic medal, but the boycott was called and he turned professional. That left me, at the age of 14, the best-known boxer on the Hollenbeck Boxing Team and our team's only hope for Olympic gold in 1984.

Those Olympics would be held in Los Angeles, only four miles from the Hollenbeck Division. If this homeboy made the cut, he would be fighting at home, in front of his friends and neighbors. In 1984, I would be 19 and the Olympics would be perfect for me.

The Hollenbeck Police Business Council completed the Captain's dream, the Youth Center, and hired Danny Hernandez to run it. I trained there every day with Al, and Danny encouraged me, pulling out all the stops to help me hold my dream together.

In February 1984, I flew to Moscow to fight the defending Olympic champion from Russia, Shamil Sabyrov. When they said I knocked him into retirement, I knew I was ready.

THE GAMES OF LOS ANGELES

I fought in the Light Flyweight division (under 106 pounds). My Olympic experience was not what I had been expecting.

I was tall for the class and because of my height, many of my opponents would drop their heads when they saw a blow coming. I would often hit them on the tops of their heads and this would do more damage to my hand than to their heads. This, in combination with my earlier street fighting, created a serious bone spur in my punching hand.

As soon as I landed my first right in my first bout of the Olympic Games against Kim from Korea, I felt a sharp pain travel up my arm. I had reopened a hairline fracture in my first and second metacarpals. Even so, I won the bout, 5-0. Al once said that I'd "...win the gold medal with one hand, if that's what it takes." Little did he know how true that statement would become.

Out of sight of the others, I kept my hand bandaged and in hot wax, refusing any medication for fear it might turn up in a random drug test.

I fought my second match with left jabs and advanced (5-0) to meet John Lyon from Great Britain. His slower style threw off my rhythm and almost put me to sleep. When he caught me with a left hook, it woke me up and I got back to business. I won (4-1) in three rounds.

———❖———

As soon as I landed my first right in my first bout of the Olympic Games, I felt a sharp pain travel up my arm

———❖———

I fought Venezuela's Jose Marcelino Bolivar in the semis, and waltzed over him (5-0 with two standing eight-counts) to earn the right to meet Italy's Salvatore Todisco for the gold. (That same day, we watched him beat Rafael Ramos from Puerto Rico. Ramos had speed and moved like a pogo stick.)

The night before the final match, I was in the video room in the athletes' village reviewing tape of Todisco's earlier fights, when one of his cornermen came over to me and gave me the "thumbs-up" sign and said (in Italian), "Paul Gonzales, Campion Olympico." I thought he was being sarcastic.

The next day, I entered the ring in full dress ready to fight the biggest match of my career, when my opponent, Todisco, came forward in street clothes with a cast on his arm. He had broken his thumb in his last match and would be unable to fight me.

I assumed I'd be fighting Ramos, his last opponent, but the official raised my arm and the gold medal was determined in a walk-over. If only I had known, I wouldn't have put on the headgear, 'cause it messed up my hair.

Actually, I was disappointed because I wanted to win the gold with a knockout. In the prior matches I was giving the fans a boxing lesson, but on that day, I wanted someone to "kiss the canvas."

I guess the AIBA referees and judges didn't need to see that last fight, though, because they awarded me the Val Barker Cup as the Games' Outstanding Boxer (in *all* weight classes). When I got back to the athletes' village, my teammates on the U.S. Boxing Team, Tyrell Biggs, Evander Holyfield and Henry Tillman were quick and sincere with their congratulations. Mark Breland had hoped to win the Cup, but it went to me...the kid from the barrio.

Yes, this Mexican-American won an Olympic gold medal. I kissed my mother, thanked my country and cried. That day I went to the Hollenbeck Youth Center to see my friends, some very old, some very young and all of us very proud. We had parades and block parties. I attended more than 100 celebrations that month.

Everywhere I went, I told my audience the backward ABCs philosophy. What you can *Conceive*, you *Believe*, then you can *Achieve*.

Today, when I go through the neighborhood where I first began my training, I look at how much change has taken place since my first run in 1976. Mexican-American kids wave at me on their way to school and these kids will stay in school and experience success. The Hollenbeck Youth Center has just added 15,000 square feet and serves more than 12,000 youngsters a year. City Hall is not the tallest building in Los Angeles any more, but in those halls are Mexican-American City Council members. In our community, we are voting and we are becoming strong and responsible. There is hope and pride.

Photo provided by Paul Gonzales

I am reminded of a remark made by my friend and fellow Olympian, Anita De Frantz. She is the president of the Amateur Athletic Foundation and when she was elected vice president of the International Olympic Committee she was asked about being the first woman to achieve such a powerful position. She said that it was not important for her to be the first, as long as she was not the last.

I think about that when people remind me that I was the first Mexican-American to win a gold medal in the history of the Olympics. I was the first, but since 1984, several Mexican-American athletes have done themselves proud and won medals too, like Oscar de la Hoya. Two Americans on the U.S. Boxing Team in Atlanta, Albert Guardo and Fernando Vargas, each came up to me and said, "You're the man! You're the one who gave us an opportunity to believe we can do things in life. Thanks, man." That was better than an awards ceremony.

There will be more, because each of us works very hard to let the youngsters living in the barrios and the ghettos know that they can *Conceive*, *Believe* and *Achieve* their dreams.

What kind of kid do you think I would have become had it not been for Captain De Leon, "Pop" Al Stankie, and Danny Hernandez—and how can I ever thank them enough? Perhaps by passing on the backward ABCs to every kid I meet and to challenge you to do the same.

Do you think in your *barrio*...your community, your company...there could be some kid like me, a *vato*, full of hope and potential, needing only encouragement and a helping hand? Can you follow in the Captain's footsteps by making your basement or your conference room or fitness center or meeting hall available to help some other kid like me? Can you take your *time* like "Pop" did to reach out and help a kid who can't help you back?

Throughout this book are more than two dozen essays explaining how to awaken the Olympian within you. I dare you to step into the ring and awaken the Olympian within someone else.

ROWDY GAINES

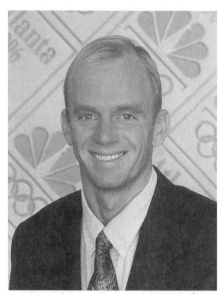

Throughout the 1980s Rowdy Gaines was the fastest swimmer on the planet. His world records confirmed his place in swimming history. The Olympic boycott of 1980 came during the peak of his career, when he set world records in the 100- and 200-meter freestyle events and he was expected to win five Olympic gold medals in Moscow. *Swimming World* magazine voted him World Swimmer of the Year.

Photo courtesy of Kimberly Butler/NBC

After a brief retirement, the allure of competing proved too strong, and he returned to the pool, where the consummate technician resumed his attack on the record books. World records continued to fall on his way to the XXIII Olympiad. At the 1984 Games in Los Angeles, no swimmer won more races than he did with his three gold medals in the 100-meter freestyle, the 4 x 100-meter freestyle and medley relays.

In 1991, the swimming world was shocked to hear that Rowdy had contracted Guillan-Barre Syndrome, an autoimmune virus that attacks the nervous system. Paralyzed for more than two weeks, Rowdy fought back, overcame the disease and one year later went to the World Masters Championships and won the glamorous 50- and 100-meter freestyle events.

He has worked with CBS, TNT and ESPN as a regular announcer for swimming events, and will call his third Olympic telecast for NBC at the 2000 Games in Sydney, Australia.

3

Ignore the Details & Miss Out on the Gold Dust

Rowdy Gaines

At the 1984 U.S. Olympic Team Trials (a meet viewed by many as the most intense swim meet in the world), I was preparing to enter the warm-up pool before the start of my race. After chatting with my coach, I took off my T-shirt, dropped my sweat pants and began to swing my arms in circles to loosen them up.

Suddenly, the crowd of about 3,000 people grew very silent. I looked around to see what was the matter, when someone yelled out, "Rowdy, look down!" As I did, I realized that I was completely naked. I had forgotten to put on a suit under my sweats. Somewhere above the crowd, the ABC cameras were recording the whole thing, while my coach just stood there, smiling and shaking his head.

I quickly pulled my pants back on, but the worst moment came, when perhaps the greatest female swimmer in history, Tracy Caulkins, who had been sitting next to where I was, stood up and whispered in my ear, "Don't worry, Rowdy, it's no big thing."

Go ahead and laugh, but in the very next race, Tracy broke the world record, and I take full credit for her performance.

I guess it's all too easy to keep looking at the bigger picture, that we tend to fall prey to the small details that are so easily overlooked. It's almost like the gold diggin' prospector who couldn't figure out where his wife was getting all that spending money, until she explained that she collected the gold dust from his laundry water.

In 1976, I was a straw-thin high schooler, growing up in Winter Haven, Florida. Mom used to say I was so skinny I had to jump around in the shower to get wet. My first coach, Bill Woolwine, said I was so small that we both would have to learn all we could about technique for me to get faster. Just working long and hard might not be sufficient. I needed more....

———❖———

He did it by technique, not power

———❖———

Three months later, I was watching the Montreal Olympics and I noticed that an American named Bruce Furniss defeated two much larger and stronger swimmers (U.S. teammates Jim Montgomery and John Naber) for the gold in the 200-meter freestyle. He did it by technique, not power. I watched in fascination as I saw him use every part of his body in the pool.

He exemplified everything I aspired to be, as far as paying attention to details. During the race, his head position never wavered—as if he were riding a rail down the pool. His hip rotation was well ahead of his time, getting every ounce of power from his legs and body, like a skinny Tiger Woods who can drive the ball 300 yards by using all of his body on the swing. Bruce was using every tool at his disposal, allowing himself to put more of his body into his stroke than just his arms. His swim gave me hope that I might also enjoy success at the Olympic level, and his methods gave me a vision of how to achieve it.

You might be surprised at all the details that champions have to think about. In my last Olympics, the shortest event was the 100-meter freestyle. This race takes around fifty seconds, and each time I swam it, I had to focus on a long list of details:

❖ As I marched up to the blocks, I would begin with an attitude of relaxation, my heartbeat slow and steady. Like a cat ready to pounce, I would wait patiently for the sound of the gun or horn. Tension here would cost me ^{2}/10ths of a second.   .2 sec

❖ With the race underway, that first stroke to the surface was always the most important because it would determine my momentum for the entire length of the pool. Done well, worth ^{1}/10th second.   .1 sec.

❖ My ideal body position: flat like a hydroplane, across the surface, not plowing through the surf with an arch in my back. If the waterline stayed between my hairline and eyebrows, I could cut another tenth off my time.

.1 sec.

❖ With a repeatable breathing pattern, I could focus on my stroke, and not my lungs. Two strokes, a breath, two strokes, a breath, four strokes, a breath and repeat. This "2-2-4" was worth $^2/_{10}$ths.   .2 sec.

❖ It doesn't matter much what happens above the surface of the water, the body moves as a result of what's happening below. The powerful pull, sweeping (we call it sculling) under the body, but never crossing the center line of the body. That might make my body wiggle down the lane which might cost $^3/_{10}$ths.   .3 sec.

❖ The end of the stroke is where I "release" the water, always below my waist, the wrist leaves the water before the fingers, otherwise I'd be pushing the water skyward and myself deeper into the pool.   .2 sec.

❖ I would never slow down for the turn, always accelerate and bounce off the wall. Just one fluid movement beginning with a tuck of the chin. As if the wall was on fire, my feet would burn if I left them on the wall too long ($^3/_{10}$ths per turn).   .3 sec.

❖ Off the turn, I would do everything possible to streamline my body. Thumbs locking my overlapped hands together, biceps pressed against the back of my ears, head down until the first stroke, "ride that glide" as far as possible, kick shallow and quick off the wall until I passed beneath the wave generated by the field coming into the wall, worth another tenth.   .1 sec.

❖ Coming to the surface, I hit the turbulence caused by the other swimmers. I must be aggressive and fight my way through like boxing my way out of a duffel bag (another tenth).   .1 sec.

❖ Remember not to breathe during the last seven meters. The oxygen I take in after that point won't reach the muscles in time to do them any good. ($^1/_{10}$th).   .1 sec.

❖ Anticipate the finish and be sure to end on a complete stroke. Touch the wall with the hand, not the nose ($^2/_{10}$ths).   .2 sec.

Total: 1.9 secs.

With almost two seconds deducted from my time, it's easy to see why so much energy and deliberation goes into the perfect race. The margin of victory for an Olympian is often determined by the man or woman who searches for just such details and gives each one the attention they deserve.

I managed a health club in Honolulu for a few years with more than 2,000 members to satisfy on a regular basis. They needed more than ample parking, a clean pool and well-surfaced tennis courts. They also noticed things such as properly pressed towels, dry counter-tops and liquid soap containers that were always full and clean. The Olympian within me realized that I still had to provide the big things, but if I forgot to work on the little details, my members would be looking for another club to join.

As an expert analyst for my sport on television, I try to look beyond what happens in the pool. I try to learn about the athletes' lives outside the water. To analyze their strengths and weaknesses, I watch them in practice, I ask about their favorite movies and music. I learn more that way. I find it's the swimmer who is still working on technique in the warm-down pool who usually ends up having the better race.

Two weeks before my last college meet, I entered a relatively insignificant meet in which, before one of my events, the elastic strap of my goggles wore through with a snap, making them useless.

I have always trained and competed wearing goggles, because they give me good underwater vision of the field, including the turning walls and the other competitors. Without them I had difficulty in that race, the blurred vision made me miss opportunities and affected my pace and confidence.

————❖————

Moments before the start of the race my goggles snapped

————❖————

A fortnight later, at the 1981 NCAA National Championships in Austin, Texas, it happened again. I was about to swim my final collegiate 200-yard race, flanked by two of the toughest competitors I had ever faced; David Larson, who would win a gold medal in 1984 and Brian Goodell was arguably the greatest distance swimmer America has ever produced.

Moments before the start of the race, after introduction of the swimmers, and as we were heading to the blocks, my goggles snapped again. My initial reaction was one of panic—until I realized that this time I'd brought a spare set to the start. I turned to my towel and grabbed the new pair, immediately returning to my routine. I'm happy to say that I won the race, and from that point forward, there was never a race that I didn't bring two pairs of goggles to the start. In fact, at the Olympics, I had three.

With so much to think about, it would be easy to do just what everybody else is doing. Looking for *more* things to focus on seems almost crazy, but it's what the Olympian does by habit.

While attending a meet in Paris, U.S. teammate Dara Torres and I had the opportunity to watch a track competition going on at the same time, and we took special interest in the runners "track start." Together, we decided to add this innovation to our starts, by placing one foot at the rear of the starting block for a better, more reliable takeoff. The first time I tried the new start, I slipped into the pool and finished last, but over time and after much practice, this technique (which has since become almost universally accepted) became a valuable part of my race.

Speaking of starts....

Swimming competition at the Olympic level always is very intense. As much as I trained for my event, others trained more. As much as I knew about the 100-meter freestyle, others knew just as much. When people ask whether winning at the Olympics is more physical or mental, I say that just to get to the final, everyone has to be about equal athletically. I needed to look for another advantage. I had to find something the others had overlooked.

———❖———

I had two days of practicing a 'quick set,' just in case
'Jesse James from Panama' ended up starting my event

———❖———

My first race occurred on the third day of the 1984 Olympics in Los Angeles. During the first two days, while other sprinters were using the warm-up pool, getting rubdowns or cheering for their teammates, I was quietly watching the officials. My college and Olympic coach, Richard Quick, had noticed a rotation of three starters. Officiating jobs at the Olympics are often "perks" meted out to member federations in recognition for volunteer service through the years. It's strange, but at the most important meet of my life, the officials were not chosen because of their competence alone. Two of the starters seemed fine (i.e., experienced and always unpredictable), but the third seemed to have a quick trigger finger. I noticed that he always fired the gun immediately after finishing the statement, "Take your marks." He was controversial because a lot of swimmers didn't even have time to get set on the blocks.

Throughout my career, I had been deliberately slow in coming down to the "set" position (Remember: relaxed like a cat, "heartbeat slow and steady...") but at the Olympics, Coach Quick said I would have to be prepared to change my cadence in getting set. I had two days of practicing a "quick set," just in case "Jesse James from Panama" ended up starting my event.

Two swimmers were faster than I was in the preliminaries. I was seeded in lane three, next to the top qualifier, 6'4" Mark Stockwell from Australia. On his other side was the top American from the morning swim, and the second-fastest overall, Mike Heath. Mike had won this event at the U.S. Team Trials. Since the fastest American in this race would earn the right to swim the anchor leg of the 4 x 100 Meter Medley Relay (an almost certain U.S. gold), I viewed this race as one in which, in my case, *two* gold medals were at stake. Beyond Heath was Per Johansson from Sweden. At 6'6", he was the tallest swimmer in the field, with less speed than the other two, but always with plenty left at the end of his races.

I noticed that the Panamanian official was loading his starting pistol as we were being introduced. You guessed it: "Jesse James" had been assigned to my race.

Standing on top of the starting blocks, I heard the command, "Take your marks." In a flash, my track foot was back and I was holding the front of the blocks. Stockwell was still lowering himself into position when the gun went off.

I was in the water before the others had left their blocks. Frankly, I was expecting a recall, but when I reached the surface without hearing a second gun, I was thinking only of one thing—how to get to the other end of the pool as fast as I could.

I carried that body-length lead all the way to fifty-meters and, because I trained for longer races than the rest of the field, by the time I surfaced after the turn I knew I had the race won. I finished first, followed by Stockwell, Johansson and Heath.

Some of the spectators made an effort to overturn the results, saying the other swimmers had been unfairly penalized, but Per also had gotten a good start, and I talked with him after the race. He and his coach had shared the same concern about the starter. We both saw it coming but, naturally, there are some details that you can't really share with everybody else.

———❖———

The little details—how seemingly insignificant sweeps of the second hand would harshly declare one man a champion and the other, a loser

———❖———

My quick reaction before the gun in my individual event was probably worth about $4/10$ths of a second. My margin of victory over the Australian had been $43/100$ths. I could have trained exactly the same distance, over exactly the same period, under the identical coaches and conditions, but if I had neglected all the attention to detail that I mentioned earlier (which added up to 1.9 seconds) I'd have lost the "big race" by more than a second-and-a-half.

Moments before my third and final event, the start of the men's Medley Relay, our team was gathered in the "ready room." Rick Carey would lead off with the backstroke, followed by Steve Lundquist in the breast-stroke. Both these men had won their individual events. Our "butterflier," Pablo Morales, was the only member of our team without a gold medal at that point and he was a bit nervous. To lighten his load, we all began sharing reflections of how far we'd come and the hours and miles we'd trained.

Four hours and five miles per day, six days a week, fifty weeks a year. We figured that because of the 1980 Olympic boycott, the last eight years had cost each of us about 9,600 hours and a distance equal to the circumference of the earth. We calculated 160 different swim meets and 1,600 different races. Big numbers, when you look at the big picture.

But I also recalled the little numbers, the little details—how seemingly insignificant sweeps of the second hand would harshly declare one man a champion and the other, a loser. No mistakes today, we agreed.

How glad I am that my coaches instilled in me the desire to look beyond the obvious, beyond the mundane to the minute details that gave me the chance to stand on top of the awards platform. It wasn't much, $^{43}/_{100}$ths of a second in the 100-meter sprint, and $^{65}/_{100}$ths in the freestyle relay…my first two gold medals won by the barest of margins.

The Medley Relay traditionally is the last race of every meet, and the four men who had endured the boycott of the 1980 Games came back in Los Angeles to demolish the existing world mark by more than a second.

After the final swimming race of the Olympics (and Pablo's first and my third gold medal), Steve ("the Lunk") Lundquist pulled a towel out of his bag and we all held it up to the nearest television camera—revealing our joy in this moment of victory to the country that we were so proud to represent. As members of the United States Olympic relay team we shared the sentiment printed on the towel: "Thanks America, for a dream come true."

Photo provided by Rowdy Gaines

Nadia Comaneci

Photo courtesy of Paul Ziert & Associates, Inc.

Nadia Comaneci is the most celebrated gymnast in history. As star of the 1976 Montreal Olympic Games, she became the first gymnast to score a Perfect 10, earning seven such marks on her way to three gold medals, a silver and a bronze. She appeared on the covers of *Time, Newsweek* and *Sports Illustrated* the following week.

Nadia continued her dominance through the 1980 Moscow Olympics, earning two gold and two silver medals. She retired from gymnastics in 1984 and was awarded the prestigious Olympic Order from the President of the International Olympic Committee, Juan Antonio Samaranch.

Except for a brief, heavily supervised appearance at the 1984 Olympic Games in Los Angeles, Nadia was rarely seen by the Western public. Romania's communist leadership considered her a prime candidate for defection. With travel forbidden, she felt she could no longer live in such repression, so in 1989, she fled across the border to freedom. Her departure was viewed by many as the beginning of the end of the Romanian communist regime. Her return years later was greeted with accolades usually reserved for a liberation army.

Nadia, who still trains and exercises daily, speaks five languages and has been a commentator at major gymnastics competitions for several television networks. In 1996, Nadia married Bart Conner in Bucharest, Romania in what became a State celebration. Together, the two perform in exhibitions, at speaking engagements and in commercial endorsements for major companies.

BART CONNER

Photo courtesy of Paul Ziert & Associates, Inc.

Bart Conner is the most accomplished gymnast that America has ever produced. He is the only American, male or female, to win gold medals at *every* level of junior, national and international competition. During the Olympic Games in Los Angeles, he won double gold with his performance on the parallel bars and as part of the U.S. Men's Team upset victory over the World Champion Chinese.

Bart began his illustrious career in a local YMCA program and won his first Junior National title by the age of 14. Three years later he became the youngest gymnast ever to win the U.S. Gymnastics All Around Championship, and one year later he qualified on to his first of three Olympic Teams.

Bart has appeared in feature films and on television shows such as "Highway to Heaven" and "Touched by an Angel" and, along with his wife, co-hosted his own television series called "Food and Fitness with Bart and Nadia."

He is co-owner of *International Gymnast* magazine and The Bart Conner Gymnastics Academy in Norman, Oklahoma. He has appeared on ABC's Wide World of Sports, ESPN and Turner Broadcasting as an expert analyst and television commentator. Bart has been a pioneer in promoting professional gymnastics opportunities, organizing exhibitions around the country, and was instrumental in relocating the International Gymnastics Hall of Fame to Oklahoma City.

4

Finding Your F.O.C.U.S.

Nadia Comaneci & Bart Conner

When I was a little girl tumbling in the park in Onesti, Romania, could I ever have dreamed that I would have the opportunity to represent my country in the Olympics, let alone write about my life in a book like this? No way. But, of course, I never thought that I would escape from my country, get married to a blond "All-American" guy and live in Norman, Oklahoma, either!

I am still surprised that many people remember me from the 1976 Olympics in Montreal. Thirteen years later, when I moved to the United States looking for a better life, I, of course, had changed a lot from the 14-year-old, pony-tailed little girl I had been in 1976. Soon after I arrived in the U.S., I started spending time with Bart Conner. Whenever we were out in public, people would recognize him and ask for his autograph. After he signed one for them, he would say, "Would you like an autograph from Nadia Comaneci?" They always went into shock. They would say, "Oh my God, you have changed so much. You were so cute when you were 14." I still don't know how to respond to that one.

Then, one day, I was on a plane returning from an appearance where I had just performed some gymnastics. I was talking to a flight attendant who did not recognize me, and she said, "Wow, your legs sure are in great shape, do you do any sports?" I said, "Yes, I am a gymnast," and she said, "Yeah, right. Who do you think you are, Nadia Comaneci?"

I said, "Well, actually I am." She got flustered, threw her arms up in the air and spilled coffee all over my T-shirt. We had a good laugh over that one.

It is true that I am the girl who scored the first Perfect 10 in the Olympics, and certainly that is a great thing to be remembered for, but for me, there are many other lessons that I learned that have helped me find my way in life. These lessons are more important than my Olympic medals.

Because of all of the attention that I received at the 1976 Olympics in Montreal, I have continued to come under a great deal of scrutiny. After those Olympics, I endured growing up, maturing, gaining and losing weight, and lots of other adolescent girl "stuff." That is all normal—except I had to do it with the world watching. Not fun!

By the time I got to the 1980 Olympics in Moscow, I had gone through lots of changes and, instead of being the little 14-year-old sensation, I was now the one to beat. Although in the six months prior to the Games I had had appendix surgery and a problem with the sciatic nerve in my leg, I still managed to get physically prepared for the meet. I did not realize that my mental resolve was not as complete—until it was too late.

————❖————

I was supposed to be the 'Perfect 10.' How could this be happening to me?

————❖————

As I was moving through my bars routine in the team competition, I had a single flash of indecisiveness, and the next thing I knew I was on the floor under the uneven bars. I had been training for a new move and I was not sure of myself. Actually, I had made the new move, but as I transferred to the low bar, I relaxed and missed one of the easy moves in my routine. *But this was the Olympics.* I was the reigning champion. I was supposed to be sailing through my exercises just like at Montreal four years earlier. I was supposed to be the "Perfect 10." How could this be happening to me?

I'll never forget the newspaper coverage of the meet the next day. The headlines read: "Comaneci Falls," accompanied by a picture of me sprawled underneath the bars in a very unflattering position.

Two days later in the All-Around competition, with more focus and intensity, I nailed my bars routine for a 10! Although I had done very well that day, because the scores from the team competition were carried over into my All-Around total, I received the silver. The Russian, Yelena Davidova, got the gold. Surprise!

By the end of the Games, I had won two gold and two silver medals. A great success by most standards, but still to this day people say, "It's too bad that you didn't do well in Moscow."

We have all heard the cliché, "Nobody is perfect." Because I had gotten perfect scores in 1976, people somehow attached that impossible label of "perfection" to me. We are not machines. I made a mistake, but I got up again and won two gold medals. I showed myself and others that I could handle adversity. Unfortunately, I had to learn that lesson with billions of people watching.

BART: Standing on the podium at the 1984 Olympics was an experience that has come to define my life. Along with my teammates, Peter Vidmar, Mitch Gaylord, Tim Daggett, Scott Johnson and Jim Hartung, we experienced a life-changing moment together. We had all come from very different backgrounds but, as a team, we accomplished something that none of us could have done alone. To this day, when we see each other, we feel a special bond because of how we helped each other to achieve a dream. For me, it was an especially emotional moment because I had come very close to not being there at all.

———❖———

I heard the strangest ripping sound, like pieces of Velcro being torn apart.
Then I felt a burning sensation

———❖———

Just seven months before that day, I was competing on the rings in an important pre-Olympic event in Japan. My world was shattered when, in the first move of my routine, my left biceps muscle ripped loose from my shoulder. When it happened, I knew instantly that something was terribly wrong. I heard the strangest ripping sound, like pieces of Velcro being torn apart. Then I felt a burning sensation, as if someone had placed a hot iron on my upper arm.

I knew immediately what had happened because I had experienced a similar injury to my other arm three years before, and it had taken me nearly a year to recover. This time I only had six months until the Olympic Trials.

I jumped down from the rings and looked around for my coach, Paul Ziert. I also saw one of my gymnastics heroes and winner of fifteen medals in three Olympic Games, Nikolai Andrianov from Russia. He knew that at 25, I was pretty old to be competing at this level, and he spoke his consoling words in broken English, "Conner, too old, I am sorry."

Coach Ziert had to stay in Japan with the rest of the delegation, but he handed me his credit card and said I was to get back to the U.S. right away. We called our friends, physical therapist Keith Kleven and Dr. Lonnie Paulos. A few days later I was in Salt Lake City having my muscle reattached and forty small bone chips removed from my elbow. These chips were a result of a previous injury, but undoubtedly had contributed to the stress on my biceps.

I don't want this to sound self-serving or arrogant, but my reaction to this potentially career-ending injury was anything but depressed. Sure, I was scared, but I remember thinking that my 1984 Olympic experience was going to be that much sweeter because I would make a terrific comeback. It never occurred to me that I might not make it.

Six months later, at the final Olympic selection meet where they announced the team of six male gymnasts who would represent the U.S. at the 1984 Olympics, I finished sixth. It was the last spot on the team, but I made it.

Our performances in Los Angeles were spectacular—every man pulling his weight, turning in solid routine after routine. By the time the team competition was over, the six of us had combined to become the best gymnastics team at the Games and America's first team champions since the 1904 Games in St. Louis (where *every* team was American). After so many years of anticipation, I couldn't hold back the tears. It's hard to smile and cry at the same time, but I did it.

A couple of days after experiencing the joy of our gold medal performance in the team competition, I had the chance to compete in the individual finals on the floor exercise and the parallel bars. Going into the floor final, I was tied for first place with the amazing Li Ning from China. He went up early and scored a 10! Fine, thanks a lot, Li! (He would end up with three gold medals in Los Angeles.) Now, it would take a 10.0 from me to tie. I had never received a 10.0 on floor and, honestly, I did not feel that I could get one. But all week long, every routine that I had performed had gone so smoothly that I really felt I was in the "zone." So, as I stepped up to salute the judges, I felt pretty cool. I already had a gold medal in my gym bag from the team competition. I was sure that nothing could go wrong.

When I landed my first tumbling run, instead of sticking the landing, I took a step backward and, as if the judges might have missed it, I heard the entire crowd at Pauley Pavilion moan, "Ohhhh." They also knew that the 10.0 was out of reach at that point. I finished the routine with a few other bobbles and, at the end of the floor final, dropped from a tie for first to fifth place. From a shot at a gold medal to no medal at all. How could this have happened?

—————❖—————

The only thing in my whole life that seemed to matter was whether
I was going to stick the landing or not

—————❖—————

I was pretty shaken up by this. When I spoke with Coach Ziert, he reminded me how hard we had worked to be here and that not only in gymnastics but in life, I couldn't "assume" anything. If I wanted to have success, I must "make it happen."

So, as I mounted the parallel bars in my last individual event final (as well as the last competitive routine of my career), I approached the exercise with a completely different focus and intensity. The moment came when I got ready for the dismount. The routine had been very clean up to that point and it seemed silly that, as I flew through the air, the only thing in my whole life that seemed to matter was whether I was going to stick the landing or not. Like being in a car wreck, everything seemed to be moving in slow motion. Even though a "double back" off of the parallel bars takes less than a second, it seemed to me that I was in the air for several minutes. I made a nice landing, and the judges gave me a 10.0 (the third and final perfect score of my career).

In the space of just two hours, I had experienced a microcosm of life. In both the floor and parallel bars finals, the situation was exactly the same. I was physically, mentally and emotionally prepared for both routines, but the only difference was that I had found my focus and, as a result, made it happen.

BART AND NADIA: Every time we make an appearance or give a speech, we write our own material and try to draw some analogies between our experiences as athletes and the challenges that our particular audience members might be facing. Do we need to focus on personal goals, teamwork, re-motivating a successful sales force, handling adversity, paying attention to details? These are the topics that many corporate groups want to key on.

Surely there are many aspects of sports training that have helped us make transitions from the gym floor to success in the business world. We call them the "Mechanics of Achievement." Most people are familiar with the championship qualities that help an athlete become a winner. These, of course, are the same attributes that help business people enjoy success. We all have the ability to make a commitment, the courage to set long- and short-range goals, the strength to lead, the guts to handle adversity, the selflessness to be a team player.

Most of us have been exposed to these principles. It does not matter where we learn them. Whether at home, in school or by playing sports, these mechanics will allow us to achieve success in almost anything! Yet how can we use these championship qualities daily?

We like to remind people that there are more than 1.5 million kids in the United States practicing gymnastics and yet only six men and six women will make the U.S. Olympic Team once every four years. Plus, if you tell five-year-old gymnasts that all they need to do is work hard for six hours a day for the next fourteen years and, if they have the talent, ability and some luck, they might make it to the Olympics, most kids would say, *Forget it!* Long-range goals tend to be very daunting.

❖

There are more than 1.5 million kids in the United States practicing gymnastics and yet only six men and six women will make the U.S. Olympic Team

❖

Yes, we need to think of the big picture, but our happiness and self-confidence can be enhanced if we focus on daily improvements. That way, at the end of every day, we feel some sense of accomplishment rather than feeling the burden of "just thirteen more years of this and I *might* get a chance to compete for my country." Even if you get to compete, you might still feel unfulfilled, because after going to the Olympics, just being there is no longer enough. You will want a medal, and then you may want to try to repeat as a medalist. So, as you can see, if you focus just on the results, it may never be enough.

Think of this analogy: There will always be someone with more money, a bigger house, better-behaved children, more opportunities and more of just about everything, so if you are focusing on that (the win, the title, always being on top) as your goal, you will never be totally satisfied. If you *enjoy* the process, then you will be constantly fulfilled and can always feel successful.

We both now feel that the most important thing we have gained from sports is the ability to focus. We use the word, focus, as an acronym to illustrate some of our thoughts on achievement.

F.O.C.U.S.

F: FIND YOUR TALENTS

You have undoubtedly found some things that you are good at and have made a major commitment to developing your skills. Whether you find yourself in sales, management, human resources or finance, it is important to continue to look for and identify your talents.

At very early ages, we (Nadia at 6 and Bart at 10) discovered that we had the "feel" for the acrobatics necessary to do gymnastics. Actually, our parents signed us up for gymnastics because they were tired of our breaking furniture as a result of doing flips off the couches. Whatever got us into the gym in the first place, we started getting positive feedback and encouragement very early. "Hey, you're good at gymnastics," was all we needed to hear—and we wanted to get even better. That nurturing environment contributed an enormous amount to our self-esteem, even to this day.

O: OBSERVE YOUR ROLE MODELS

The young gymnasts in our club learn by watching others perform the skills. Observe talented and gifted performers and watch how they achieve the results you seek. Let their experiences guide you. Observe other people who seem to be on the right track. Hang around success-minded individuals. Read biographies and profiles about the kinds of people who are already successful in your chosen field. That alone will help you find inspiration and guidance, as well as motivation.

In addition to our supportive (but not "pushy") parents, we also were lucky to latch onto terrific coaches who were role models as well as teachers. Who are your role models? Do you have top performers around you to show the way to be even better?

C: CHALLENGE YOURSELF

The same routine that earned Bart a gold or Nadia a Perfect 10 is no longer sufficient to even qualify for Olympic competition. The sport is constantly developing and becoming more challenging. We need to be the same way, always pushing ourselves beyond the comfort zone.

We set long-range goals, but we remember to set daily goals as well. Every day we try to come home feeling like we are "getting there," making progress, instead of getting stressed out about how much we still have to do. A good practice last week is no excuse to slack off today.

Sometimes, closing the sale takes several months, but if it is important, try to accomplish one small thing toward that goal each day. As gymnasts, we used to concentrate on getting the details right. Today "I want my handstand to be a little straighter and my back somersault to be a little higher." Those were tangible goals that allowed us to experience daily success.

In Romania, they have a saying, "Don't say 'Whoop' before you jump the fence." This is like the American saying, "Don't count your chickens before they are hatched." Whatever your language, try to improve slowly but consistently. Everyday, you should get a sense that you are getting better at what you do.

U: UTILIZE YOUR RESOURCES

We are all very lucky to grow up in a time where the world provides enormous access to information and opportunities. There are examples of people all around us who have done impressive work and who can help us enjoy similar results. Do not be afraid to ask for some help. Log on to the Internet, scan the library, get a trainer. You will be surprised how many people will mentor or lend a hand when they realize you have dedicated yourself, and that you are passionate about a goal. People will want to help you, and you will, in turn, be inspiring to them.

I (Bart) remember telling my parents that I wanted to be a gymnast. They said, "How can we help?" Even today, as professionals, we continue to search for people and resources that can help us get where we want to go.

S: STRIVE TO MAKE A DIFFERENCE

This is the best part. By equipping ourselves with all the tools we need, we can discover where we can make our contributions and where we can have an impact. We were not put here to accumulate wealth, we are placed on this planet to be agents for change. So, what do you believe in? Where will you make a difference? And remember it doesn't *have* to be at work.

Will you be on a team of researchers that discovers the cure for AIDS? Will you start a charitable organization to help underserved kids? Will you raise a future artist or start the world's largest computer software company? Will you travel the world and help fight hunger or will you become a professional athlete? A college professor? An accomplished entertainer? A community leader? An elementary school teacher?

When Romanians want to remind themselves that life is not always easier for the other guy, they say, "Not every dog has a bagel on his tail." It's not easy, but if you find your F.O.C.U.S. you will have given yourself

Photo courtesy of Paul Ziert & Associates, Inc.

a better chance to succeed. That is all most of us ask and that is all most of us need. Only you can decide who you will be and what you will do.

Although for me (Nadia), that was not always the case. Growing up in a totalitarian regime, during the days of Communist Romania, I was not allowed to choose my direction in life. So, in the fall of 1989, I performed my riskiest move ever when I crawled through snow and ice in the middle of the night to cross the border and escape from Romania as a political refugee. Eventually, the Romanian people revolted and gained their freedom. Today in Romania, life is still difficult, but at least for the first time in more than forty years, people have hope that they can improve their lives because they can choose for themselves. This may be difficult for Americans to understand because most of you have enjoyed freedom your entire lives. Do you realize how lucky you are?

———❖———

I performed my riskiest move ever when I crawled through snow and ice in the middle of the night to cross the border and escape from Romania

———❖———

As athletes dedicated to lofty goals, we realize that even if we had not won our Olympic medals, we still would have gained much value from the process of trying to become champions. Those life skills and attitudes define who we are.

Our coaches taught us that "There is nothing wrong with chasing dreams, you just might catch one." What you do with those dreams—that's up to you!

JEFF BLATNICK

For many, the most heartfelt victory at the 1984 Olympic Games in Los Angeles came at the hands of Jeff Blatnick, a man who just two years earlier had been diagnosed with Hodgkin's Disease, a form of cancer that attacks the spleen and lymph nodes.

His last-second, two-point victory in the gold medal wrestling match brought tears and cheers, when he knelt on the mat and raised his arms in a prayerful

Photo provided by Jeff Blatnick

thanks. Later, in the post-bout interview, he tearfully spoke the words that were to become his trademark for years to come, "I'm a happy dude!"

Jeff's victory was America's first-ever Olympic medal in the super-heavyweight division of Greco-Roman wrestling, and he received an Olympian's highest honor when he was chosen to carry America's flag in the Closing Ceremony of those Games.

He has distinguished himself as expert analyst and commentator for freestyle and Greco-Roman wrestling and Japanese Sumo events on cable and network television, including three Olympic Games. He addresses many of the Fortune 500 companies and shares the podium with athletes, politicians and entertainers. His message of overcoming the nearly insurmountable is inspiring, empowering and motivational.

5

Escape, Counter & Attack

Jeff Blatnick

The significant tournaments in wrestling are all held in the spring, but it's the harsh cold months of winter when wrestlers prove their devotion to the sport and their willingness to train. Although we endure running, technique drills, cauliflower ears, cutting weight and lifting weights all year long, the winter begins our long hours of actual combat on the mats, where preparation meets reality.

On January 23, 1980, I was practicing in Fargo, North Dakota, training with 1976 Olympian and World medalist, Brad Rheingans, when President Jimmy Carter announced the boycott of the 1980 Olympic Games scheduled to take place in Moscow eight months hence.

"What the...? Oh, no! It can't be! Why this? Not now, not me!" I thought.

Who was this distant politician to turn my life on its head? What right did he have to so impact our lives? And for what? The instant President Carter decided to mix politics and sport, he forced hundreds of devoted athletes like me to abandon their dreams. The boycott was a tremendous blow both to Brad and to me. Brad was the best Greco-Roman athlete in the country and was a shoo-in to win America's first-ever medal in Greco-Roman wrestling. His dream of Olympic achievement vanished with that boycott. He retired and I lost a training partner and a mentor.

Now, if there's one thing wrestling teaches you, it's *not* to be a victim—not to allow the other guy to determine what's going to happen. I had to find a way to stop the self-pity and to forge my own future out of the circumstances that were handed me.

It was only after I shed the idea that I was without options that I was able to discover my real power. I still had a healthy body and would very likely be around four years later. I just had to refocus my goals.

Growing up in Niskayuna, New York, I was the middle of three boys. I tried out for lots of sports with little success. In basketball, I wasn't even good enough to start and frequently found myself watching from the sidelines.

My older brother David introduced me to his shop teacher and the school's wrestling coach, Joseph Bena. After David tipped him off, the coach said, "Jeff, you can get splinters in your butt watching from the bench while others play hoops, or you can get some mat burns on your elbows and knees and be our heavyweight wrestler."

I showed up for practice the next day and quickly discovered I had found my passion. Coach Bena taught me all the moves in wrestling, and specifically how to score points with an *escape*, a *counter* (like a reversal) and the *attack*.

The first move necessary when facing a superior foe was to learn how to *escape* (survive); in the sport of wrestling this is worth one point. If I couldn't learn how to remove myself from the danger of being bent, twisted, extended, compressed, taken down and pinned, I would forever be unsuccessful—and that was not an option.

———❖———

Jeff, you can get splinters in your butt watching from the bench while others play hoops, or you can get some mat burns on your elbows and knees and be our heavyweight wrestler

———❖———

The second and more advanced stage was to learn how to *counter.* I had to keep my opponent at bay and, *at the same time,* put him on the defensive. Countermoves, like a reversal, are worth two points.

After I learned how to escape danger and to counter the existing circumstance by taking control, the real fun began! The next step was to *attack.* This is where the big points were earned. A good throw can be worth up to five points and if it leads to a pin, you've won the match.

These wrestling moves became a formula, simple and straightforward. Looking back, I used this same formula to deal with the emotional blow of the boycott. I *escaped* from self-pity, planned a *counter* to my circumstances and, finally, I *attacked* my task with all the enthusiasm of a Trojan gladiator heading into war (now you know why I like Greco-Roman wrestling). This formula would serve me well again when I faced the battles that lay ahead.

❖

My brother had brought me to my sport,
but he was taken away before he could see my success

❖

In my first year on the high school wrestling team, it seemed like my opponents' personalities ranged from master craftsman (those with skill and prowess) to those with a bad attitude who seemed to have a percentage deal with my dentist or physician.

Quickly growing in speed and strength, I flourished on the mat. Soon I was defeating people who had beaten me months earlier. I was improving and motivated. My brother David and his buddies started showing up at the gym whenever I had an important match and, if I did well, I heard them pounding their feet in unison on the bleachers, the sound echoing off the walls. Even after he joined the Air Force, David would come home on occasion and stomp on the bleachers with his pals.

In 1977, David was a passenger on a motorcycle that didn't negotiate a sharp turn and he was thrown. He died shortly thereafter. My brother had brought me to my sport, but he was taken away before he could see my success.

In the spring of 1982, I was in the best shape of my life, both physically and emotionally, working toward my goal of making the 1984 Olympic Team and winning a medal. Primed, focused and determined, I was defending National Champion when my world was again upended and slammed to the mat.

I found some bumps in my neck and, thinking they were from the stress of overtraining, I had them tested. The doctors said I had a lymphatic disorder known as Hodgkin's Disease.

Cancer.

Here I was, a 6'2" wrestler, stopped at the peak of my career by an almost invisible, yet frequently fatal disease. I felt I was no longer the master of my destiny; cancer was now in control. This was way more than a wrestling match. How in the world was I going to remain focused on winning an Olympic medal while I sparred with this unfamiliar opponent? My life had changed.

Gradually, the shock dissipated and I was able to regain a proper perspective. I *could* take action. My formula for success in wrestling could work in this arena as well. Escape, Counter, Attack!

THE ESCAPE!

As my world-class athletic instincts kicked in, I saw the cancer not as unbeatable, but as a worthy opponent. I was sick, no doubt about it, but I would not be reduced to the level of sparring partner to a greater foe. I hadn't given ten years of my life to wrestling just to give up because life threw a big obstacle in my path.

I escaped the role of victim, of self-pity, because *I* decided on the outcome. I would not lose.

THE COUNTER!

The countermove to cancer was a bit trickier. I knew I wanted to fight, I just didn't know how.

I found an oncologist whose professionalism and positive attitude helped replace my fear of the unknown with a battle plan. Our first move was to rid my body of as much of the enemy as possible.

I had major surgery to remove my spleen and began radiation treatments that lasted for more than a month. My strategy included a combination of diet and exercise. Too much work and my body would be too weak to fight off infections. Too little work and my dream of medaling in the Olympics would evaporate once again, possibly forever. There were risks associated with every course of treatment and, with the added stress of concerned family and friends, I had a situation filled with more anxiety than the Olympic finals!

It was clear to me that other people had a harder time with my situation than I did. Their fear of my failure (my death?) was far greater than mine. If I told them about my illness, I was treated like Jeff-with-cancer. If I held back the news, I was just treated like Jeff-the-wrestler. I decided to keep my problems to myself. Fear is restrictive and limiting. I had to think of myself as Jeff-the-wrestler.

THE ATTACK!

At the time, surgery and radiation were the recommended forms of treatment for Hodgkin's Disease. This combination killed the remaining cancer cells in my body. The treatment took precious time from my training schedule and it also weakened me and interrupted my life, but it was worth it for the possibility of a cure.

I attacked by taking control *inside* my mind.

———❖———

I escaped the role of victim, of self-pity, because I decided on the outcome

———❖———

I visualized the cancer being eradicated by the treatments. I thought of myself as a proud medieval knight looking to slay the cancer dragon. I began to see myself as strong and invincible. I was a general marshaling the forces of every blood cell in combat with each invading cell. If the doctors removed something during surgery, it had cancer. If my hair fell out, it had cancer. If I was constantly running to the toilet to vomit, well so be it, that had cancer too. Good riddance! There would be no mercy for the little invaders—no safe haven, no compromise.

The treatment worked. After six months of battling the disease, the doctors pronounced the cancer in remission. I could return to normal life and, for me, that meant wrestling.

What happens when we face such a dragon? Perhaps it takes the form of a pink slip, a lost sale, being passed over for a promotion, the breakup of a marriage. The tendency to feel like a victim is understandable, but we must never allow ourselves to give up. By figuring how to keep danger at bay (settle with creditors, check into rehab, undergo radical surgery), we must also reassert our control (schedule meetings, rewrite a resume, start prospecting all over again, go back to school). Finally, we'll see the day when we can once again attack our world with confidence and a workable strategy.

———❖———

There would be no mercy for the little invaders—no safe haven, no compromise

———❖———

With the cancer dragon slain, my next opponents became my fellow wrestlers. I returned to competition with a vengeance, only to suffer some embarrassing losses. I was thinking as I used to, training as I used to, approaching matches as I used to, but the results were anything *but* what I was used to.

Before the Hodgkin's, I had become accustomed to winning. It dawned on me that I had forgotten the fact that I was no longer in any *condition* to win. In the aftermath of the cancer, I had lost touch with the formula that had led me to the victories of so long ago and that had helped me face my last dragon. I would have to treat my Olympic quest in the same fashion that worked with the cancer…escape, counter and attack!

Again, I had to escape from that nemesis of self-pity. I found it isn't enough to survive cancer. To defeat cancer you must win at life. Unlike my brother David, I had received a second chance and it gave me an added sense of responsibility. I came to realize that I had been given an *opportunity*, when most people believed it was a bum hand. I regained perspective.

————❖————

I found it isn't enough to survive cancer. To defeat cancer you must win at life

————❖————

With eighteen months remaining to make the Olympic team, I was starting from ground zero. Many people told me I was in a "no-lose" situation. After all, cancer was the best excuse in the book. If I lost at the Olympic Trials it wasn't going to be my fault. Life had dealt poor Jeff Blatnick a bad hand. It was almost as if they were saying it was okay to feel like a victim. I thought to myself, "What planet were these people from?"

Just because I had cancer, it didn't diminish the investment I had already made in wrestling. From my perspective, I had trained half my life, endured one Olympic boycott, lived on less than $3,000 a year for eight years, made sacrifice after sacrifice and it was a *no-lose situation?* No, sir. Just as in my battle with cancer, I had too much at stake to give up the commitment I had made long ago....I would not be cancer's casualty, so I could not let cancer make a casualty of my Olympic aspirations.

I would *counter* my circumstances (lost matches, lost strength and lost training time) with complete and total dedication. I conducted an inventory of my strengths and needs and created a new battle plan. I watched videotapes and learned the moves to counter each opponent's efforts. If he were stronger, I would be faster. If he were more experienced, I would be better conditioned.

The entire scoring system in wrestling is based on the premise that the greater the risk that an athlete takes, the greater the points awarded (if successful). This premise doesn't just apply to sports. In life, just as in business or sports, we are defined by and rewarded for the risks we take. We can't advance without taking risks. The greater the risk, the greater the opportunity for reward.

So I went back to the beginning. I took risks. I went on the attack. I asked Brad to oversee my training and I moved back to the Midwest to train. Eighteen months later, I made the Olympic Team as the American Super-Heavyweight (100+ kilograms) and couldn't sleep for three days. I was pumped when I won the Trials because people would identify me as "Jeff-the-wrestler" again!

THE OLYMPICS IN LOS ANGELES

Becoming an Olympian in 1984 and having the chance to compete was nirvana for me. I lived in the athletes' village with the likes of Michael Jordan, Evander Holyfield, Mary Lou Retton, Carl Lewis and many more. I wore the national uniform and kids asked for my autograph.

My first match was against the Yugoslavian, Refic Memisevic, the 1982 World Champion. If I could defeat this pre-tourney favorite, I would be in the hunt for the gold. When Brad and I saw him smoking a cigarette outside the arena, we decided our strategy would be to outlast him and the tactic worked perfectly. I avoided his early attacks with speed and counters. By the second period, he was so tired that he stopped attacking altogether. When I attacked, dropping him to his back as he retreated, he was disqualified for passivity.

This win set the stage for the finals and my shot at the gold!

I would face Thomas Johansson of Sweden for the title. He was younger, stronger, heavier and (unbeknownst to me) later that week would test positive for steroid use.

Before my match, I sought out a quiet place to relax, and from my hidden alcove, I could watch the coaches and athletes move around the floor. I smiled when I noticed the Swede walk by, because he looked more nervous than I felt. Stepping from the shadows, I saw my family smile as they saw me coming. In an age-old ritual, my Dad said, "Get mad, son!" and I responded as I always had, "If you get mad, you get stupid." He patted my shoulder and I thought my family had given me all the encouragement possible, until, as I walked toward the mat, Mom whispered in my ear, "Do it for Dave."

Almost as if by magic, I felt grounded—centered in the knowledge that I was in control. I felt calm and at peace. And there was Brad, my mentor and friend, warming me up, keeping me loose, sitting in my corner during the match.

Once again, our strategy was simple: Let him run out of gas. Avoid his power early and wear him out. Keep him off-balance at all times and try to score late in the match. (You know: Escape, Counter, Attack!)

I was focused, intense and ready. I had my plan. The stage was set. The heralding trumpets sounded (no joke—the great movie composer, John Williams, wrote the score). I marched out of the backstage area to stand next to my opponent in the most important match of my life.

Then, at my big moment in front of the television cameras, just before I reached the mat, I tripped on a loose TV cable! I smiled as I thought, "Yes, ladies and gentlemen, I *am* an elite world class athlete!"

———❖———

I responded as I always had, 'If you get mad, you get stupid'

———❖———

I had to quickly refocus. The match seemed to move in slow motion. Every time he tried to turn me, I resisted. We were scoreless after the first three-minute round, and when the official warned him for passivity, I elected not to place the Swede on the mat below me, but kept him standing. I didn't want him to rest, I wanted to attack him.

With a minute left on the clock, I dove under his long arms and I threw the tiring Swede to the mat with a twisting bear hug. The score was 1-0. Thirty seconds later I attacked and scored again. When the referee raised my arm in victory, I fell to my knees and released the powerful emotions of eight years of hopes and dreams. Brad and I had finally earned our Olympic medal. The television cameras caught me in another defining moment...as the Olympic champion Greco-Roman Super-Heavyweight wrestler, I cried and cried and said, "I'm a happy dude!"

On August 2, 1984, I became the second American in history to win an Olympic medal in Greco-Roman wrestling and it was gold. I won 2-0, scoring both points in the last

Photo provided by Jeff Blatnick

minute of the match. I had come out a double winner with my victories over Thomas Johansson *and* cancer.

Perhaps it was just my imagination, but as I stepped up to receive my gold medal, amid the clapping and cheering of the partisan American crowd, I thought I heard the sound of feet pounding in unison on the bleachers, echoing off the walls.

JOHN NABER

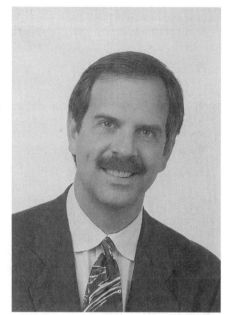

Photo provided by John Naber

At the 1976 Games in Montreal, John Naber became the most highly decorated member of the U.S. Olympic Team, winning four gold medals and one silver, setting four world records in the sport of swimming. In the process, he became the first swimmer in Olympic history to win two individual medals on the same day. In 1977, Naber won the James E. Sullivan Award as the nation's outstanding amateur athlete.

In 1984, he was inducted into the U.S. Olympic Committee Hall of Fame, just two days before he carried the Olympic torch, and later the Olympic flag into the Los Angeles Olympics Opening Ceremony.

Quickly moving into the broadcasting field, Naber worked for all the major networks and almost every cable channel covering his sport. In 1986, he began working as a play-by-play announcer covering sports as varied as motorcross, skiing, gymnastics, football, bowling and equestrian events. He has hosted coverage for more than thirty-four sports and for six Olympic Games, both Winter and Summer. He is a featured author in *The Power of Character* and is president of the U.S. Olympians, the alumni association comprised of more than 6,000 of America's Olympic athletes.

As a keen observer of excellence, he has discovered the method that champions in all walks of life use to reach their goals. He shares this "Gold Medal Process," along with other personal insights, with audiences all over the globe.

6

No Deposit, No Return

John Naber

I was enjoying a bottle of root beer from an ice-filled Styrofoam chest. When I pulled out the glass bottle, the label came off, but four words remained visible, words that taught me a life-changing lesson.

The words said simply, "No Deposit, No Return."

I'm certain the maker of that bottle was thinking something else, but as an impressionable 11-year-old, the words carried a lot of weight. I thought to myself, "To enjoy the flavor inside, I have to pay the price. I have to invest in my dreams if I want to see those dreams come true. What am I depositing," I asked, "in order to see my dreams come true? What price am I willing to pay?"

Every Olympian feels the same way. It is the act of paying the price "up-front," the willingness to invest in ourselves, the understanding that we have to feel tired to get stronger, that has allowed us to reach the medal platform. Some call it delayed gratification. I call it common sense.

In the course of my career (swimming ten miles a day, six days a week, eleven months a year), I have traveled the equivalent of twice around the planet's equator. Each winter morning I walked across an ice-covered cement deck, steam rising from the pool's surface, bleeding the top three inches of water of their treasured temperature. The first swimmer in the pool (usually me) was the "ice-breaker" who stirred up the water for the guys who followed. They often teased me about my eagerness because I sprinted the warm-up, crammed the "free-swim" periods with thousands of yards and was often the last one out of the pool.

Viewed from the perspective of a deposit or an investment, the long hours in a pool or weight room were no longer a punishment, sacrifice, penalty or even an inconvenience. The hours of training now seemed like an *investment* in my future.

At an Olympic fund-raising event, I had the chance to meet one of America's top speed skaters, Sheila Young, after her three-medal performance in 1976, and she gave me my first evidence of how an Olympian thinks.

"I remember how glad I was that I had worked hard enough over the last five years, so that I wouldn't have to stand *there*," she said as she pointed to the floor beside her, where the silver medal platform would have been.

-------❖-------

The hours of training now seemed like an investment in my future.
You can't cram for the Olympics during the three weeks prior to the
Opening Ceremony the way you study for a college midterm

-------❖-------

The Olympian views each day of practice, each party unattended, each distraction withstood or temptation resisted as a part of the price gladly paid to experience that wonderful feeling when the national anthem is played. The Olympics require a concrete investment of effort *prior* to the actual competition. You can't cram for the Olympics during the three weeks prior to the Opening Ceremony the way you study for a college midterm, any more than you can rescue a business relationship after months of neglect with one quick phone call.

The understanding that the prize must be paid for in advance includes the realization that for the prize to mean anything, it must be earned *fairly*. To win a race, I must follow the rules and compete honorably against the competition. One of life's greatest lessons is one that should still be taught in the athletic arena: The lesson of character.

As I write this, a trial is underway in Germany to determine an appropriate penalty for the coaches who administered performance-enhancing drugs to members of former East German Olympic teams. It seems that these coaches forced young women to take massive doses of steroids and other drugs, which produced remarkable athletic results at the Olympic level. But the consequences were equally remarkable: unwanted body hair, physical deformities and the inability to have children.

If winning is *all* that matters, then cheating becomes an option. I've heard it said that if we're unwilling to lose, we had better be willing to do *anything* to win. At the time of their victories, the German athletes appeared pleased with their Olympic successes, but their gold medals are tarnished and their internal suspicions and eventual exposure have robbed them of the pleasure of winning fairly.

No one honestly thinks cheating is right, but they want to win so badly that they'll try to justify their actions. Eventually the truth will surface, just as it did in Seoul in the case of Ben Johnson, the Canadian sprinter and, when it does, there's no putting that genie back in the bottle.

Even an unselfish gesture can backfire, as was the case in February 1998 when the coaches of two basketball teams agreed to allow Nykesha Sales, an injured senior from the University of Connecticut to limp off the bench to score an uncontested basket so that she could break her school's scoring record. Afterward, she admitted, "I think it would have been better if I was actually playing," thereby telling the world how unfulfilling that basket (and that record) actually was.

------❖------

If winning is all that matters, then cheating becomes an option

------❖------

Our willingness to invest in our dreams is inevitably related to our confidence that the dreams are actually attainable. It's hard to bet confidently on a long shot, but once we feel the *possibility* of success, the work involved is more easily produced.

My folks were supportive, but not pushy, parents. Instead of attending every meet, shouting for his son's victory, Dad chose a more valuable method of encouragement. Before the existence of computerized spreadsheets, he created a personal "best times chart." The column headings listed the various events in the sport (100 back, 200 back, 200 free, etc.) and the rows down the page were labeled by the meets I attended. After each contest, we would enter that day's results in the corresponding boxes and, whenever the time was a personal best, we would circle the number with a brightly colored felt-tipped pen. Gradually, the page filled with numbers and circles and I began to see a trend in the right direction, even though my resulting times were not spectacular. A sixth-place ribbon was no cause for disappointment because I was, instead, focusing on the progress.

My faith in my ability to improve led to an increase in my willingness to set personal goals. As a senior in high school, I could look at past Olympic results and estimate how fast the current world record holder (an East German named Roland Matthes) might be able to go at the next Olympics. I extrapolated his gold medal performances from 1968 and 1972 and decided that by 1976, he'd be able to swim my event in approximately 55.5 seconds. That allowed me to shoot for a specific time, rather than to focus on an intimidating champion.

————❖————

$1/1,200$th of a second was less than the blink of an eye

————❖————

At the time, I was covering the distance in just under a minute—59.5 seconds, to be precise. I had to drop four seconds, which amounted to one second a year or one-tenth of a second per month or $1/300$th of a second per day or $1/1,200$th of a second for each hour of training. Four seconds seemed huge, but $1/1,200$th of a second was less than the blink of an eye. I can do that, I thought. "If I can keep up this level of improvement for three years, I'll be breaking world records by then," I said to myself.

Is it *ever* realistic for an 11-year-old to imagine him or herself as an Olympic champion? Probably not, because the possibility of becoming an Olympic champion certainly isn't likely. More Americans buy lottery tickets that eventually win million-dollar jackpots than Americans who win gold medals in Olympic competition. But I didn't have to be realistic to be *optimistic*.

To awaken the Olympian in each of us, we have to look at negative evidence as *temporary*. Just because I can't swim the 100 meters in less than a minute doesn't mean I'll *never* do so. Just because this job seems beyond me now doesn't mean it always will be.

A wealthy socialite saw a man carrying a cello on the streets of New York and asked him if he knew how to get to Carnegie Hall. She heard the following reply, "Practice, lady, practice."

Peter Daland, my head coach at USC, conducted regular team meetings before each workout, and I can still recall his admonition to the incoming freshmen: "Gentlemen," he said, "the secret to swimming is not how far you swim and it's not how hard you swim. The secret to swimming is how *far* you're willing to swim *hard*." It's the combination of quality and quantity that determines our results.

As a result, every day at the end of workout, he gave us "speed sets," which required short bursts of energy, usually with ample (but not generous, etc.) rest in between. It was important to go fast, but also to see what the pace felt like when we were actually tired. That way, speed and fatigue could coexist, and the pain we felt toward the end of a race would not be so debilitating. We learned to expect the pain and learned how to deal with it.

The wise coach never says, "Practice makes perfect." What he actually says is, "Practice makes permanent. Only perfect practice makes perfect."

———❖———

More Americans buy lottery tickets that eventually win million-dollar jackpots than Americans who win gold medals in Olympic competition

———❖———

I've worked on six Olympic broadcasts as a television announcer and each time the viewers remember our stories of determination—where Olympians had reasons for giving up, but never did. Dan Jansen's career was plagued with bad luck. Greg Louganis cut his scalp when his head hit the diving board. Dan O'Brien "no-heighted" in the pole vault, knocking himself off the Olympic team when he had been a virtual "lock" to win the gold medal a month later. Kerri Strug had injured her ankle when her team needed her to vault once more.

I often refer to legendary Olympic heroes, such as the Hungarian army sharpshooter, Sgt. Karoly Takacs, who lost his shooting hand in 1938 when a hand grenade exploded prematurely. He trained himself to shoot with his other hand and won two gold medals. Or the swimmer, Jeff Farrell, who qualified to be a member of the 1960 Olympic Team just six days *after* undergoing surgery for a ruptured appendix. Or Silken Laumann from Canada whose doctor recommended the amputation of her leg after a rowing accident, three months *before* she earned a bronze medal in Barcelona. These athletes may not have been rational or realistic, but they are champions.

What do these Olympians share in common besides their medals? They share an undying faith in the eventual positive outcome and an unwillingness to give up.

Winston Churchill, Great Britain's prime minister during the Second World War, was invited to speak at an American university's commencement exercises, where he delivered perhaps his most oft-quoted speech.

He began, "Never give in, never give in, never, never, never, never— in nothing, great or small, large or petty—never give in except to convictions of honor and good sense." And then he sat down.

The final step of an Olympian's dream always includes a dose of what I call "performance under pressure"—the ability to deliver the goods when it actually matters most.

In 1988 and again in 1992, the United States entered backstrokers in the Olympic Games (David Berkoff and Jeff Rouse, respectively) who were capable of winning the gold. In each case the swimmer left the Olympic Games having broken the world record, but on both occasions the swimmer went home with the silver medal. David broke the world mark in a preliminary heat and Jeff broke the record, leading off the country's Medley Relay the day *following* his individual event. At the time of the actual championship races, however, their performances were not up to their capabilities, and others won the gold medals.

My summer coach, Mike Hastings, would often remind me that I didn't have to deliver 200 percent or swim twice as fast as ever before. In fact, I didn't have to do anything differently. I only had to do the job I had been training to do and try for a personal best time.

At the 1976 Olympics in Montreal, the 100-meter backstroke event featured a heat, a semi-final and the championship race. I had broken the world record in the semi- and was seeded in the center lane. On my left was the defending champion from East Germany, Roland Matthes, who had not lost a backstroke final in the last two Olympics, earning four gold medals. On my right was Peter Rocca, my American teammate who finished ¹/₁₀₀th of a second behind me in the most recent NCAA Championships.

Though each was capable of a great swim, I was confident that I could win if I just performed to my potential.

We hopped into the water and it felt colder than expected, droplets running easily off my shaved arms and chest. The buzz of the crowd slowly diminished when the starter called us to our positions: feet on the wall; back to the pool; arms extended grasping the starting blocks.

My start had always been a powerful part of my race. I practiced the start, jumping backward through the air, arching my back and diving into the pool hands first instead of plowing through the water like a boat being launched at dry dock. At 6'6", when I powered my way through the air before slicing into the water, I almost always came up a few feet ahead of the field.

According to the rules, each swimmer was allowed two false starts that would be charged to the field, but I had never seen anyone false-start in the backstroke before. It's hard to slip when you're hanging on to a metal bar.

"Take your marks!" the official's voice echoed throughout the indoor arena.

I folded my body into a tight little tuck, coiling like a spring in anticipation of the gun. Out of the corner of my eye, I saw Roland begin moving an instant *before* the gun sounded. "He's jumped," I thought, and calmly waited in position for the official to call back the field.

Silence.

For what seemed like an eternity, I was left alone, hanging on the wall, as the rest of the field splashed into the water. Eventually, I heard the retort of the false-start pistol and the race was stopped.

———❖———

I saw him suppress a crafty little smile. He did it on purpose!

———❖———

I was in shock. I realized that I had almost single-handedly thrown the race into the trash by stupidly assuming the official had seen what I saw. Glancing at Roland when he resumed his position on the wall, I saw him suppress a crafty little smile. He did it on purpose!

When he repeated his trick a second time, I went with him at the gun and the officials stopped our race once again.

Never before had I *seen* a backstroke false start and now in the most important race of my life there had been two. If it happened again, someone would be disqualified so I would have to play it safe.

An often overlooked advantage of "No Deposit, No Return" is the reassuring effect of knowing the price has been paid. I had ultimate confidence that the prior two false starts had not exhausted me and had not lessened my potential. Even with my most powerful tool (my quick start) diminished, I knew that it didn't matter. Just swim the race the way you've trained, I thought.

Bang! went the gun and off we leapt, flying backward over the water. Magically, when I pulled and kicked myself to the surface I could no longer hear the crowd. In fact, I couldn't even see the swimmers on either side. I felt as if I were looking through a tube, ignoring everything that was happening outside my lane. I focused on the starting block, swimming away in a straight line from where the race had begun. With each pull, each rotation of my arms, I moved across the water like a rowing shell slipping across the Thames.

Midway through the race, as the water roared past my ears, the backstroke turn flags flew across my line of sight and I counted my regular three strokes to the wall. Initiating my turn, I threw my body into a spin, ricocheting off the wall. Some swimmers stop, turn around and push off the wall, but I thought of myself as a rubber ball bouncing off the turn, changing direction but maintaining speed.

———❖———

I moved across the water like a rowing shell slipping across the Thames

———❖———

As I began the final lap of the race, I could see the challengers swimming at my feet behind me. Not a time to get cocky, I returned my concentration to my kick, pull and recovery.

When tired, a swimmer's technique begins to suffer. The only way my arms would maintain their form was if I thought of myself as arm-wrestling with each handful of water, across the length of the pool. Thanks to the prior "perfect practice," every pull was precise and powerful, each kick fully functional. No wasted breath, no wasted motion.

I lunged at the wall, stopping the clock with a hard touch. The crowd's cheers had been building in volume as I approached the finish, but when I struck the electronic touch pad, they let loose with a burst of applause and their cheers washed over me like the wake that followed me into the finish.

Rocca touched next followed by Matthes in third. The timing system registered a new world record, 55.49, almost exactly what I had privately predicted almost four years earlier.

———❖———

Their cheers washed over me like the wake that followed me into the finish

———❖———

When I looked into the crowd, I saw Coach Daland, Coach Hastings, my parents and thousands of others, all thrilled to have seen me reveal the fruits of my years of labor.

Photo provided by John Naber

I often try to describe the thrill of receiving an Olympic gold medal, but I can't do the moment justice without recalling the months and sometimes years of effort that went into its achievement. To paraphrase Tom Hanks' baseball manager's character from the movie, "A League of Their Own"—"The *hard* is what makes it great."

DICK FOSBURY

Photo courtesy of Sydney Conger

The name Fosbury is synonymous with the high jump because Dick Fosbury was the man who innovated one of the most radical changes in the sport. He introduced the world to his "Fosbury Flop" on his way to winning the 1968 Olympic gold medal, setting new American and Olympic records. His technique is now the global standard in the event. He also demonstrated his control over his mind when pressure was greatest, with his "psyche-up" and concentration techniques.

The French magazine, *L'Equipe*, lists Fosbury as one of the top 100 athletes of the 20th century. He was inducted into the U.S. Olympic Committee Hall of Fame and he is currently serving as the General Secretary of the World Association of Olympic Winners.

Professionally, he is the co-founder and president of Galena Engineering, Inc., a civil engineering and land surveying company that specializes in land development and public works projects in the Sun Valley, Idaho area. He is a licensed civil engineer and land surveyor, and has served as the city engineer of Ketchum and Sun Valley, Idaho, and is the chairman of the Ketchum Area Rapid Transit Board.

Dick Fosbury shares insights from his athletic and business experiences when speaking to business groups, coaches and athletes about innovation, success and hard work. He has worked with many of the Fortune 500 companies in their marketing efforts and is active with both the National and International Special Olympics.

7

Maybe You're Right & Everyone Else Is Wrong

Dick Fosbury

In the 1950s I discovered my sporting love—while trespassing. As a 10-year-old school kid in Medford, Oregon, I walked home past the local junior high school, where some track and field equipment had been left out overnight. I hopped the fence with a buddy and we ran the hurdles and high-jumped into the sawdust pit over and over again. I can still recall the delight of competing against my imaginary opponents without having to follow any rules.

That experience led me to join the local track team, where I learned how to high jump. I was taught both forms of jumping—the straddle and the scissors.

In the straddle style, the athlete rolls over the bar, face down, like a cowboy throwing his leg over a saddle, with the hips crossing the bar at the same height as the head.

In the scissors version, the athlete runs and jumps across the bar with the torso in the vertical position, alternating each leg as it comes up, almost like pedaling a bicycle as he drifts sideways across the bar. Done correctly, the legs look like a pair of scissors, snapping together and opening again. With the body position erect, the head travels much higher than the hips.

When I started out with the straddle, the target was below my shoulders and I felt awkward, jumping down at the bar. I felt much more comfortable, more "springy," running at the bar and jumping with my body upright. Yet the thinking at that time was that the straddle offered more potential.

I discovered my sporting love—while trespassing

In high school, Coach Dean Benson took a look at the new sophomore athletes coming out to join the veterans. When he reached the high jump pit he watched me take a couple of tries with the scissors technique and asked if I was just playing around. I told him I'd always felt more comfortable with the scissors and that I had been using it since grade school. He explained that the scissors may have been okay then, but now it was time to work on the straddle technique "like all the best jumpers." We had a couple of weeks before the first meet, so I worked on the straddle every day.

In the first big meet of the season, about twenty different schools were competing. Our opening height was 5'0" and my personal best was 5'4" but with the new straddle technique, I missed three times and was out of the meet at the opening height. I had *never* done that since I was 10 years old!

Even so, I continued to follow my coach's advice and instructions for the entire year. I felt I was uncoachable and, at 6'4" and 165 pounds, I was too tall and uncoordinated—or so I thought. At the end of the season with two meets left, I expressed my frustration, and Coach Benson sympathized but encouraged me to stick with it. I asked him if I could return to my scissors in a meet, for the sake of my confidence level. Reluctantly, he agreed, but suggested that I not give up entirely on the straddle.

The next competition was the Grants Pass Rotary Meet, an invitational with top athletes from around southern Oregon. I decided to give the scissors a go. I jumped 5'4", my old record, and felt very good. Now, facing a new personal record height of 5'6", I knew I had to do something more. As I faced the bar, I knew my weakness with this technique was knocking the bar off with my butt. If I could just lift my hips a little, I might make it. I concentrated on lifting my hips and leaning back a bit on the jump and I cleared the bar. Next height —5'8"—I tried the same thing, only more so. As I lifted my hips to clear the bar, my upper body reacted by laying my shoulders back. I cleared 5'8" to everyone's surprise and even the coaches took notice. As they raised the bar to 5'10", I realized I was competing with the good jumpers and could contend for a place and some points.

I missed twice at 5'10" but on my last try I did the same movement with even more intensity and made it. I had bettered my best height by half-a-foot! By this time the other schools' coaches were pulling out the rule book to see if what I was doing was a legal technique, since it was certainly not usual. They found no rule to disqualify me, so they just had to watch.

I placed third and finally felt redeemed. I went out at 6'0" with a smile on my face. The coach spoke to me on the bus ride home, saying he had seen a couple of jumps and was pleased and, oh-by-the-way, could I meet him before practice the following Monday?

On Monday, Coach said that he couldn't figure out what I was trying to do. How would I like to watch some films of other jumpers' techniques? We went into the film room to check out his old movies and these super-eight film strips showed a variety of styles, each with a common denominator...all the jumpers crossed the bar on their stomachs or on their sides. He was trying to allow me to maintain my individualism, but also tempt me away from the scissors with anything that could eventually be a transition back to the straddle.

I was quite amazed at some of the contorted styles that I had never known existed. After studying the styles, I picked out a couple that looked interesting. It was a good way to break up the routine of practice drills. I had fun trying them out, but I never quite felt as comfortable as I did doing my own thing.

I jumped the following Saturday in the District Meet and repeated the laid-back scissors technique, jumping 5'10". I didn't place because I was competing against a superior level of athlete, but I proved to myself that I had discovered something that was mine to work on and improve. That was key. I began to trust my instincts when it came to jumping. Within each of us lies a form, a talent or a gift that we can develop if we just pay attention.

My style continued to evolve slowly over the next two years. Earlier I had learned to run my approach in a slight "banana" curve, first heading toward the bar and gradually turning and running parallel to it. I began to lead more with my shoulder on the takeoff. With my new technique I was, as a junior, able to break the high school record of 6'3". As a senior, I was jumping 6'5-1/2" and had developed the "flop" technique—going over head first, with my back to the bar, arched, lifting my hips and kicking my feet clear at the last moment. It was not as though I set out to make up a new style or form of jumping. Instead, I found it while solving my problem.

When I showed up for my first practice at Oregon State University, Coach Berny Wagner watched me jump and invited me to his office for a talk. He told me he had coached a couple of "near seven-footers" and he thought I had potential, but might need to work on that style I was using. In fact, he told me he could teach me to straddle to reach my true potential! I didn't object at the time since he had the credentials and I was just a green freshman. I trusted him.

------❖------

Within each of us lies a form, a talent or a gift that we can develop, if we just pay attention

------❖------

The deal we struck was that I would "flop" on the weekends during meets to maintain my confidence and score points, but all week long I would practice with the straddle. Eventually, he felt, I would catch up with the other straddlers and make the transition.

I was an obedient, willing student but, unfortunately, my skills were just not suited to that technique. I worked on the straddle style for the next year-and-a-half, not coming within 6″ of my personal best and not improving in the flop (I was jumping 6′6″ to 6′6-3/4″—all year long).

During spring break in 1967, the varsity team went to California for a couple of meets. I was excited to be out of school, out of the Oregon rain, and I felt great. I don't know whether it was the California sunshine, but *Pow!* I jumped a personal record of 6′10-1/4″ and in the process, broke the school record.

After the meet, Coach took me aside and told me we had a *new* plan, no more straddle for me and from now on he would watch, film and analyze my technique to help me develop into the best "flop-jumper" I could be. He converted to this new religion and from that day forward neither of us ever looked back. Two years after I had first discovered the new style of high-jumping, I had been given the green light to develop the technique fully. That suited me fine.

It seemed that my patience and devotion to the style finally paid off, because now I had persuaded the experts that I was on to something. I had enough faith in my discovery to know that eventually it would pay off. I didn't try it to be different, I tried it because it worked!

Even successful coaches (or bosses) can learn from their students (or employees) by providing a healthy environment in which they can share thoughts and ideas and eventually develop their full potential.

———❖———

He converted to this new religion and from that day forward neither of us ever looked back

———❖———

In my mind, I began to imagine what worked during a successful attempt and to recall what it *felt* like. By practicing the skill in my mind, it just seemed to happen more naturally in real life. Under stress, I used this mental technique to keep my focus on the goal, to remain calm while the storm of competition raged all around—and it seemed to help my results. I added it to my routine immediately before taking each jump.

While I was confident in my technique, I could not rely solely on my unorthodox style. I began weight-training in combination with plyometrics (bounding exercises). I was gradually changing into a higher class of athlete so that by the NCAA Championships in 1967, I went from being in the top fifty in the country to finishing fourth. I was building a foundation of skills that would enable me to compete against the best in the world. Practice and preparation created the confidence I needed to be the best I could be.

THE "FOSBURY FLOP"

In 1964, the *The Medford Mail-Tribune* showed a picture of me clearing the bar with the headline "Fosbury Flops Over the Bar." I liked the irony because the word *flop* connotes failure. The flop motion is similar to what a fish does when it lands in the boat. To the naive, that headline could have been taken as derogatory.

By January 1968, when the journalists were asking me what name I gave to my unorthodox style, I said, "I don't know what to call it, but back home they called it the 'Fosbury Flop.'" The name stuck.

At the NCAA Championships of the Olympic year, I cleared 7'2-1/4", establishing a new NCAA record. The crowd laughed at first, but cheered when I won. I began receiving invitations to compete at other meets around the country. I think they just wanted to see me "flop."

THE OLYMPIC GAMES

At the Olympic Trials in South Lake Tahoe, I noticed that many jumpers were curious about my style but were reluctant to attempt it because they had invested up to twelve years perfecting their straddle techniques. At that point, the top jumpers wanted to reduce their risks, not increase them.

Three jumpers qualified at 7'3" and it was a personal record for all three of us. I qualified behind a 1964 Olympic veteran, Ed Caruthers, and a 17-year-old high school phenomenon, Reynaldo Brown. The "flop" made the team.

Mexico City was the site of the XIX Olympiad. Twelve jumpers qualified to advance to the finals, which were held on the last day of track and field.

By this time most of America's heroics had already played out at the track. Those Olympic Games have gone down in history as one of the greatest track and field meets of all time, and that American team is considered by many as the best our country has ever assembled. Bob Beamon made his "leap into the 21st century," Lee Evans shattered the world record in the 400, Al Oerter captured his fourth consecutive discus gold medal, and Jimmy Hines was the first Olympian to finish under 10.0 in the 100. Real excitement existed at the track, to say the least.

———❖———

I could hear them laughing whenever I took a practice jump

———❖———

On Sunday, at around 1 p.m. the twelve jumpers made their way to the infield to begin warm-ups. It was a classic fall day, with a clear sky and the temperature in the mid-seventies. The crowd was eager to enjoy the afternoon and I could hear them laughing whenever I took a practice jump. Most track and field meets are like a three-ring circus, with many events taking place simultaneously (the marathon, the 4 x 400-meter relays, announcements, award ceremonies, etc.). I noticed that in spite of the other events, whenever I stood on the apron, scattered conversations would subside, people elbowed each other and pointed toward me, as if to say, "Hey, check this out."

I was to jump fifth and my main competitors, Valentin Gavrilov from the Soviet Union and American Ed Caruthers, had the last two spots— eleventh and twelfth, respectively. The Olympic record was 7'1-3/4" set in 1964 by my hero, Valery Brumel from the Soviet Union.

The opening height was set at 6'8". At the lowest height, I just sailed across the bar and the laughter that followed my jump was very loud as the spectators wondered at this *"loco"* American. With each successive jump, the laughter abated and the cheering began to grow. I cleared 6'8", 6'10-1/4", 7' 1/4", 7'1-3/4", 7'2-1/2" without a miss. They actually enjoyed seeing the flopper do well.

Ed and I, the two Americans, and Valentin, the Russian, all cleared 7'2-1/2", which bettered my hero's Olympic record. The crowd was watching a spectacular contest—and they knew it.

At 7'3-1/4", I cleared on my first jump, Ed on his second, and Valentin missed his third attempt. At 7' 4-1/4" it was just Caruthers and me, going for the gold.

By this time, the afternoon shadows were beginning to reach the outside of the track and the air had cooled a little. It was almost five o'clock, and the entire stadium was silent before my first attempt at 7'4-1/4". It was as if we were at a funeral. When I realized that the spectators were looking at me, I used that attention to draw inside myself and focus. They drifted off into the background.

I made a good run to the bar, veered off and launched into the air. My body cleared the bar, but it caught on my heel. The crowd let out a collective gasp, but I felt good about the attempt because it proved that I actually could get that far off the ground. The spotlight now focused directly on Ed. He made a great first attempt, but the bar fell down.

❖

The entire stadium was silent, as if we were at a funeral

❖

On my second try, I went through my normal mental process, rocking back and forth, visualizing what I was going to do. I ran at the bar and missed again. Caruthers' second attempt was similar to his first and just as before, the bar fell to the pit.

On my final attempt, I realized the seriousness of my position. I hadn't missed once at any other height, but now I was looking at my last chance. It wasn't just me on the line, the flop style also was being watched around the globe. If I failed, everyone might say it was because I was foolish enough to try something that could not ultimately work.

The stadium was absolutely silent…with all eyes on the high jump. The quiet was eerie, but I was totally focused and took nearly my full two minutes. I ran at the bar, threw my body into the air and watched as the bar glided beneath me. Looking up from the pit, I saw it was clean. The crowd erupted in *"Ole's!"* and I bounced out of the pit, arms raised.

Photo courtesy of Track & Field News

Coincidentally, Kenny Moore (another Oregonian and an Olympian who would later write for *Sports Illustrated*) entered the stadium at the end of his marathon, noticed the crowd's celebration and looked up at the scoreboard to see that I had cleared 7'4-1/4" (new American and Olympic records). He began to dance a jig down the straightaway after having run twenty-six miles. His reaction told me how exceptional the jump was. I smiled at him and we both began to celebrate.

Ed Caruthers still had to complete his final attempt and I knew that he had the ability to make this height. I had to return to the contest and mentally prepare myself for the chance that I'd be called to jump again.

———❖———

Kenny Moore entered the stadium at the end of his marathon,
noticed the crowd's celebration and began to dance a jig down the straightaway

———❖———

Ed ran at the bar and took off. He had the height, but came down too soon, rattling the bar. The crowd sighed for him and realized that the championship had been determined by his miss. Their attention turned to me and they began to applaud. The gold medal was mine.

The flop had won the gold and established the new Olympic mark. Subsequently, by 1980, thirteen of the top sixteen jumpers in the world were using the "Fosbury Flop."

Perhaps you're frustrated with some policy or requirement at work that prevents you from reaching your full potential. Perhaps someone who works for you wants to "draw outside the lines" on occasion. To awaken the Olympian within, we have to look at what works now, not just at what's worked in the past.

By having openminded coaches and by focusing on what worked for me, I was able to add an innovation to the sport that has eventually pushed the world record to more than eight feet.

That's how you make a winner out of a "flop."

SINJIN SMITH

Photo courtesy of Leanne Robinson

Christopher St. John "Sinjin" Smith is a dominating force on the Pro Beach Volleyball Tour where he has claimed twelve World Championship crowns and was the all-time winner with more than 130 victories. With partner Randy Stoklos, they had won more games and prize money than any other team in the sport. It's no wonder his nickname on the tour is "King of the Beach."

He has served his sport as president of the Assn. of Volleyball Professionals (AVP), as player's commissioner for the Federation of International Volleyball (FIVB), and president of the FIVB Beach Volleyball World Council. He was instrumental in getting beach volleyball accepted as a medal sport in the 1996 Centennial Olympic Games, where he and Carl Henkel represented the United States at those Games in Atlanta. It was a remarkable achievement for a 39-year-old.

He is a part owner of Sideout Sports, a popular apparel company, and his All-American good looks have led to opportunities in modeling, television and feature film roles, as well appearances in national publications, including *Rolling Stone* magazine and as one of *People* magazine's Fifty Most Beautiful People.

He authored *King of the Beach*, an historical account of the evolution of his sport. Sinjin is still competing on the World Tour and he also serves as an expert analyst for his sport, commentating on ABC, ESPN and Turner Broadcasting.

8

Seize the Opportunity

Sinjin Smith

I told my wife, Patty, that I had to go to work, gave her a kiss on the cheek and drove the thirty-minute commute to Hermosa Beach. Parking is always difficult on weekends, but my pass allowed me easy access, right below the grandstands. I slipped into my Speedo shorts, sandals and sunglasses, and made my way toward the sound of the public address announcer, who was blaring the names of the Federation of International Volleyball World Tour sponsors. Their names were plastered on banners that surrounded center court: Budweiser, Coppertone, Reebok, Mikasa, Ford, BodyGlove and ESPN. These were my customers and this was my office.

It sounds like an idyllic career, right? Lots of sunshine, funding sources, and drinking water in abundance; casual Friday every day; tanned women in skimpy bikinis and lots of fresh air to boot. Well, when I first visited this same beach, twenty-three years earlier, I witnessed the same tournament, the same weather and the same excellent level of play, but not a single sponsorship banner was in view. Not one.

Since then, I've grown proud of how the sport has flourished, both in revenue and exposure (I am, after all, a professional volleyball player). But my greatest memories in the sport revolve around the moments that I played for free.

When I was growing up in the 1960s, beach volleyball (two men to a side) was a sport for amateur enthusiasts. There was no significant prize money or publicity. The tournaments were confined to Southern California. The athletes playing the game all came out of the beach communities—from San Diego to Santa Cruz.

Back then, names like Gene Selznich, Ron von Hagen and Ron Lang were much bigger than life. In my eyes they were superstars who never missed a block or a serve, could jump to the moon, and always smiled for the crowd. They were cool and clean-cut at the same time, and they were playing within arm's reach. I would sit by the court for hours watching them play, and I'd run after their loose balls all day long—just for the privilege of handing them back.

———❖———

My greatest memories in the sport revolve around the moments that I played for free

———❖———

As big as the stars were to me, they virtually played for tips. Those who competed beyond their college years were considered "beach bums." They got part-time jobs waiting tables at night so they could play beach volleyball all day, every day. If you want something enough, you'll find a way.

Players' careers would only last about four or five years because they would eventually have to support their families with full-time jobs but, in the meantime, they seemed to be having fun.

I'm certain my parents thought my attraction to the game was a phase I'd grow out of. All members of the Smith family were avid athletes, but they hoped I'd find a real job in the real world where I could make some real money and support a real family. None of this mattered to me because all I wanted to do was play volleyball. I was too young to be concerned about those grown-up problems.

My first organized competition in indoor volleyball (six on a side) came in high school. The sport was in its infancy and the school could only afford a volunteer coach. I was barely able to spike the ball over the net, but this didn't stop me from wanting to play and improve. I'd run and jump in the sand, developing the muscles and skills I'd need later on.

Through a combination of training, discipline and devotion to the sport, I became stronger, able to jump higher and hit the ball harder. Three years later, I turned down scholarship offers elsewhere, just to "walk-on" to UCLA where many of my beach volleyball heroes (like Jim Menges, Greg Lee, Tom Chamales and Ron von Hagen) had been students.

Playing well and playing with other good players are what mattered to me, not the financial reward of a scholarship. Together, under UCLA

Coach Al Scates (a perennial NCAA contender), the Bruins and I developed our game to the point where we were able to win the National Title in 1976 and 1979. Lest you think it was all my doing, Al Scates has coached teams to seventeen National Titles since 1963. There was no better coach.

During summer, I always returned to the birthplace of my fascination with volleyball, the beach.

In the late 1970s, there were only eight tournaments on the calendar and winners at these events earned a free dinner, plus an occasional six-pack of beer. A win in the "Grand Finale" at the end of the season was worth a meager $1,000. But since college-eligible athletes couldn't take the money anyway, I played for the love of the game. I was still young and looking forward to my sophomore year in college and I didn't need much in the way of financial help. After all, I thought I might be able to survive for at least three or four more years if I found work in a restaurant at night (just like the "beach bums" who came before me).

―――❖―――

*Playing well or playing with other good players is what mattered to me,
not the financial reward of a scholarship*

―――❖―――

When my scholarship kicked in during my sophomore year, I had my expenses covered so I could devote myself fully to earning an economics degree and practicing volleyball.

At the time, beach volleyball was pretty much of a "cult sport," but as a young 19-year-old newcomer, playing on center court was everything I thought it should be: large crowds of loud and enthusiastic supporters, the excitement of competition and the thrill of victory. We often drove overnight to get to the events, slept on a friend's floor or in the car, all for the sake of competing for a trophy. I had discovered my true calling.

In 1980, USA Volleyball decided to move its National Training Center from Dayton, Ohio to San Diego, which is one of the most beautiful places in the world—if you happen to dig the beach. I could train for both indoor and beach volleyball.

As an elite member of the USA National Indoor Team, it was hard to concentrate just on the indoor game with the beach so nearby. After practicing for four to five hours in the gym, I would sneak away to play a few more hours on the beach with U.S. teammate Karch Kiraly. My mentor, Ron von Hagen, often said the only way to play *good* beach volleyball was to play *lots* of beach volleyball.

Later, we'd return to the Training Center and lift weights for a few hours as part of the National Team. This "double duty" was very demanding physically, but I needed my beach game to stay sane. By enjoying something this much, I didn't even think about how hard I was working. It was "volleyball until you drop!"

------❖------

We often drove overnight to get to the events, slept on a friend's floor or in the car, all for the sake of competing for a trophy

------❖------

Along with my various partners such as Karch, von Hagen, Mike Normand, Jim Menges and Randy Stoklos, I was successful right away, winning early and often. Money was not necessary; I played for an elusive feeling of excellence, something many athletes refer to as "the zone." Basketball players refer to the feeling as when the ball seems smaller and the hoop seems to grow. Golfers say the cup gets bigger and the ball seems to have eyes. In football, ball carriers say the linemen slow down and holes appear as if by magic. Baseball players claim to see the seams on a fastball.

The "nirvana" of beach volleyball came to me at a tournament in Boulder, Colorado. I was paired with Stoklos, and we were playing against Karch and Kent Steffes. We all had trained in equal measure and were in top condition, but for some reason, the "volleyball gods" smiled on our team that day, because we found ourselves in "the zone."

On the sand, it seemed as if everything were moving in slow motion. The ball seemed slower on defense and faster on offense, the net seemed lower, and my jumps provided more than enough "hang-time." While in the air, I not only could see the ball, but I could also see the blocker and the defensive player at the same time. Wherever I hit the ball seemed to be the one place they couldn't reach. It was magical and we easily controlled the game.

A frustrating thing about sports is that in spite of the training or preparation, reaching that "zone" is not always possible. Just as a golfer can't easily repeat a hole-in-one, that feeling of perfection does not appear on command, but that's reason enough to play again. The desire to experience that feeling is what awakens the Olympian within. If you want something enough, you'll find a way.

It was my love of the game, this "passion to play," like someone's devotion to a hobby, that prompted me to find ways to make playing the sport affordable. A few years later, I was able to see the game grow in dramatic ways, providing me the opportunity to keep playing.

During the early 1980s, the sport began to enjoy an increase in viewership. We saw local events draw in excess of 10,000 spectators, all without an on-site structure, a television package or local promotion. Many of the fans would sleep outside the night before for the privilege of sitting courtside. We realized that fans this devoted had to be on to something.

Under the direction of a former player-turned-sports agent, Leonard Armato, we organized the players into a union that became the AVP (Association of Volleyball Professionals). We negotiated directly with sponsors and television. We sold signage, built arena seating and received exposure on the local news.

As president of the AVP, I was able to join Leonard in securing larger rights fees and more influence in the promotion of the sport.

Perhaps my attention to the business of beach volleyball might have had something to do with my greatest sadness in the sport. Although I had been a member of the U.S. National team for years and had consistently played well, I was not selected to play at the 1984 Olympic Games in Los Angeles. The coaches felt I was less committed to the indoor game than they thought I should have been but, regardless, after suffering the boycott of 1980, this came as a doubly disappointing blow.

———❖———

Perhaps my attention to the business of beach volleyball might have had something to do with my greatest sadness in the sport

———❖———

When the American men won the gold in 1984, I was thrilled for the team. The exposure of the six-man game built substantial interest in the outdoor game, as many of the Olympic champions such as Pat Powers, Karch Kiraly and Steve Timmons began to play professionally on the beach as well. Their Olympic credentials established widespread acceptance for the sport overnight.

Even so, much of the country doesn't have a beach, so we had to devise a way to get the sport seen in landlocked cities across the country. To increase our fan base, we had to think in different ways to find methods of reaching a bigger market.

The sponsors who aligned themselves with the sport felt this was an ideal vehicle to expose their products, so we had the AVP Beach Tour make stops all over the country, erecting nets and trucking tons of sand to the banks of rivers, the edges of lakes, outside bars and saloons. We even built sand courts indoors. If you want something enough, you'll find a way. It worked! People across the country came to see volleyball played on the sand.

------❖------

We had to think in different ways to reach a bigger market

------❖------

I enjoyed hanging around after the games, chatting with the spectators, signing autographs and answering questions from the media. I guess you could say I was a self-appointed public relations campaign. I found that the quality of play mattered to the viewers, but they also wanted to *experience* the California lifestyle. They wanted to talk to a guy with wraparound shades, who used words like "cool," "dig," "stoked" and "totally awesome" without sounding self-conscious.

Just as I had been searching for "the zone," they were searching for a feeling as well.

With all the time I was investing in the sport (I also opened my retail store and helped launch a national brand of beach apparel), my conditioning suffered, and I found myself more injury-prone as the years went by. The pain I felt while jumping off the sand almost pushed me into retirement. I spent so much time with my orthopedic surgeon that I probably put his children through private school.

But one personal dream would not die: I wanted to play volleyball in the Olympics.

It took the president of the International Volleyball Federation (the FIVB), Dr. Ruben Acosta, to make my dream come true. Olympic status is only granted to a sport after a long and involved process that usually takes many years, but in 1992, at the Barcelona Olympic Games, Dr. Acosta arranged for a beach volleyball exhibition for members of the International Olympic Committee (IOC).

Randy Stoklos and I volunteered to play, incurring the wrath of the AVP. Those years I had spent developing the AVP helped solidify its control over the professional sport, but the FIVB was the international governing body responsible for Olympic competition. Each had its agenda, but mine was simple. I just wanted to play in the Olympics and I was understandably torn when I "crossed swords" with the group I helped create. Shortly after that demonstration event, we were able to gain the approval of both Juan Antonio Samaranch (IOC President) and Billy Payne (president of the Atlanta Olympic Games).

❖

But one personal dream would not die: I wanted to play volleyball in the Olympics

❖

When the FIVB began its own tour, the AVP threatened any players who "crossed the line" with sanctions. Fifteen months before the 1996 Olympics, the day my first son, Hagen, was born, my partner, Ricci Luyties, informed me that he wouldn't be able to play with me in the Olympic qualifying season due to AVP pressure. Immediately, I grabbed a list of players from the four-man sport (another event altogether) and called the top four ranked players, leaving messages on answering machines from San Diego to Santa Cruz. The first to respond was Carl Henkel, a tall player and a very strong hitter who was twelve years my junior. We didn't have much time to learn how to play together but we were eager to climb the rankings of the FIVB, so we hit the FIVB tour with a vengeance. If you want something enough, you'll find a way.

You may have heard about some of the controversy surrounding the selection process of the U.S. Olympic representatives in beach volleyball. Some of the AVP players were saying that I didn't deserve to be on the 1996 Olympic Team because I was too old, hadn't proven myself and recently

Photo courtesy of FIVB

had undergone two different surgeries, making my game ineffective. My partner, Carl Henkel, though an excellent four-man player, was also judged to be lacking experience in the two-man game. The criticism stung. Sure, I wanted to play in the Olympics, but not if I didn't deserve to be there.

In spite of the basis for their allegations, Carl and I made a formidable team. We met and trounced the team from Portugal, sending them into the losers bracket, 15-7. The Cubans (viewed by some as the most athletic team in the Games) played us to deuce before we eventually won the hard-fought contest.

———❖———

Some of the AVP players were saying that I didn't deserve to be on the 1996 Olympic Team

———❖———

This set the scene for a much-anticipated match-up between us and perhaps the greatest player in the game at that time, Karch Kiraly, and his equally talented partner, Kent Steffes, of the United States. While many thought this meeting would be a blowout, we enjoyed the lead on numerous occasions and even "served for the game" a couple of times, before Karch and Kent took the match, 17-15. They won the game to enter the medal round (where they went on to win the gold). We had to play again just ninety minutes later and were eliminated by the same Portuguese team we had defeated a few days before.

No, I didn't win the gold medal or the silver or the bronze. My partner and I finished in fifth place, but because of my devotion to the sport and love of the game, I was able to enjoy a remarkable comeback and proved to myself and to the naysayers that I *did* belong in the Olympic tournament.

I was bummed that I didn't win, but I walked away knowing I had accomplished something unique and praiseworthy. I made it to the Olympic Games sixteen years after the boycott and twelve years after losing my spot on the 1984 Olympic Team (my greatest disappointment) with a shot at a medal at the advanced age of 39. Back in 1984, when I was accused of lacking commitment, I thought my chances of playing in the world's greatest volleyball tournament were lost forever, but because of my efforts, and those of a few excellent people, I finally realized my dream. If you want something enough, you'll find a way.

I don't think the Olympian within can ever lose that competitive drive, we just redirect it, but there is still so much more to do. I'll continue to play as long as I feel I can compete with the best, but what excites me most, what awakens the Olympian in me, is to see the rest of the world fall in love with the sport that I fell in love with when I was just a boy.

BONNY WARNER

Photo courtesy of Michael P. Masuka

While Bonny Warner's main passion is aviation, she is most noted as America's foremost luge racer, having competed in three Olympic Games: 1984 Sarajevo, 1988 Calgary and 1992 Albertville. Her dynamic and effervescent personality has lifted the sport throughout the 1980s to its current status as a very popular Olympic event. During the 1994 Winter Olympics in Lillehammer, Norway and again, in 1998 at Nagano Japan, she continued to bring the sport into America's living rooms, as an expert commentator for CBS Television.

Bonny began luge racing in 1980 and was a National Team member for eleven straight years, during which she earned five National titles. She has introduced 1,500 youngsters to the sport of luge, dozens of whom have gone on to National and Olympic teams, including one of America's first Olympic luge medalists, Brian Martin.

In addition to her luging triumphs, she earned a degree in broadcast journalism from Stanford University, where she was a scholarship field hockey player. She spent three years as a reporter for ABC-TV in San Francisco before changing careers to pursue her love of aviation. She's now a full-time pilot for United Airlines and recently was promoted from Boeing 777 co-pilot to captain of a Boeing 727. Bonny is now training for the Salt Lake 2002 Olympic Winter Games in the new sport of Women's Bobsled.

9

It Might as Well Be Me!

Bonny Warner

Mt. Baldy, California, was a town so small that the phone book had only one yellow page. It was here that my single mother raised her three children on an elementary schoolteacher's salary. Toys were expensive, so we had to make do with just our imaginations. And that was good because I look back on my athletic and professional career and realize that my imagination allowed me to hope for things others wouldn't dare dream about. Whenever a package came, I was the one who ran breathlessly to the door, because it might be for me. If someone was going to win the ball game, I thought, it might as well be me.

At 14, as an impressionable high school student, I came home from school and announced that I wanted to become an Olympian.

ABC sports had televised the 1976 Montreal Olympics and the following week our school held an assembly where a professional explorer named Dr. John Goddard challenged the school to write down what we wanted to accomplish during our lifetime, what our dreams were.

With all the enthusiasm I could muster, I wrote down the following:
- ❖ To go to a top college
- ❖ To become an Olympian
- ❖ To work for ABC-TV
- ❖ To obtain a private pilot's license.
- ❖ To build a log cabin

Looking back, I realize how lucky I was to have such an assignment at an early age. Even now, twenty years later, I benefit from mini-versions of that assignment. How many people go through life, just one day at a time drifting along with the tide? I was left unsatisfied with that approach. I wanted to establish my direction, to take control of my life, but I just didn't know how.

Perhaps I had a hidden, unfulfilled potential, an Olympian trying to break out—if only I could awaken the untapped resources inside.

Awakening that Olympian within has been the most satisfying part of my life, leading me to successes in other areas as well. When I speak to audiences now, I try to share the thoughts and decisions I made growing up, which I call my "Olympic Rules for Living."

RULE NO. 1:
YOU HAVE TO HAVE A DREAM
TO HAVE A DREAM COME TRUE

The first key is to have a clear destination. We wouldn't jump in a car or a plane without a destination in mind. Nor should we begin a project at work without knowing what we want to accomplish. Yet, why is it that most of us merely plug away at life, without heading toward a specific goal?

Imagine for a moment that there were no obstacles. What would we want to accomplish in the next year, ten years, thirty years? Don't worry about failure, just dream for a second.

———◆———

We should expand the list and not limit ourselves to what we know we can do

———◆———

Perhaps we want that elusive promotion, maybe even the title of CEO of the company (if we're going to dream, then we might as well go for the top). If we sell a product, what would be a "dream" level of market share? Is a comfortable retirement enough to shoot for or are we capable of more? How is our family life? Are we as physically fit as we'd like? Have we seen enough of the world? We should expand the list and not limit ourselves to what we know we can do. *This is about dreams.*

Mine was a rather "uninhibited" list, considering the circumstances. As a family, we had no money for such "dreams" and although I was a rough and tumble tomboy, I was not exactly Olympic caliber in any particular sport. I was the perennial junior varsity athlete in a variety of high school sports and the only blue ribbon I ever won was in the fifty-yard backstroke, racing in a pool with only one contestant—me.

Yet, when I told Mom of my "dreams," she didn't laugh, bless her heart. Instead she said something that has stayed with me ever since. "Now that you know where you are going, how are you going to get there?" I had dreams, but I needed plans. That was the first glimpse of what I call:

RULE No. 2:
CHAMPIONS SET A SERIES OF INTERMEDIATE STEPS TO ACHIEVE THEIR GOALS

Once I had a dream, I had to turn it into a goal, something tangible, something measurable, and then I broke it down into smaller steps.

Swimming and track were not in my future, certainly not if I couldn't even make the varsity team in high school. However, field hockey was a sport I loved and one where I showed "great potential." Furthermore, there were lots of college field hockey scholarships available and perhaps I could get one to pay for the top; i.e., expensive, school of my choice. I realized I could accomplish two of my dreams—to go to a top school and to become an Olympian—by marching down the same path.

I wrote to the Field Hockey Association and discovered the steps required to make the Olympic team. If I played in a good college program, I could get the training I needed to move up the ranks. It all seemed so simple once I knew the path.

What are the intermediate steps required that would turn our dreams into goals? The dream may seem impossible, but is the first step possible? When I accomplished the first step, how much easier the second appeared. My sense of accomplishment began to build, feeding the next attempt.

We should make a list of the steps and visualize achieving the first one. Almost before I knew it, I was halfway there.

———❖———

The dream may seem impossible, but is the first step possible?

———❖———

Sometimes when our path takes an unexpected turn, we should remain flexible and ready for it. The plan should be a living, changing document, which leads me to the next rule:

RULE No. 3:
CHAMPIONS NEVER SAY NO TO AN OPPORTUNITY

Who said that when there is a fork in the road, I *couldn't* try both paths? I tried the one path in my plan—field hockey—but I tried the other—luge, too. I never stuck so rigidly to a plan that I couldn't see other possibilities springing up around me.

When I was 16, I entered an essay contest about the Olympics and was chosen as one of fifty torchbearers for the 1980 Olympic Winter Games!

That winter, I was a freshman at Stanford, pursuing my path to the Olympics through field hockey, and I had taken the winter quarter off to watch the Games in Lake Placid. Yes, I watched the U.S. Hockey Team beat the Soviet Union. I watched Eric Heiden win all five of his Olympic medals. I also saw a crazy sport called luge: athletes on their backs on a flimsy sled, zooming eighty miles per hour down an ice track with thirty-foot-high steeply banked turns. I remember thinking they must be nuts, but it sure looked like fun.

The Games concluded at the end of February, but since I didn't have to be back for spring quarter until April, I had a month with nothing to do and no money with which to do it. I heard of a beginner's luge camp with top coaching that only cost $8 for two weeks! Who can turn down an opportunity like that?

The one catch (there's always a catch) was that I needed my own sled. The going price for sleds was $450, ten times more than I had! Fortunately, the sled owner happened to run a deli shop called "Captain Billy Wizbang's," so we struck a deal. I worked as a sandwich maker for free for three weeks and he gave me a sled. It took some creativity, but I was headed down a new, parallel path. I kept playing hockey to see whether it would pan out, but I also started luging. I made the USA Development Field Hockey Team (one level below the Olympic Team) but later had to choose between hockey and luge, since both required year-round commitments. I chose to focus on luge, although I did stay with hockey long enough to finish college on the hockey scholarship.

Before you start thinking that my life was charmed, that everything came easily, perhaps we should discuss the "toughest" of the rules.

RULE No. 4:
ALL CHAMPIONS HAVE TO START SOMEWHERE AND QUITE OFTEN IT IS AT THE BOTTOM

Perhaps it's ironic that I would learn this rule, especially since luge, bobsled and Alpine skiing start from the top and end at the bottom, but I think you'll get the idea.

Michael Jordan didn't start his career in the NBA. Bill Gates' first job wasn't as CEO of Microsoft (well actually it was, but he began in his garage). Many corporate presidents began in the mailroom, and most champions began as "second stringers." Almost every winner's path has a humble beginning and, since most of them began their journeys as individuals with no more promise than I had, I realized the same results might be true for me.

By the time I had sliced enough deli meat and spread enough mayo to earn the luge sled, winter had come to an end in Lake Placid. I had to wait until the following season to try out my new toy.

I wanted to keep playing hockey at Stanford (to pay for school) and I wanted to train for luge to make the next Olympic Team. Stanford's hockey coach, Janet Luce, doubted I would have enough time in the day to do everything, so I wrote a fourteen-page "term paper" explaining how it could be done and dropped it on her desk. She let me keep the scholarship and, from that moment on, I knew my commitment had been put in writing and was sitting in some file in someone else's desk. Stanford's policy allowed me to take one quarter off per year so I could train to make the Olympic luge team.

I didn't *have* to write a fourteen-page paper to figure out the steps necessary to convert my dreams to goals; a few notes probably would have done just as well, but it does help to write them down and give them to someone, such as a spouse, co-worker, boss or friend. It's far too easy for us to stray from our chosen path if we are accountable only to ourselves.

Earlier that year, I entered another Olympic drawing, with the theme, "Be All You Can Be." Out of 1.8 million entries, I won the $5,000 First Prize. Hey, if somebody's gonna' win, it might as well be me! Since everyone had been telling me that the only way to excel at luge was to go to Germany and since East and West Germans had comprised half the Olympic final each year since 1972, I chose to spend the prize money on a plane ticket. I left for Germany after the hockey season the following October.

Having flown so far to train, the Germans assumed I was one of the best lugers in America. Because my German was limited, I couldn't explain that I was just a beginner and had never even met the "best in America." Furthermore, I was so naive, that when they invited me to start from the top, I jumped at the chance. What a fool! Even today, with twelve years of training, I would never go from the top on the first day of the season.

On that fateful day, October 15, 1980, I launched off the top of the most challenging track in the world, on the fastest sled I had ever ridden. I survived about two turns, before crashing spectacularly. In fact, I crashed run after run, fifty-two times in a row. My arms and ankles were so swollen from slamming into the walls that my skin stretched until it shined. But I had a dream and I had a path, and I wouldn't give up.

I was a mess, but bit by bit I learned, advancing to three turns, then seven, then twelve, finally making it to the finish line on my fifty-third try. Of course, my determination was aided by the fact that I had a non-changeable plane ticket home, and I didn't have the money to buy another one for an earlier date!

In luge, if you never crash, thereby eliminating the mystique, then you'll always be afraid of crashing and, as a result, drive the sled too cautiously in competition. In life, too, if we don't fail on occasion, then we're too cautiously choosing our path. Enter the lottery of life now! Don't worry about taking baby steps and don't be afraid of tripping. If we choose a challenging path, we will have some failures, yet if we don't, then the path is not challenging enough. We really are capable of much more than we think.

Perhaps the most important side effect of trying something beyond our abilities is that eventually we'll earn the respect of others. If we have faith in ourselves, others will soon come to our aid. This help from others is the final key to success. No matter how good we are, we cannot succeed alone.

RULE NO. 5:
IF YOU TRULY BELIEVE IN YOURSELF, OTHERS WILL, TOO

After crashing so many times and coming back for more, the Germans thought I was crazy. They saw very quickly that I didn't know what I was doing, and that I certainly was not one of the best in America. Soon they also realized that they either had to help me or bar me from the track. I wouldn't give up, and they knew I could really get hurt. I found that the Germans really did want to help me. They wanted me not just to survive, but to succeed.

———◆———

If you never crash, you'll always be afraid of crashing

———◆———

They couldn't bear to kick me out of town; I was trying so hard. They figured since I was such a rookie, I could be no threat to the great West German team, and so they took me under their wing. Three months of coaching from the Germans allowed me to quickly become one of the best Americans in the sport. Without their help, I surely would have broken more than just my sled. Yet, even when I started showing promise, the German coaches still helped me. They considered me one of their own. Silently I developed a new dream, to one day beat a German in Olympic competition.

There are two types of people who attract truly qualified help: those who try hard and fail but get back up again, and those who are successful, but are always open to suggestions. If we begin in the first group and transition to the second, our mentors will follow. Everyone loves to help someone who actually follows his or her advice, becomes successful and attributes that success in part to those who helped. I certainly wouldn't be where I am now if I had tried to do everything alone.

Is there someone above us on the corporate ladder who can "coach" or mentor us? Maybe a networking organization that we can join with professionals who are at or above our current level and who can act as mentors? When striving for our goals, first we should do everything we can on our own and then reach out when we deserve outside help. Go to a coach or mentor with your plan laid out and ask for criticism, rather than approaching them for advice on a blank piece of paper. We should make our mentors part of our success plan and let them know how much we value their help.

My first Olympic experience in Sarajevo in 1984 was more valuable than I had imagined. Marching in the Opening Ceremony was both magical and inspiring. I was fulfilling the dreamlike wishes of a 14-year-old girl. I was *part* of the ABC broadcast coverage rather than merely being a viewer of it.

------------ ❖ ------------

There are two types of people who attract truly qualified help:
those who try hard and fail but get back up again, and those who are successful,
but are always open to suggestions

------------ ❖ ------------

Luge requires that each athlete take four runs down the course, and the sum of the times determines the winner. The only other rule is that the rider must cross the finish line "with the sled." After three runs, I was in eighth place, with a realistic shot at fifth. I could play it safe and finish ahead of at least one German or I could go all out and see what the time would be. I went all out, of course.

With two turns to go, I felt the sled take a path that was slightly different from mine and I began to slip off. It took all the strength and experience I had acquired over the previous eight years to keep one hand on the sled, while using the other to cushion the blows of the ice walls. Together, we slid through the final turn and across the finish line. I dropped in the standings to fifteenth place. No medal, but a higher Olympic finish than any American woman in history.

The experience had been so rewarding that I couldn't help but want to do it again, but now I wanted to reach a higher standard. At that time, no U.S. athlete had ever won a medal in Olympic luge competition. By resetting my goal for the 1988 Games in Calgary, the next four years just flew by.

My results in Calgary were even more impressive, if not as picturesque. I rode smoothly to a sixth place finish, improving on America's best-ever result, male or female, and placed higher than one of the Germans in that meet.

I had reached another dream and my success in the sport opened up another opportunity—to become my sport's expert analyst for (you guessed it) ABC's "Wide World of Sports." (Dream No. 3)

To see how these rules apply to life in general, I would sacrifice my dream of an Olympic medal at the altar of another dream....

You may recall that in high school I had listed "To obtain a private pilot's license" as something I wanted to accomplish. The basic goal of just getting a pilot's license was actually very easy. I just needed the money, which I earned quickly as a sports reporter for the local ABC-TV affiliate in San Francisco.

To learn the steps, I turned to a mentor friend and fellow pilot, Dr. Peter Bing. Once I started flying in April 1988, I realized I wanted much more than a pilot's license—I wanted to be a *commercial airline pilot.*

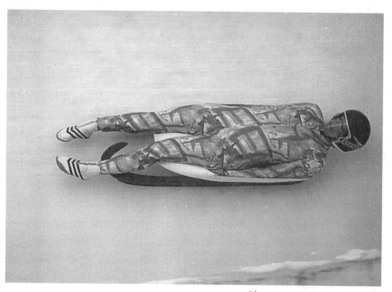

Photo courtesy of Nancie Battaglia

With Dr. Bing's encouragement, I gained the confidence to try and reach for the top.

I dared to dream that I might become an airline pilot in today's job market. Oh, it's difficult for a nonmilitary trained pilot in this extremely competitive field. The odds are slim and many qualified pilots never even attempt the application process. I figured someone had to get hired and it might as well be me, but it would mean abandoning my career as an athlete.

After getting my private pilot's license, I did some research to determine what the intermediate steps would be. I needed eight different licenses and ratings, ratings in all three classes of aircraft (the single engine, multi-engine and turboprop) to become a commercial pilot. I needed to log a significant number of hours to pass certain tests and to undergo a very demanding interview.

Still keeping my options open to any opportunity, I moved up through the ratings and licenses to become a flight instructor. I started booking every student I could, gathering hours for my flight log. Some instructors didn't want to work nights or weekends or holidays, but I didn't mind. I never turned away a student. A couple of those weekend/holiday students had good connections to other flying jobs that, in turn, gave me even more varied experience, all of which enhanced my credentials in the eyes of those who later interviewed me for an airline job. They *wanted* to help me.

When I finally reached the experience level required to apply for an airline job, I approached a friend with the hope that she might be willing to help me out. It turned out that Sandra Fisher, who was a pilot herself, had been following my career with interest, and was eager to help. She offered to prepare me with some coaching in airline industry interviewing skills. Two weeks later I went for the real test and passed with flying colors. Without her help, I'm not sure that I'd have received the offer from United Airlines.

Yes, I started at the bottom. It may seem hard to believe, but many of the pilots who are flying jumbo jets started their careers in puny two-seater prop jobs, too.

I still remember my first lesson. I got in the little Cessna 152 and looked at all the dials and gauges and told the instructor it looked much too complicated for me. He laughed and said, "Just give it a try."

Ten years later I find myself at home as captain of a Boeing 727 for a major airline.

I call it my dream job. However, I have one more dream to go…Remember the log cabin? I'm setting up the plan now.

MILT CAMPBELL

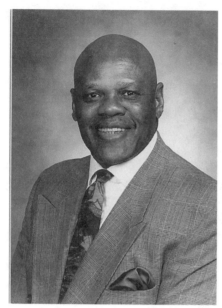

Photo provided by Milt Campbell

After a stint in the navy, he claimed the title of "The World's Greatest Athlete" when he won the gold medal in the decathlon at the 1956 Olympic Games in Melbourne, Australia.

In Milt's case, that title is more than a convenient handle to honor his decathlon success. During his varied athletic career, he was an All-American swimmer, a national champion hurdler and a professional football player for the Cleveland Browns and two teams in the Canadian Football League. He has been inducted into ten different Halls of Fame, including halls for National Track and Field, the U.S. Olympic Committee and even the International Swimming and Diving Hall of Fame.

As a businessman, Milt founded the Chad School, which serves inner-city youth; ran the Milt Campbell Community Center; and has created Milt Campbell Enterprise, a personal development and motivational company.

He addresses children and adults across the country, speaking on various motivational topics from "overcoming the hurdles of life" to "you don't have to quit at second place."

Milt stands alongside the other great decathlon champions—Bob Mathias, Rafer Johnson, Bill Toomey, Bruce Jenner and Dan O'Brien as a true American sports hero.

10

How to Win Your Personal Decathlon

Milt Campbell

Some athletes are bigger, faster, stronger and smarter than others—
but not a single person has a corner on dreams, desire or ambition.

—Duffy Daugherty, Decathlon Coach

When I was 18 years old, I competed in the 1952 Olympic Games in Helsinki, Finland. I had only competed the decathlon once before (at the Olympic Trials). Now here I was, still in high school, up against the 1948 gold medalist, the great American champion (and future Congressman), Bob Mathias. Too inexperienced to accept the concept of defeat, I never thought I wouldn't win. In fact, I came close, earning the silver as part of an American sweep behind Mathias' second title. To me, it was only a momentary setback. I knew that I still had a dream to realize, a prize to win. I was the greatest athlete in the world—at least in my own mind. But I had to win the Olympic decathlon for the world to agree with me. I made the commitment right then to be ready four years hence to stake my claim on that elusive gold medal.

My journey to the Olympics began when I was about 12. My junior high coach told me that if I was willing to put in the effort, I could be a really good athlete…maybe even the best athlete in our town of Plainfield, New Jersey…maybe even the best athlete in the whole state.

Well, that wasn't enough for me. I didn't want to settle for good. I decided that I wanted to be great! I told everyone that I was going to be the greatest athlete in the world. That title, "The Greatest Athlete in the World" goes to the gold medal winner of the Olympic decathlon. That became my dream. Members of my family shook their heads in disbelief. My brother laughed out loud. Later on, my girlfriends got angry because I was more focused on my goal than I was on them. I didn't care. I knew what the prize was going to be and I was out to get it.

————❖————

I had to win the Olympic decathlon for the world to agree with me

————❖————

All Olympic athletes know that total fixation with, and focus on, our goals is absolutely necessary if we're going to succeed. Whether we're going to win a medal or get the promotion we desire, there's no magic to the formula. We simply have to keep our attention centered on what we want, play by the rules and pay the price necessary to achieve it.

While I only participated in the ten-event competition a total of five times (twice at the Trials, twice at the Olympics, and once at the 1953 U.S. National Championships), the discipline of the event has stood me in good stead throughout my life. In fact, the individual events of the decathlon have become a metaphor that I use to illustrate the techniques I used when playing professional football, and that I still use in my speaking career.

The decathlon requires speed, strength and versatility. The winner is the person who's been shown to be stronger and faster and able to jump higher in ten major track and field events. Once we master the mind-set skills we need for the individual events, we've mastered the mind-set skills required for success in every area of our life—even if we never compete in any sport.

THE 100-METER DASH
(GETTING STARTED BY STAYING HEALTHY)

The 100-meter dash is the first event and, to me, it represents our first priority…to take care of our body and our health. It is an explosive event and if we are not in tiptop physical shape, we will fail. Likewise, if we do not exercise and watch what we eat…if we are not in good physical shape, we will fail in the world of business. There's no way we can succeed in anything if we're sick and run-down. That means staying away from liquor, cigarettes and the other excesses that look like sophisticated fun but that destroy the remarkable machine that houses our brain. Like anything valuable, we want to keep it safe.

In 120 A.D., the Roman lawyer, Juvenal, wrote about *mens sana in corpore sano*, "a sound mind in a sound body." Any prize we want begins with making certain that our body and mind are healthy and ready to do the work.

THE LONG JUMP
(THE LEAP OF FAITH)

The second event is the long jump, which represents the big picture of our life. If we're going to go from where we stand to where we want to land, we've got to visualize where we're going and how we plan to get there. Sometimes people will accuse us of daydreaming. If they do, that means we're on the right track! Without daydreams, there is no growth. We can only become what we can imagine.

Look at the big picture, plan your steps, and then take the long jump…that leap of faith…that takes us out of our comfort zone and places us on a path to accomplishing our goals.

Someone once gave me a copy of the book, *Think and Grow Rich* by Napoleon Hill. It changed my life, as it has changed the lives of thousands of other people. In the book, Hill says, "Whatever the mind of man can conceive and believe, it can achieve," or in other words, we become what we think about.

In 1992, I shared some of these ideas with Dan O'Brien, then America's next gold medal hope in the decathlon. Immediately after his victory at the 1996 Centennial Games in Atlanta, he credited that conversation with helping him earn his title.

THE SHOT PUT
(GET RID OF ALL NEGATIVITY)

The next challenge for a decathlete is the shot put. In this event, we throw a sixteen-pound lead ball as far away from us as possible. Off the playing field, that ball represents all of the negative weight we carry around with us everyday. If we're going to achieve our goal, we've got to see that ball as a round container into which we've stuffed every depressing, negative thought we've ever had. Take all those comments from others ("You'll never be able to do that! You're deluding yourself. Get real!") and push them into the ball. Now, mentally toss that ball far, far away. The winner is the person who puts the shot the farthest, who can most completely rid himself or herself of the negative elements that spell defeat.

THE HIGH JUMP
(SET INTERMEDIATE GOALS, RESET THE BAR OFTEN)

Now we're ready for the fourth event, the high jump. This is when we concentrate on the goals we've set for ourselves and, as we train, we accomplish intermediate goals. Each time we clear the bar—or achieve a goal—we raise the bar a little bit higher, never for an instant believing that we've gone as far as we *can* go. If every athlete thought that the record couldn't be broken, then we'd no longer have competitions. In everything I do, I challenge myself to be just a little better than anyone (including me) who has done it before.

THE 400-METERS
(WILLINGNESS TO PAY THE PRICE)

This event takes commitment and endurance. It marks the halfway point in the decathlon and it is the first test of how firmly we are focused on winning, how well we're keeping our eye on the prize. This is the first event of the decathlon that is truly grueling, because for the first time in the contest, we are feeling tired *before* we can see the finish line. At the end of the first day, the pain is real and it lasts a long time. It is at this juncture that many decathletes wonder why they didn't concentrate on only one event, so they wouldn't have to go through so much agony.

In the business world, hard work is required to accomplish our goals. Work is seldom easy, and often it is painful. In the quarter-mile, the *talkers* are separated from the *doers,* just as in business, the eager workers naturally pull ahead of those who just punch the clock.

THE 110-METER HIGH HURDLES
(OVERCOME ALL OBSTACLES)

The first event on the second day of the decathlon is the 110-meter-high hurdles. It takes confidence and coordination to overcome these obstacles. In high school I had it easy, because the hurdles are set three inches lower than they are at the Olympics. I felt I could sail across 'em.

There was no obstacle too tough (remember my attitude in Helsinki?). At 18, I hadn't failed often enough to be afraid of losing. Nobody is as self-confident as a high school athlete. They feel they're at the top of the food chain. It's later in life that the hurdles get tougher.

The challenge taught by the high hurdles is to keep that youthful enthusiasm and confidence, even after the years have dealt us a few blows. With that "spring" in our step, we can smoothly clear just about any hurdle, any obstacle that keeps us from attaining our dreams.

THE DISCUS
(PROPER TECHNIQUE AND MOMENTUM)

Have you ever thrown a discus? It's like a very heavy Frisbee. In this event, form and momentum are the keys to winning. When I throw the discus, I'm actually throwing a circle within a circle. It's the circular motion, the windup and the spinning revolutions that precede the release, that propel the discus through the air. Once I get going, if I slow my circular movement because of a distraction or slip in concentration, I'll lose my throwing power and the disc won't travel very far.

In business, not only must we know what we're trying to do, we must do it correctly. Learn the skill, practice the craft, understand the customer's needs. Not only must we do the right thing, we must do all things right.

THE POLE VAULT
(FLY HIGH WITH THE HELP OF A MENTOR)

The pole vault is the only event where I needed a boost from an outside source (the pole), and, consequently, it was a real test of faith in both myself and the pole, which I used to propel me through the air and over the bar.

———❖———

Not only must we do the right thing, we must do all things right

———❖———

This event reminds me of the importance of a mentor who will help teach us the techniques to succeed and provide valuable advice to keep us moving forward. The advice is so much more credible when it comes from someone who's already been where we seek to go.

My coach and mentor was George Rhoden. Born in the West Indies, he won two gold medals for Jamaica in 1952. After I enlisted in the Navy, I continued my training on the nearby campus of the University of Southern California under his supervision and guidance. Every morning, he'd come into my room and say, "Get up, get up. You're the greatest athlete in the world."

I'm looking up into the face of a two-time Olympic champion, and *he's* telling me how great *I* am? I ask you, after such a buildup, who wouldn't conquer the world? He worked on my form and helped me keep up the enthusiasm necessary to attain my goals. The fact that he had already won Olympic gold didn't hurt, either.

No one can be a winner alone. It takes teamwork, the other people who give us a boost when we need it, something to inspire us to reach higher than we've ever reached before. By the way, all this should also remind us of our obligation to help others.

THE JAVELIN
(DON'T LET UP, KEEP THE PRESSURE ON)

While in competition, I wanted to be both fast and strong, accurate and powerful. By the time I reached this next-to-last event of the contest, I was filled with confidence. This confidence, just like the sharply pointed spear itself, could be dangerous. Having come so far, and having proved myself successful to this point might allow the "normal me" to think I could relax, let up just a bit, but the Olympian within needed to keep going strong.

Persistence is obvious when things go poorly, but sometimes we overlook its value when things are going well. The secret is to recognize our ability without losing our concentration.

When the president of the company invites you to play golf on Saturday or the vice president of sales asks you to attend a high-level meeting, all the signs point to the promotion you've worked for. This is the time to maintain your focus on the goal. Don't assume you've made it. Even though you're almost on the winner's stand, you still have one more event to run. In life, there's always one more event. No matter how far you go, how much you earn, how impressive your position, there is always "one more event," one more obstacle, one more rung on the ladder.

THE 1,500 METER
(FINISH THE JOB)

The metric mile is the final event in the decathlon. At this point, a decathlete is pumped. The end is in sight and the goal is at hand. I could almost feel the medal bouncing against my chest as I ran. It was now time to put this question to rest, get the job done and go home. All I had to do was stay the course and victory would be mine. I made it a point to save some extra energy for this last event and to keep racing until I crossed the finish line.

———❖———

There is always "one more event," one more obstacle, one more rung on the ladder

———❖———

The danger comes if we let down because the competition is almost over. We've all heard the motto, "The job's not finished until the paperwork's done." What a shame to come so far, and forget to ask for the order, confirm the guarantee or get signatures on the document. For goodness sake, close the sale!

So, if we begin with a healthy body, make the commitment, lose all negativity, establish stepping–stones and challenge ourselves, work hard, overcome obstacles, hone our skills, take advantage of advice, keep up the pressure and eventually finish the job, there's virtually no limit to how far we can go.

THE GAMES OF MELBOURNE

I used all these ideas in my training and preparation during the years that followed my silver medal in Helsinki. Since the Olympic gold medal is only awarded every quadrennial, I wanted to be ready, even if very few people would be paying me any attention.

The 1956 Olympics were scheduled to take place in Australia between Thanksgiving and Christmas—definitely not when Americans were accustomed to watching summer sports! In fact, the broadcast networks decided so many people would be gift shopping or watching football that there wouldn't be enough viewers (or advertising revenue) to justify televising the Summer Games.

As the rest of the world looked toward the Melbourne Olympics, most of the talk was all about a young black athlete from Los Angeles named Rafer Johnson. He was everyone's pick to win the decathlon because he was the current world record holder and had won the U.S. Olympic Trials earlier that year. The top international star was Vassily Kuznyetsov from the Soviet Union.

Since Bob Mathias had retired, and I wasn't training with a traditional track club, I had been pretty much forgotten. Most felt that the kid from Plainfield, New Jersey, who had finished second in Helsinki, was just a fluke—a name in the record books.

———❖———

After nine events, I almost could have walked the metric mile and still have earned the gold

———❖———

In my ten events, I was quick off the blocks and had plenty of power but lacked endurance. Rafer was skilled in the technical events, especially the long jump, and the Russian was known to have an overpowering second day. If I were to win the title, I would need to have the gold "locked up" before the last event.

Photo provided by Milt Campbell

Over two days, I won four of the ten events outright, and beat Rafer in six. In Rafer's best event, the long jump, he only beat me by one centimeter. In the hurdles, I beat all the field but one by more than a full second, earning more than 1,100 points. Mathematically, after nine events, I almost could have *walked* the metric mile and still have earned the gold.

As I stood on the awards stand, below me to one side was Kuznyetsov with the bronze, on the other was Johnson with the silver and between them, on the highest platform, the gold medal was draped around my neck.

Afterward, headlines around the world confirmed that I had achieved what I had set out to do so many years before. In 1956, the winner of the decathlon, "The Greatest Athlete in the World," was *me*!

PAM FLETCHER

Photo provided by Pam Fletcher

Pam Fletcher is a 1988 Olympian and nine-year U.S. Ski Team veteran who grew up on skis at Nashoba Valley ski area in Westford, Massachusetts. Pam was a six-time national champion and a gold medal winner at the 1986 World Cup Downhill in Vail, Colorado. At the 1988 Olympics in Calgary, she was "America's most likely candidate for a medal in Alpine skiing" until a freak accident shattered her leg and her Olympic dreams. Though she did not return from those Games with a medal, the U.S. Ski Writers awarded her the title of "Outstanding Competitor" for her courage and sportsmanship.

Her life continues to revolve around the slopes, working on promotions and corporate ski outings with many of the world's top companies. She gives motivational speeches throughout the country, delivering her Olympic story to inspire her audiences to stay positive in the face of adversity. She has covered Olympic skiing events for Turner Broadcasting in Albertville and Lillehammer, and has worked with ABC, CBS, ESPN and the Outdoor Life Network covering World Cup Alpine races, as well as outward bound adventures. She is also a contributing fitness editor for *Snow Country* magazine.

Pam brings her personal experiences, dynamic personality and boundless energy to everything she does, including her fun-filled presentations to audiences large and small.

11

Don't Play the Blame Game

Pam Fletcher

It was my sixth year on the Alpine World Cup Circuit. I had been improving steadily, but had yet to win at the World Cup level. Oh, I'd post hot results in the training runs, but when the actual day of competition arrived, it was always a different story. The European veterans would take their fast skis out of the closet, blow off the cobwebs and smoke me in the race.

Sleep was something ski racers cherished, especially at the end of the season. On the morning of the 1986 World Cup Downhill event in Vail, Colorado, the phone rang at 7:30 a.m., shocking me out of a deep sleep. Whoever was calling better have a good reason, because I didn't have to get up for another hour. It was Steve Sheridan, a good friend and forerunner in the downhill. "Fletch, I had to call you!" he said breathlessly, "I had a dream last night—it was snowing and you *won* the Downhill race here in Vail! Look out the window!" It was snowing. Great! I thought sarcastically…Flat light always makes ski racing so much more interesting, because at seventy miles per hour when you can't see, you feel like you're skiing by Braille!

In Alpine Downhill competitions, the earlier skiers leave ruts in the snow, making the course more difficult for those still to come. In an attempt to "level the playing field," the top fifteen ranked skiers were randomly assigned the first fifteen spots and the rest of the competitors came down the mountain according to their international ranking. In most races, the fastest of the first fifteen would win the event, as the later starters wouldn't stand much of a chance on the slower snow.

My start number was 30.

I had visualized myself skiing that downhill course from start to finish through every turn and over every roll. I had rehearsed the course so many times in my head that I could almost feel the G-force on my body through the run. I could even smell the flowers on the victory stand.

When my turn came, I had the run of my life. Everything seemed so simple, almost as if I were moving in slow motion, although I was traveling at more than sixty miles per hour into bumps. Compressing myself into a tight ball, I would fly a hundred feet down the slope, ten feet off the ground; waiting to extend my landing gear so I could land like a cat and make the touch down, subtle, quiet and smooth. All through my run I kept saying to myself, "Look for speed! Stay aerodynamic!" I thought: *Concentrate! Anticipate the gates. Set up well in advance.* My muscles were burning. My legs were pumping through the bumps like a car's shock absorbers cruising down a cobblestone street.

---❖---

I would fly a hundred feet down the slope, ten feet off the ground

---❖---

When I crossed the finish line, the stadium erupted in a chorus of cheers. I knew I must have had a good run but I didn't see the scoreboard. I actually had to ask someone in the finish area how I did. It was an honest-to-goodness win at the World Cup! I was elated. I'd worked so hard. Finally, I found myself standing on the top platform above the best in the world. It was awesome! My friend Steve was blown away by the connection between his dream and my victory.

The next day was a different story.

I raced in the World Cup Super G, a shorter, tighter turning downhill. I was starting No. 46. Once again the race should have been over after the first fifteen racers, but midway through the course, my time was only a couple of tenths behind the leader, Marina Keihl of Germany. Coming toward the finish, I hooked my ski tip on the second-to-last gate. My leg was yanked from under me and I was launched out of the course. It was over. I tore ligaments in my right ankle and was out for the rest of the season. Later the television coverage showed a split screen image of my run and the winner's run up to the point where I crashed—I was leading.

In a two-day period, I went from being the best in the world to being on crutches and sidelined for six months. Only my Olympic hopes and my parents' words gave me reason to look ahead.

My father has always motivated me. He tried to encourage me to look through my problems toward the future. He ought to know. He runs one of the most volatile of businesses, a recreational ski area, called Nashoba Valley in Massachusetts. His business can be drastically affected by the weather. Just one warm, snowless season and the attendance and profits can be influenced negatively for years. I remember being blown away at how often he had to put up with fickle weather, unreliable labor, fluctuating energy costs and other adverse conditions. In times of difficulty, Dad would comment that if we focused on the past, it would only set us back further. He would always encourage me to think positively and move forward. Dwelling on the negative, he would say, only puts you in reverse. Even when it rained all night one New Year's Eve, and the forecast showed no cold weather in sight, Dad had something positive to say. He said, "You can't change the situation, so there is no sense in dwelling on it."

Well, what better way to test his theory? Here I was with a torn ligament, off the snow just when I was beginning to enjoy great results, and the Olympics were less than two years away. Instead of staring at my ankle, I looked inward. The skier, the Olympian inside, hadn't changed. Only my circumstances had. It would do me no good wasting valuable energy on self-pity. The "woulda', shoulda', coulda'" attitude needed to be shaken quickly. What I needed was to look ahead and begin the preparation for my return to the slopes. Dad was saying my future was up to me, and I gave him my first smile since the accident.

------❖------

Good things come to those who wait
—Harrison Dillard

------❖------

Six months of rehab put me back on snow. Hard work and two seasons of racing on the Alpine World Cup, including the 1987 World Championships in Crans Montana, Switzerland, brought me to the 1988 Olympics in Calgary. In the pre-Olympic publicity materials, I was depicted as the athlete (male or female) most likely to medal for the U.S. Olympic Alpine Team. I credit much of that comeback to my father's words.

Some call the Calgary Games the most accident-prone of the Olympics because of a long series of tragedies. Speed skater Dan Jansen's heart-wrenching slip on the ice, the Austrian Alpine coach who was brutally killed when he ran into a snowcat between runs at the men's Giant Slalom race, and the warm, prevailing Chinook winds that not only postponed Alpine events, but sent a Nordic ski jumper flying into a camera tower, breaking his arm. Little did I know that I was to become another such statistic.

❖

I was depicted as the athlete most likely to medal

❖

I drew the No. 1 bib in the Olympic Downhill, one of the most coveted start positions. It was great to be in the top fifteen in the world and I was excited about my draw.

The Downhill is the "sexiest" of all the Alpine events. Imagine a steep, icy track that winds down a mountain over bumps and rolls. The world's best downhill ski racers can hit speeds of ninety miles per hour. These athletes negotiate tight turning arcs, long-radius, high-speed turns and big bumps, all with the intention of carrying as much speed as possible. Risks are high and injuries are prevalent. One tiny pilot error can cause a crash that might put you out for the season. Since the Olympic Games come along only once in four years, staying healthy and injury-free is a high priority on the World Cup Circuit.

I felt confident on the morning of the Olympic Downhill race. My warm-up went without a hitch. About an hour before the start of the competition, I took an additional run on the practice course to get used to the speed. At the bottom of the training hill, there was a "cat track" (a narrow trail providing a short-cut between two slopes). All of the athletes used this cat track to get back to the base of the mountain and the main lift. As I entered the cat track, an

Photo courtesy of Vail Resorts

Olympic volunteer course worker came into view heading toward me, up the trail. There was neither space nor time to slowdown. I moved to my right and I saw him move to my right. I moved left—he moved left. I threw my skis sideways trying to stop and *smack*, we crashed.

Sadly, he was big, about 6'2", 220 pounds, and I'm only 5'4" on my best day with mousse in my hair. What ripped my heart out was that the course worker merely collected himself and skated away, leaving me in a heap on the side of the trail, unable to get up. It seemed like a half-hour (it was probably only about five minutes) before anyone found me. A Swiss coach came by and immediately radioed for my coaches. They arrived in seconds. One coach, Chip Woods, thought the damage wasn't that bad and we could grab my running shoes and jog around in the parking lot to loosen up my leg. A great, positive attitude, but I barely put some weight on it and crunch…I felt the bones move. Dr. Steadman arrived on the scene and confirmed my worst thoughts: "The Agony of de Fibula"— a spiral fracture. My Olympic dream was over.

I could only cry when I first saw my parents as I lay on the ski patrol sled. In some ways I felt I had let them down, even though I knew the situation was out of my control. "Why did this have to happen?" everyone asked. Sometimes there is no answer to that question.

———❖———

You gain strength, courage and confidence by every experience in which you stop to look fear in the face. You are able to say to yourself, 'I lived through this horror, I can take the next thing that comes along.' …You must do the thing you think you cannot do

—Eleanor Roosevelt, *You Learn by Living* (1960)

———❖———

My dad was so positive in the patrol room. He encouraged me to remember how hard I had worked to make the cut. He said that the dream of becoming an Olympian was a goal in itself for me, and I should be proud just to be a part of the 1988 Olympic Team. My mom tried to assure me that these things sometimes happen for a reason, even though it seemed impossible to imagine what the reason could be.

Being in Calgary, in itself, was a goal accomplished and my inability to ski in the event did not make me less of a person. Winning a medal there would not make me a better skier, it would only prove how good I was to those who didn't already know. The people whose opinions really mattered to me already knew and loved me for who I was.

———❖———

Winning a medal there would not make me a better skier,
it would only prove how good I was to those who didn't already know

———❖———

I recalled the other accomplishments in my life and the person I had become through them. Looking back, I was glad that I had the opportunity to endure the rough spots, to have been good enough to be picked as a medal favorite. If I had dwelled on my misfortune in 1986 in Vail, I would never have persevered to get this far.

Gradually, my attitude changed. I decided to make the best of it and push onward. Members of the media were hovering around outside the first aid building at the base of the mountain, awaiting my reaction to the accident. Finally, with my parents' help, I was able to crutch outside to address the gathering. I told the media the details of the accident as I remembered them, but stated emphatically that I held no one responsible, that accidents sometimes happen.

I could almost feel a sigh of relief from the Olympic officials who had roped off the "cat track" moments after the accident. There was also a sense of disappointment encircling the media when it became evident that there was not going to be an ongoing story about a pretty young American girl with tears in her eyes, surrounded by lawyers taking depositions and threatening legal action.

I remember my reaction to the events on the Olympic track in 1984 when American Mary Decker fell during the women's 3,000-meter run against Zola Budd from South Africa. To me, it appeared that Decker blamed Budd for the tragedy. Watching her cast blame, almost implying the girl did it intentionally, I wondered how much psychological damage was being done to Mary's running career by her negative stance. I'm happy that Mary eventually returned to top form, but I think she must regret the time wasted on her indulgent self-pity. Sometimes, it's just bad luck.

———❖———

Things do not change; we change
—Henry David Thoreau

———❖———

Athletes hear the words, "Good luck," all the time before they compete, and I feel luck is a significant variable in most day-to-day challenges. Everyone has encountered people in business who seem to have all the luck in the world. Their stock picks are always winners. They start up a small business just as that new field takes off. Or maybe they climb through the company ranks, seemingly with little effort. Certainly luck exists, but while bad luck can sideline achievement, I never felt my good results were entirely due to good luck. We are the ones who truly make things happen.

I wanted to cheer-on my teammates, so I chose to wait to go to the Calgary Hospital until after the race. It was tough to watch the event I had worked so hard for take place without me. I waited with anticipation at the bottom of the mountain for the Olympic Downhill to start. After just one competitor skied the course, the Downhill event was postponed due to high winds. Some days it just doesn't pay to get out of bed.

The next day, on crutches, I went back to the mountain with my mom and dad to support my teammates in the Alpine events. I traded Olympic pins and went to as many hockey games as I could. I hung around the Village and met with many remarkable athletes from all over the world. With so much of my life invested in the Olympics, I was determined to have a positive memory of the Games.

———❖———

The spirit, the will to win, and the will to excel are the things that endure. These qualities are so much more important than the events that occur

—Vince Lombardi

———❖———

Arriving home, I was greeted with stacks of mail. I received so many letters from all across the country, but the vast majority came from kids in grade school. Many stated that they were moved by my positive attitude in the face of adversity and found it refreshing. Two-thirds of the people who wrote commented on how relieved they were that I was able to respond with such an upbeat nature. Those letters supported my decision, reassuring me that in times of crisis, we have to remember the person we are, and how we got there. Our positive attitude builds our confidence and helps us move forward.

Sometimes bad things happen. The boss's son-in-law takes over the business, the company is consumed by some conglomerate or the bottom drops out of the market. It's easy to look at a pink slip as a slap in the face, but we need to remember that the bad break doesn't have to reflect on our view of ourselves. Just because this company doesn't want my skills doesn't mean that my skills aren't any good. It certainly doesn't mean that I'm a loser, either.

In times of crisis, we have to remember the person we are, and how we got there

The lessons learned from our mistakes or the bad breaks that come our way can leave solid impressions upon which we build character. We can learn from each setback, even if it occurred as a result of a freak accident.

Casting blame for our lack of success only diminishes our ability to take credit for our achievements. Sometimes the circumstances might be out of our control, but if we assess the situation and find that we did everything we could to achieve our goal, well, that's all we can do. Maybe it just wasn't meant to be.

Dwelling on a bad incident only promotes negative thoughts. Instead, try filling that void with something inspiring. Push yourself into the future. Do something you really enjoy to get on a positive plane: play golf, read a good book, go for a hike. Do anything you can to get yourself back on track.

❖

Casting blame for our lack of success only diminishes our ability to take credit for our achievements

❖

I came back from the second injury healthy, strong and upbeat. I went on to compete at the World Championships in 1989, even though I was already looking for other mountains to climb. One day my dad asked, "Are you having fun? Because if you're not, get out of it. There are too many other things to do in life." I chose to retire from ski racing that spring.

My ski racing career opened the door to an opportunity in television as a color analyst for Alpine skiing. I love developing an angle and educating people about what is happening on the slopes. Because I have experienced first-hand the highs and lows of the sport, as a television commentator I can effectively tell the story and set the stage for the viewers at home.

The lessons I learned competing on the Alpine World Circuit are invaluable. I achieved a level of recognition, not because of an Olympic medal, but through my perseverance and character. I now understand how important it is to stay positive when faced with adversity.

———❖———

The real glory is being knocked to your knees and then coming back.
That's real glory. That's the essence of it

—Vince Lombardi

———❖———

Greg Barton

Photo provided by Greg Barton

At the 1984 Games in Los Angeles, Greg Barton became the first American man since 1936 to win an Olympic medal in kayaking. Four years later he became the sport's superstar when he earned two gold medals on the *same day* (the individual 1,000 meter and the pairs event with teammate Norman Bellingham). What makes his story even more impressive is that he was born with a physical handicap that made participation in sports much more challenging than for most.

Greg won four World Championship titles and, in 1994, he won the Finlandia Clean Water Challenge (a race over lakes from Chicago to New York City). He is the recipient of the Olympia Award and a Sullivan Award finalist.

A member of the National Honor Society and salutatorian of his high school class, Greg went on to become a Summa Cum Laude graduate with a B.S. degree in mechanical engineering from the University of Michigan in 1983. He is currently the president of Epic Paddles, Inc., a supplier of high performance kayak paddles.

A member of the USOC Board of Directors through the year 2000, Greg has assisted the U.S. Olympic fund-raising efforts as a member of Team Xerox and was a part of the 100 Golden Olympians. Greg was also the venue announcer for his sport at the Olympic Games in Atlanta and speaks to audiences around the country on a variety of subjects.

12

Just One Race at a Time

Greg Barton

I was born with club feet. My toes pointed inward and I had to walk on the outside of my feet. After a series of unsuccessful childhood surgeries, I ended up with limited motion in my ankles and one leg an inch shorter than the other. It often hurt to run and sometimes even to walk. It would have been easy to say, "I can't do sports," and let my feet be an excuse, but I am thankful that my family kept me from sinking into self-pity.

Perhaps it is simplistic to point out that even the longest journey begins with a single step, but when each step hurts, you become aware of every part of the journey. I could not yet see myself winning a marathon, but at age 14, one year after my fourth and final surgery, I decided that I was going to run again. I went out in the evening three or four times a week. At first, I would only make it a quarter-of-a-mile before my feet began to ache, and eventually the pain, almost arthritic, would force me to stop. I'd sit down and massage my feet for a few minutes, get up and walk a bit, and eventually begin running again. A short distance conquered, I would then look ahead to the next milestone. After two months, I was able to complete two miles without stopping. A few months later I could go three miles, then eventually up to five miles at a time.

When I was a sophomore in high school, I decided to go out for the cross-country running team. My older brother Bruce had competed for the school a year before and I knew about the dedicated athletes on the team. I had no illusions of becoming the *fastest* runner. I simply wanted to challenge myself to become part of the team and share their winning attitude...one step at a time.

❖

Even the longest journey begins with a single step, but when each step hurts,
you become aware of every part of the journey

❖

Predictably, I was one of the slower runners on the team that year, but I ran as hard as I could in every meet, and I was having a wonderful time with my teammates. Our coach, Chuck King, was great and had a winning attitude. I learned a lot from Mr. King that year. He was the one who pointed out that each goal reached must be followed by setting a new goal.

I remember riding back to school in the bus after a successful dual meet. At one point, Coach King told the driver to pull over to the side of the road. We all wondered what was going on when Coach King got up and said, "I'm proud of you. Great job in winning the meet tonight. However, we need some more training mileage if we are going to continue to improve. We're about three miles from school, so I'd like you to get off the bus and run the rest of the way back."

Immediately my friend and training partner, Tim Bush, got up and said, "Awww, Coach, do we all have to run back to the school?" Coach King replied, "No, I don't want everybody to run back. I only want those of you who want to be state champions to run back to the school."

You can guess what happened. Everybody on that bus, including my friend, Tim, and me, got off and ran. Later that fall, our cross-country team won the school's first-ever State Championship! Coach King helped me reach all my goals in running, so I began to look ahead. I wanted more.

I had taught myself to run and I could play other sports. However, I also realized that I would never compete at the level necessary to go to the Olympics in sports that required a lot of running. Biomechanically, I was still at a disadvantage. Luckily, a few years earlier, I had discovered kayaking. It is an upper body sport. Your feet are used only minimally in the kayak to brace yourself in the boat so the upper body can apply power to the paddle. Kayaking is the perfect sport for me.

I first paddled a canoe at 5 years of age when visiting my aunt and uncle at their cottage in central Michigan. For me, it was a treat to visit them and get a chance to paddle their aluminum canoe. A few years later, my brother Bruce bought an aluminum canoe and kept it at a pond in the woods one-half mile behind our house. I can remember, at 8 years of age, riding my bicycle to that pond all by myself and sneaking out in the canoe.

First, I would practice paddling as quietly as possible, taking very slow and precise strokes with minimal splash on each stroke. I'd try to make no sound as the paddle dipped into the water and I'd try to sneak up on the ducks that lived on the pond. It was truly a joy to paddle.

Then I would practice paddling as fast as I could. I'd take hard strokes, aiming for maximum acceleration from the old canoe. I didn't have a coach telling me to do this. I did it because it was fun! I'd pretend that I was the fastest paddler in the world, even though it would be two years before I even considered entering a race.

At the Olympics, kayaking is contested in singles (K-1), doubles (K-2) and four-man (K-4) over a variety of distances.

When Charles Lindbergh attempted to fly solo nonstop across the Atlantic Ocean, the common belief was that he should use a three- or four-engine plane for greater safety and reliability. At that time, Lindbergh knew that even with a multi-engine plane, if any one engine were to fail, the remaining engines would not be efficient enough to allow a safe completion of the crossing. Multiple engines just made for multiple possibilities of failure. Therefore, the chances of success were greater if he focused all his attention on just one machine by flying a single-engine plane. History proved Lindbergh right.

As in Lindbergh's case, many people thought that America's best chance for Olympic success in the kayaking event would be to put our four fastest paddlers into a four-man boat. I felt that was our *least* likely scenario. Countries such as Hungary, the former Soviet Union and the former East Germany had very strong kayaking programs. They had a large pool of talented athletes, so it was relatively easy for them to assemble a team of four world-class paddlers. Since the U.S. was not a kayaking powerhouse, I knew it would be difficult enough to get myself into world-class condition, much less have my chances depend on three other Americans also reaching that level. I decided to put most of my emphasis on the single kayak event.

My strength in kayaking has always been my endurance and pacing ability. Once I got to the race, my main strategy was to win—not by blowing the competition away at the start with speed (many competitors were still faster than I), but rather to use my ability to pace myself to stay close to them at the start and then make my move later in the race.

It was that focus of attention or *taking the race one step at a time* that I credit with allowing me to become the first American male to win an Olympic medal in kayak in forty-eight years. During the 1984 Olympics in Los Angeles, I finished third in the K-1 (1,000 meters), winning America's first-ever medal in that event. Although an American named Frank Havens won gold medals in canoeing in the 1948 and 1952 Games, no American male had won an Olympic kayak medal since the 1936 Games in Berlin. No American male kayaker had even made the finals in decades.

——❖——

Each goal reached must be followed by setting a new goal

——❖——

As Coach King taught me, when one goal is reached, set a new one. I set my sights on Seoul, South Korea.

My roommate at the Los Angeles Games was a 19-year-old newcomer to the sport, Norman Bellingham, who had come out of the sport of whitewater kayaking. Norm, like me, enjoyed focusing on one thing at a time. His training was impressive. By 1987, Norm was beating me at the shorter distances and pushing me in the 1,000-meter singles, my specialty. Norm had become a world-class competitor in his own right, and we saw this as an excellent opportunity to combine our efforts for a doubles team. Though I continued training for the singles, a new goal was added— a pairs gold medal at the next Olympics in Seoul.

At the major meets, for as long as I could recall, my two events had taken place on the same day. I remember watching the 1975 World K-1 1,000 champion, Gregorz Sledziewski from Poland, attempt both the K-1 and K-2 at the Montreal Olympics, where he finished out of the medals each time. The two events fell only ninety minutes apart, so the unfortunate timing of the races was never a shock, but it was an ambitious challenge just the same.

Norm had a huge stake in whether I should attempt both events, since his only race would come *following* my effort in the singles. We spoke to physiologists and other experts about the consequences of the difficult double. Both events (1,000 singles or doubles) take about three-and-one-half minutes, not unlike running the mile. At the 1987 Worlds, we attempted to complete this difficult "double" and, sadly, after winning the singles event, I was unable to repeat a good performance in the pairs, in which we finished fourth. After reviewing those races, we decided the prime factor was not my conditioning but something in my blood. The intensity of the first race would produce lactic acid throughout my system. Jay T. Kearney of the U.S. Olympic Committee suggested it would have to be flushed from my body by paddling a short distance at medium- to low-intensity during the limited time between events. *That* I could work with…okay, it could be done.

————❖————

Working on two jobs at once can appear a daunting challenge,
but our efforts on one project can often be applied to the other project as well

————❖————

Kayaking requires a combination of strength, endurance and technique. The skills needed for the singles correspond precisely to the skills needed for the doubles event of the same distance, so the training I did in one boat transferred directly to the other. The only difference was my technique—I needed to train in two slightly different strokes. My singles stroke was strong and long compared to most of my competitors. Since the double kayak travels faster than a single, it requires a higher stroke rate. Norm preferred to paddle at a faster rate than I, even when he was in the singles. Therefore, I had to use a slightly shorter paddle and increase my stroke rate whenever we shared a boat.

Working on two jobs at once can appear a daunting challenge. It may feel as if we have twice as much work to do, but our efforts on one project can often be applied to the other project as well. This way, instead of seeing two separate and distinct assignments, we can look at them as one project plus another smaller task that utilizes much of what we are already doing. Thankfully, Norm had faith in me and in our plan. We agreed to take the chance.

When I awoke on the morning of my two Olympic races in 1988, I told myself, "Today, I have only one event—and that is the singles." To perform to the best of my ability, I knew I would need to focus solely on one event at a time. Since the singles race was first, I did my best to block the doubles event from my mind. I didn't worry about it or even consider backing off to save something for later on.

Shortly after dawn, while the water was at its smoothest, the gun sounded and I headed down the 1,000-meter course, seeking my first Olympic gold medal. I came from behind and the finish of my singles race was so close that it required a photo finish. The film revealed that I had beaten the Australian, Grant Davies, by $^5/1000$ths-of-a-second, equal to the distance of less than an inch.

After crossing the finish line, I glanced over to the dock. Norm was there, waiting patiently with our doubles kayak. Right at that moment, I told myself: "Today I have only one event, and that's the K-2."

The singles race was over and there was nothing more I could do about it. Now was the time to start concentrating on the doubles. I paddled over to the dock and gave my singles kayak to the officials so they could verify that it was within specification. Immediately, I jumped into the doubles kayak. Norm and I paddled for twelve minutes before I was called in for the awards ceremony for my first race. That short paddle was both a recovery from the previous race and also a warm-up for the upcoming one. Even more important, it put me in the right frame of mind for our doubles event, a bit more than one hour away.

---❖---

The film revealed that I had beaten the Australian by $^5/_{1000}$ths-of-a-second, equal to the distance of less than an inch.
I told myself: 'Today I have only one event, and that's the K-2'

---❖---

Our main competition was the pair from New Zealand. Ian Ferguson had won the 500-meter "double" in Los Angeles with a win in the 500 K-1 and the K-2 along with his partner, Paul MacDonald. In Seoul, they were the winners of the pairs over 500 meters, and in the 1,000 they were the defending World Champions.

With the shot of the gun, Australia jumped out to an early lead, but Norm and I tried to remain calm, stroking according to plan. We were a bit worried that I might tire out too soon and not have enough to "reel in the field," but we stuck to our race plan. At the halfway point we became worried. New Zealand was a full boat ahead of us, approaching Australia. It was time to change gears. I was in the front of the boat, with Norm seated behind. He was following my cadence, looking for any change in stroke speed or power.

At the 800 mark we still had not closed the gap much, but after I yelled a quick "Hup!" we dropped in a couple of hard strokes to increase speed. We then began to pick up the rate and length of our strokes. We passed Australia within 100 meters, and were neck-and-neck with New Zealand all the way to the finish. I was tiring, but not unexpectedly so.

As we passed the final buoys, we looked over and saw New Zealand's bow cross the finish line. We'd done it! Norm and I had won the gold, defeating the world champs by a comparatively "huge" margin of slightly less than three-tenths of a second.

Wow. America's first and second gold medals in kayaking in forty-eight years…all within the span of an hour-and-a-half!

People everywhere face numerous responsibilities and distractions on a daily basis. For our most important projects, the Olympian within each of us tells us that it is necessary to focus on the task at hand to maximize our performance.

❖

Would it be possible to win a medal in three consecutive Olympics?

❖

It didn't take us long to cool down and prepare for the second awards ceremony—and this time I didn't have to keep glancing at my wristwatch. I was relieved that the battles of the day were over.

After returning home from Seoul, I couldn't help but allow my mind to look ahead to my next goal. Would it be possible to win a medal in *three* consecutive Olympics?

Photo provided by Greg Barton

Each step of the way, the road has been made easier by looking just as far as necessary—yet not beyond that. I was fortunate to represent the U.S. in Barcelona in 1992 and, yes, I was able to win that fourth medal, a bronze in the K-1 (1,000). Once again, after the race, my mind began thinking about the future.

Looking back, it's amazing what was accomplished by focusing on one step at a time...one race at a time. I learned how to walk, then run, then run a long way. I paddled for fun, then for competition, then at an international level. Eventually, after reaching Olympic caliber, I followed that with something that no American kayaker has ever done before. Two gold medals in fewer than ninety minutes. Four Olympic teams and four medals, all made with one goal followed by another, one race at a time.

When life seems to be coming at us head-on, with both barrels blazing, when our schedule can't handle even one more thing, when we feel we've got more plates spinning in the air than a circus performer, don't panic. Focus on one thing at a time, give each task your undivided attention, and you'll be surprised at what you can accomplish. You can do more than you ever dreamed possible.

ERIC FLAIM

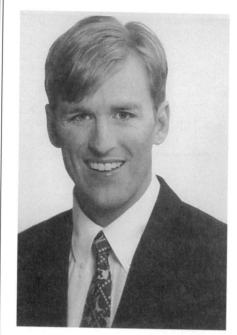

Eric was a member of the U.S. Olympic Team in *four* Olympic Winter Games; Calgary, Albertville, Lillehammer and Nagano. At the 1988 Games in Calgary, Canada, Eric won the silver medal in the 1,500-meters speed skating event, the same year he won the World All-Around title. In 1994, Eric switched sports and competed in *short-track* speed skating, a completely different format and venue. Eric helped the U.S. men earn a silver in the 5,000-meter relay in Lillehammer, becoming America's first-ever medal winner in two different Winter Olympic sports.

Photo provided by Eric Flaim

Revealing his consistency over time and circumstances, Eric held the world's top ranking for more than sixty consecutive months (a longer duration than any other skater in history) and was voted the U.S. Olympic Committee's Athlete of the Year in his respective sports, both in 1988 and 1995. He was rewarded for his tenacity and revered as a leader and spokesperson for the Olympic movement when he was elected by his peers as the flag bearer for the U.S. team in Nagano.

Eric has served as an expert analyst for television coverage of short- and long-track skating, as well as the sport of in-line skating. His television assignments have also included the "X Games" and the "Ultimate In-Line Challenge" on ESPN.

13

Have *And* Be a Role Model

Eric Flaim

A short-track speed skating relay is possibly one of the most excit-ing team events in the Olympics. Forty-five laps around a small "Planters Peanut"-shaped course. Hairpin turns and widening straightaways—bursts of acceleration followed by the sharpest of left-hand turns. Even the skates' blades are set on the left side of our feet to allow a steeper lean to port.

In every other sport's relay, each athlete gets to be in the limelight one time. The anchor leg of a short-track skating relay, however, carries his country's hopes *eight different times.* In the 5,000-meter relay (forty-five laps) each member of the team sprints for one-and-one-half laps and, instead of passing a baton, he gives his teammates a push-off from behind to start the next leg.

In my case, it was fifteen seconds of sprinting, followed by thirty-six seconds of anticipation before it was my turn again. I was always looking ahead to the man who will make the exchange with me. I watched his speed and pace, so I'd know how to be in the perfect place at the perfect time, traveling the perfect speed. It was not easy, because three other teams had their nine other skaters also jockeying for position inside the race course. To the uninitiated, we looked like a swarm of bees, buzzing in a counterclockwise direction.

This is in sharp contrast to the way long-track skaters move around the ice. A long track is a 400-meter oval compared to the short-track's 110 meters. On the *big* surface, they don't have relays and each skater stays in his own lane, with only two athletes on the ice at any one time. Hearing Dan Jansen skate is like listening to Dad slowly sharpen the turkey knife. At short-track, the sound is like Ginsu blades flying at a Benihana's.

------❖------
We can look like a swarm of bees, buzzing in a counterclockwise direction
------❖------

I'm not putting long-track down. In fact, before I was an Olympic short-track skater, I spent several years traveling to the same ovals every year, eating Wiener Schnitzel and leek soup, too. I grew up admiring Eric Heiden, whose performance in 1980 is perhaps the greatest athletic feat in Olympic history. His victories in the 500, 1,000, 1,500, 5,000 and 10,000 are the track equivalent of Carl Lewis winning the marathon as well as the sprints. I sat glued to my family's TV set as "the man in the golden suit" displayed a combination of raw power, pure grace and extreme endurance that epitomized athleticism at the Games in Lake Placid. Speed skating (as Heiden pursued it in training videos) sparked a deep passion in me. He is one of the reasons I wanted to be an all-arounder and skate all the distances.

In 1988, I was prepared to skate on the U.S. Olympic Team in the same five events, but since the sprinting spots were "coach's choice," they elected to allow someone else the chance in the 500 because I had so many other races in which to earn my medals.

I skated four events in those Calgary Games and placed fourth (the "better-luck-next-time" position) in my first two races, the 5,000 meter and the 1,000 meter. Each "near-medal" performance intensified my desire. Both times I had given it my all, even so, I didn't want the "hardware" to elude me any longer. The 1,500 meter was my best event and I came to the line confident and smiling, like a bookworm to a semester final. Since I was close in my "off events," I *expected* to win a medal here.

I knew that a world record was necessary to have any chance at winning—and skating in the first pair forced me to put a big number on the scoreboard. I kept the skating form of my role models for the entire race (almost four laps), and after completing the distance, I looked up and saw the letters "WR" by my time. I had accomplished my goal and was now the man to beat. Sadly, two pairs later Andre Hoffman from East Germany beat my time by $^6/_{100}$ths of a second (the length of a skate). I ended up with a silver medal but knew that I had done my best. I won a medal in the Olympic Games and broke a world record in the process! I skated four events in Calgary, placing no worse than fourth.

Looking up to Eric Heiden allowed me to keep what was good and right in the forefront of my mind. I would imagine his determination whenever I began to feel tired or discouraged. Watching Dan Jansen maintain his dignity and composure after the toughest of breaks helped me keep my disappointments in perspective. I guess that's why I always remember that whenever I'm on the ice some little kid might be watching me as well.

A balance needs to exist between seeing the way life *should* be and the way it actually is. That's one reason Olympic hopefuls study videotapes of the current champions and also watch tape of themselves in competition. Most Olympians look at others to pick up what they are doing well and view their own tape to see what they could be doing better. I want to take the best parts from a variety of people, without losing myself in the process. Using an Olympian as a role model in a particular area can awaken the Olympian that resides in each of us.

---❖---

Whenever I'm on the ice some little kid might be watching me as well

---❖---

During the summer when ice was hard to find, I would train on a slide board (you may have seen these on television). Wearing slippery socks, I would slide across a plastic sheet, bouncing side-to-side between two wooden bumpers. I watched the mirror in front of me to make sure my form didn't change. In my mind's eye I would try to recall the perfection of Nick Thometz or Eric Hendricksen, two of America's greatest technicians. Having them to emulate helped my form improve more quickly and stay correct during the long and monotonous hours of training.

The truly great athletes aren't just exceptional performers; they also are exceptionally positive. They make no excuses, take the blame when results don't meet expectations and congratulate their teammates on every shining performance. Picking a role model (or picking the correct attributes to model) requires some discernment. Many of today's sports superstars have displayed questionable motives with morally inept conduct. Working toward a goal means more than winning at all costs; it means keeping to the higher ideals and values as well. I tried to pattern myself after the good guys—the great athletes with strong will. I found that whenever I thought of myself as being like them, my races would turn out well. If instead I spent time worrying about my shortcomings, my performances suffered. I realized that a positive attitude matched with careful preparation and dedication worked best every time.

That's one reason I didn't want to quit the sport after 1988. After undergoing knee surgery because of an earlier car accident, my technique suffered. I felt as though I was limping my way around the curves. Even so, I knew that obstacles like this were made for overcoming. Even when I didn't make the 1991 National Team (*after* being the world record holder), I just couldn't give up. That's not what Eric Heiden would do, I thought.

———❖———

Many of today's sports superstars have displayed questionable motives with morally inept conduct. I tried to pattern myself after the good guys

———❖———

I rebounded nicely and by 1992, I was back in top form. I won a World Cup 1,000-meter event in a pre-Olympic meet, and came to the Games in Albertville filled with confidence.

The Americans had ice time between 5 and 7 p.m. on the day before my event. Trying to stoke the furnace before training, I made a quick trip to the athletes' cafeteria around 3 p.m. The French are known for their superb cuisine, but when feeding thousands of hungry skiers and skaters, some things are compromised.

The selection was poor that day and, needing to eat quickly, I served myself from what I later called a "Fishloaf." It was either that or a "Mystery Meat," which didn't seem all that appetizing, either.

You can probably guess the rest. On the ice that afternoon, I began to feel weird, sort of unsettled. Later that night, the food poisoning hit me full force. It was a double whammy—vomiting and diarrhea all night long. By the time the sun came up, I was dehydrated and exhausted.

What was I going to do? I didn't think they'd reschedule the event on my account, so I washed up and decided to make the best of this awful situation.

My 1,500-meter race was scheduled for 4 p.m. and I hoped that I could recover in time. I didn't want to tell anyone about my problem except my coach, Stan Klukowski. He was raised in Poland, under the shadow of the Soviet regime, and he knew all about skating. He suggested I drink lots of fluids and try to get some electrolytes back into my system. (Perhaps he was joking, but he also suggested that the Russians had conspired to poison me before the race).

I tried skating around the ice a couple of times, but quickly realized that my gold medal would not happen on that day.

Even so, I felt like the last finisher in the 1968 Olympic Marathon, John Stephen Akwari from Tanzania. In the finish area, he said, "My country did not send me to Mexico City to start the race, they sent me to finish the race." Following the examples set by the role models I'd chosen, I felt compelled to skate the one race I knew I could not win.

The gold that year went to Johann Olaf Koss from Norway, who skated a 1:54.81. Though my best time ever was a 1:52.1, I skated a 2:01+ and finished 24th.

My folks had tears in their eyes when I explained the reason for my poor showing, but by the end of the evening, I was surrounded by loved ones and began to look forward to the rest of my life. So what if I didn't win the gold? I've got lots of other things to look forward to, I thought.

———❖———

I had to skate the one race I knew I could not win

———❖———

Within a few months I was racing professionally…no, not on the ice, but with in-line skates on the road for Team Rollerblade. The sport was very similar in style to short-track and my conditioning was in place. It didn't take very long for me to draw the conclusion that I was going to attempt my third Olympics, but in a new sport. The bug was still there. I just needed a change of scenery with a new sport.

In 1994, I won the U.S. Olympic Team trials in short-track speed skating and we headed off to the Lillehammer Olympic Winter Games.

Though I didn't make the final in either of my two individual short-track events, I did qualify for the relay where I was teamed with Randy Bartz, John Coyle and Andy Gable. Andy was a former long-track skater with whom I had trained in the past. He had been on every World Team since 1986 for short-track and competed in the previous two Olympics. I looked to him as a model in tactics and strategy.

The U.S. team finished seventh at the prior World Championships and just barely qualified for the Olympics. Naturally, we were not expected to medal.

In the heats, we surprised the field by finishing second behind Australia. This allowed us to join the Aussies, the Italians and Canadians in the Olympic final race for the gold.

The race covered forty-five laps and, with twenty-five to go, the field was tightly bunched when the Canadian fell and slid into the pads. With no lanes to separate the teams, there is always a lot of drafting and fancy footwork. Teammate John Coyle jumped over the fray and into the lead. We led for the next fifteen laps, but not by much, when suddenly Italy streaked by and quickly built an insurmountable 10-meter gap. When the Australians passed us with five to go, I thought, *Andy will be there on the last exchange. I have to come out perfect, tight to the blocks, then go like a bat out of hell.* On the final exchange, Andy Gable gave me the perfect push past the Aussies. I held them off for the final two laps and we won the silver.

The fact that I then became America's first Olympian to win medals in two *different* winter sports escaped me for the longest time. It was not until 1998, when I qualified for my fourth Olympic Team, that I realized the significance of *being* a role model, as well as having one.

In the winter of 1998, as I was about to board my flight to the Olympics in Japan, I placed one last call to my fiancee, Marci. She was excited and said the newspapers were reporting I had been nominated to carry the American flag into the Opening Ceremony in Nagano.

The American flag bearer has always been elected by the captains of each of the various sports teams (i.e., hockey, luge, figure skating, skiing, etc.) and they always seem to choose the one person whose character and dedication to the Olympic ideal stands out from the crowd. Athletic success rarely has anything to do with the selection. Each sport nominates its candidate and the team captains meet privately to reduce the nominees until only one remains.

When I got off the plane in Osaka (site of the American processing center where we receive our uniforms, credentials and all the other freebies that come with being an Olympian), a staff person handed me a fax. Amid the jet-lag and sheer exhaustion, I asked her to tell me what it said.

I thought I heard her say, "You've been nominated to carry the flag!" and I thought to myself, "I already heard that news fifteen hours ago. Right now, I just want to go to bed."

"No," she said, "You don't understand. They had the election and they voted for you!" Immediately, my teammates surrounded me with big grins, pats on the back and whoops that bounced off the walls.

——❖——

You don't understand. They had the election and they voted for you!

——❖——

It dawned on me that, without knowing it, my life had quietly become worthy of role modeling, too. By patterning my life after quality

Photo courtesy of Duomo/Paul J. Sutton

people and quality traits, it was inevitable that some would choose to pattern themselves after me. I never set out to be a role model, but luckily there were enough Olympians out there who appreciated what my career stood for, that I was elected to represent them at this special occasion. I was speechless.

I've never won an Olympic title and was not expected to do well in Nagano. I never received the commercial endorsements or sported a memorable haircut. I had a full-time job *outside* of the Olympic world and planned to earn my living off the ice. I do not consider myself a hero by any stretch of the imagination, but my peers had chosen to bestow on me the greatest honor an Olympian can receive.

Two days later, the American Chef de Mission, Paul George, placed the flagpole in my hand and I marched behind a sumo wrestler, leading the entire 1998 U.S. Winter Olympic Team through the tunnel and into the light.

NANCY HOGSHEAD

At the 1984 Olympics in Los Angeles, Nancy Hogshead concluded eight years as a world-class swimmer with three gold medals and one silver medal—the most decorated swimmer at the Games.

Photo courtesy of Bill Frakes

In recognition, Nancy has been inducted into eight Halls of Fame, including the International Swimming Hall of Fame. She graced the cover of *Newsweek* and was featured on a ninety-foot billboard in New York City's Times Square in an ad for Jockey International.

Nancy began working at the Women's Sports Foundation (the national advocacy organization for girls and women in sports) as an intern while in college at Duke University, eventually becoming the Foundation's fourth president in 1992. During her presidency, the WSF tripled its budget and secured the resources to build a Hall of Fame. She continues to write and lecture extensively on women in athletics. The Olympics also brought a diagnosis of exercise-induced asthma. Nancy authored *Asthma and Exercise*, a book that combines stories of how world-class athletes control their asthmatic condition. As the national spokesperson for the American Lung Association, she addressed the subject of asthma management skills on "Good Morning America," "The Today Show," "CBS This Morning" and "Nightline."

Nancy is currently an attorney at Holland & Knight LLP, one of the world's largest law firms, after having attended Georgetown University Law School. Her practice includes commercial, employment, and Title IX litigation. This super-achiever speaks regularly to corporate and civic groups, with an emphasis on her fundamentals of success.

14

Success Is a Learned Skill

Nancy Hogshead

Everyone knows that Olympic athletes train very hard. But I've found that very few people grasp the enormity of the physical and emotional commitment. To get this point across when I speak around the country I mark off the room to demonstrate the size of an average high-school pool, which is twenty-five yards in length. Then I ask the audience, "How many laps do you suppose you'd have to swim every day to become the best in the world?" Most groups start guessing at around fifty laps. Fifty laps? That's just warm-up!

In the hard part of the season my teammates and I would swim *800* laps a day. That's 20,000 yards or about twelve miles.

Not everyone wants to be an Olympian, but everyone has *some* goal that they want enough to perform the *equivalent* of swimming 800 laps to achieve: to be good at a profession; to be part of a winning team; to have a solid family life; to be able to help others in a meaningful way.

There is no shortcut, no "luck" and no way to manipulate the system to your advantage *without* hard work. Improving your attitude will not relieve you of having to work hard, although it does make the effort easier. If you're not willing to give consistently, half-hearted trying will just create another disappointment. Try the lottery instead!

Why should you push yourself? The answer: Because the rewards of *reaching* for excellence truly are profound. I'm not talking about a pay raise, a plaque or even a gold medal. It's *living into a purpose or a calling* that enlivens even the most mundane tasks. It's a deep pride in the life we are living.

———◈———

Half-hearted trying will just create another disappointment. Try the lottery instead!

———◈———

Today, I'm an attorney working on commercial litigation and gender equity in university athletic departments. Every day I depend on the same skills that took me to the victory platform at the Olympic Games. I haven't stopped learning because I haven't stopped setting new goals. While I don't pretend to have all the answers, I do know something about what it takes to achieve a big goal over the long haul. It starts with a daily commitment to the goal and continues with hard work, which is the underpinning of any achievement.

My goal for this chapter is that you, the reader, will give yourself over to a purpose and then see yourself grow in unexpected ways as you pursue that dream.

DAILY COMMITMENT

There is a lot of emphasis on *making* the commitment or the big decision: "I'm going to be in the Olympics!" "I'm going to be a doctor!" "I'm going to sell twenty percent more than last year!" "I'm going to be the best parent ever!" "I'm going to start a business that makes a difference in the world!" But getting there requires making the same choice every day—for *years*, like getting up at 4:45 a.m. to go to morning practices or working on a weekend when you already had plans or tackling labor strikes, volatile markets, obsolete products or legal entanglements. At home, it's when we take the time to answer our four-year-old's questions (even when it's been a tough day) or eating healthy when we crave ice cream.

For example, the Itchnatucknee is a spring water river that flows through some of the most beautiful Florida landscape, winding around cypress trees and through chalky banks. Every kind of wildlife calls this place home.

One day, my coach got the bright idea to have us swim against the current, *up* the Itchnatucknee River. Sounds like fun, right? Yeah, we thought so, too, but the reality was a little different.

For starters, spring water is *cold*, even in Florida. I saw teammates' faces turn every shade from white to blue. Although the water is lovely when viewed from a raft drifting downstream, a thundering herd of swimmers thrashing up the river brings silt up from the bottom, blinding all except the lead swimmers. Nobody wants to lead, either, because the lead swimmer (like a lead cyclist on the Tour de France) "pulls" everyone else. If I was lucky enough to get right behind one of the big guys, (like 6'6" John Naber), I got a nice ride, but the lead swimmers knew what was happening and didn't appreciate it. They'd often stop abruptly, causing a multi-swimmer pile up.

The slimy green grass wrapped itself around my arms and shoulders and (my favorite part) *where do you think the bugs live?* My swimsuit was cut with a scooped "V" below the neck, so where do you suppose those bugs went? You got it! Right down the front! Where did they go out? Well, they didn't. Swimming the river was like an entomology lesson—afterward my suit was filled with beetles, granddaddy long legs, grasshoppers, all going crunch, crunch. Once, training partner and Olympic medal winner Billy Forrester turned to me and said, "What's that on your hip?" It was a dead frog.

Remember, this was a training exercise to increase our lung capacity, endurance and strength—not a peaceful field trip. Swimming up the river was hard work. It took five hours to go up and back. We did this every Wednesday for two years.

❖

'What's that on your hip?' It was a dead frog

❖

If I had depended on that moment when I made the big decision, I wouldn't have made it. It was the daily decisions, such as the choice to swim up a river when you're slightly "bug-phobic" that go unrecognized and frequently unrewarded, but which make the big goals possible. If you can keep that goal in front of you in spite of all that life throws at you, you've mastered the *daily* commitment, not just the commitment of the moment.

Now that you've made the decision and you're making the same decision every day, let's talk about staying true to your decision.

EXPECT OBSTACLES

Ever wonder why it seems as if every Olympian has to overcome something? The media love to give us these heart-tugging stories of injury, disease, violence, family tragedy and financial limitations. Other obstacles that aren't as media-friendly can interfere with a commitment just as easily, including: lack of support from family and friends; being told we are "foolish" or "not realistic"; personal disputes with coaches or teammates or even the doubts about whether attaining the goal is worth the effort.

I hate to be the one to burst the myth, but most Olympians do *not* have perfect bodies. They are not in perfect health, are not rich, do not live right next to the world's greatest facilities or coaches, are not exempt from the effects of racism, sexism and poverty, do not have conflict-free relationships with their coaches, teammates and support systems.

It shouldn't be surprising. The world doesn't give people exactly what they need to achieve their dream on a silver platter. Going up, down and around obstacles is *normal*, something to be expected when pursuing a big goal. *The Road Less Traveled* by Scott Peck has been on the *New York Times* bestseller list for more than two decades. It begins with the sentence, "Life is difficult." What I find perplexing is not that Olympians have to deal with these hurdles, but that people are perpetually surprised that Olympians have to overcome *anything at all*.

———❖———

Most Olympians do not have perfect bodies, are not in perfect health, are not rich, and are not exempt from the effects of racism, sexism and poverty

———❖———

A 90-year-old man came up to me after one of my talks and said, "I could have been in the Olympics. It's just that I got in a fight with my coach." I was raised to respect my elders, but I wanted to tell him, "If you let a fight with your coach get between you and the Olympics—you *weren't even close.* You've been kidding yourself for the last seventy years."

The fact that life isn't going to hand us our big reward is precisely why achieving it requires us to grow in unimaginable ways, to move far outside our comfort zone, to stretch our ideas of what we think of as possible. Expect the obstacles and embrace the struggle of growing.

WINNING WITH *YOUR* CIRCUMSTANCES

Right after the Olympics, many people wanted to know, "How did you do it?" I would recount how my parents did thus and my coach motivated me in a particular way. But soon I realized that I was doing a disservice to my listeners because no one else on the planet was ever going to have circumstances exactly like mine.

Also, if my achievement was contingent on the occurrence of precisely those circumstances, then my achievement amounted to plain luck— and I knew that I didn't get to the Olympics through luck.

To begin with, my parents are truly wonderful people. My father is an orthopedic surgeon and my mother was a teacher until the kids came along, at which time she moved into very meaningful volunteer work. But swimming was not their gig.

I was just 14-years-old when I broke my first American record at our National Championship meet in Canton, Ohio. I broke the record in the prelims and I still had to swim the race again in the finals later that night. I was so excited that I was crying when I called my parents in Jacksonville to tell them my big news:

"I broke the American record," I said between big sobs.

"Good. Good. Did you make it into the finals?"

"Yes, Mom...I was first." *You know? I just swam faster than any American ever had before!*

"Good. Good. What stroke did you swim?" *Oh, please.*

"I swam the butterfly, Mother."

"Oh. I like it when you swim the backstroke so I can see your face."

Get the picture?

———❖———

Both Tracy and I could have justified quitting

———❖———

Contrast my parents with Tracy Caulkins' parents. Tracy is the "winningest" swimmer ever, having won forty-eight National Titles and at different points in her career held American records in every stroke, both in sprint and distance events. She had an amazing athletic career.

Tracy's parents drove her and her teammates to practice, sat through many practices, clocked her split times during workout and were involved in the United States Swimming National Governing Body. Her father was a starter for many of her races.

Both Tracy and I could have justified quitting. Tracy could have said she was pressured too much and I could have said I wasn't supported enough. Even though we came from completely different circumstances, we each won three Olympic gold medals. We both won *with* our circumstances.

BEING COACHABLE

Everyone talks about finding a mentor or mentoring others, but few talk about the skills needed to be *mentorable*, to be coachable. I define being coachable as giving another person permission to demand the very best of you. I don't mean following someone blindly, ignoring your ideas or principles. I'm talking about having a goal big enough that you're willing to step outside your comfort zone—in your relationships with others—and to allow someone else to contribute.

—❖—

I whispered, 'I don't care.' Big mistake!

—❖—

Being coachable/mentorable is a learned skill that will serve you in your quest for high goals. I would not have made it to the victory stand without my coaches. Not even close. As a lawyer, I now actively seek out those within our law firm with high standards, who might push me and help me develop my legal skills.

I have been fortunate to work with several world-class coaches, and each one has contributed to my success. One afternoon, my coach made me race a fifty-yard backstroke (two laps) against a swimmer who had missed morning practice and (as far as I was concerned) had just loafed the afternoon workout (as much as one can coast 400 laps). I felt that after swimming my 800 laps, I was "done for the day." I was bone tired and didn't want any part of this unfair race at the end of practice.

We raced, she won and under my breath, I whispered, "I don't care." Big mistake!

My coach hauled me up out of the water by the strap on my suit and chewed me out good. Meanwhile, my suit was giving me a wedgie and my coach's face was just two inches from mine—and he had the worst breath.

The mind can do many things with this experience:

How dare he! How could he humiliate me in front of my teammates! I'm his best swimmer and hardest worker! It was just two laps out of 800! I do NOT deserve to be treated this way! I'm outta' here!

Or:

What's wrong with me? How come I gave up? Maybe I really don't want it. Maybe I don't have what it takes. Maybe I'm just wasting my time. What's the use? I'm outta' here!

But that's the great thing about high goals. My goal of gold medals gave my coach the permission to "get in there" and interrupt that conversation inside my head. He shook my perfectly rational, reasoned belief that I had done enough. But *that* thinking was only going to get me to a certain level, and not to the victory stand at the Olympic Games.

❖

If the people around you have to do it perfectly according to you, you will probably have a hard time finding effective mentors

❖

After telling this story, I've had people say, "I don't respond to that kind of motivation." Let me be clear: I am *not* recommending that particular coaching technique. But when I tell this story, it makes the point that if the people around you (your mentors) have to do it perfectly *according to you,* you will probably have a hard time finding effective mentors and what you can achieve will be limited.

It's the Journey

Note that my chapter does not contain a paragraph describing "the thrill of victory." That's because, for me, the honor and glory of the Olympics come from the journey, not from any one event. Throughout my career I probably swam with a thousand other swimmers from some of the country's best teams, and only a handful of us made it to the Olympics. But all 1,000 of us went through a process that taught us the fundamentals of success and prepared us for the big challenges in life. I am altered by the Olympic experience, not because I stood on a victory platform, but because I went for it without holding anything in reserve. There was no "What if?" because I knew I had gone through the struggle and had done everything I could do.

Throughout this journey of years of workouts and competitions, there were moments of true mastery, of bliss, of a oneness with myself and the world. All the splashing and chaos of workout life were muted and my soul was very still. Truly effortless. During these times, it felt like my soul hovered about two feet above my body and it condensed into a sliver, a needle. These were my shared moments with God.

Photo courtesy of Heinz Kleutmeier

In the yin and yang of life, I don't know whether I could have had such spiritual moments without also experiencing the downside of going for a big goal: the slumps and discouragements; the feeling that I could not make myself get in the water another day; the agonizing questions about whether this was the right path; the feeling that my goal was dominating my life, rather than vice versa. I endured a two-and-one-half-year period in which I did not improve a single time. And still, I got back in the water, every day.

—————❖—————

I am altered by the Olympic experience,
because I went for it,
without holding anything in reserve

—————❖—————

Ultimately, I felt that developing the talents God gave me was a noble purpose. I was proud of what I was doing. I've heard people share their visions of leadership, excellence, pregnancy, parenthood and community in much the same way. That sense of purpose gives us the ability to move beyond what we otherwise might have thought possible.

To awaken the Olympian within, we must have faith in the noble purpose of our life's goals. We must learn the skills of success to achieve our noble purpose. We'll be amazed at what we are capable of achieving.

TIM DAGGETT

At the 1984 Olympic Games in Los Angeles, for the first time in modern Olympic history, the United States men won the gymnastics team competition, and they clinched it with the high bar routine of Tim Daggett. His dismount went fifteen feet in the air with a double-back, laid-out full twisting somersault, and his perfect landing earned the maximum score...a 10.0, guaranteeing that the American underdogs would wear the gold medal.

Photo provided by Tim Daggett

While most of his teammates chose to retire in the wake of the fanfare, Tim elected to go back to the gym. Injuries plagued his career but they did not stop his resolve. Tim's willingness to dream and his tenacity in the face of adversity are the messages audiences love to hear. His book, *Dare to Dream*, is a poignant and motivational autobiography. His lectures, accompanied by videos and gymnastics performances, keep him in great demand across the country.

Tim Daggett has been the voice for gymnastics on ESPN, Turner Broadcasting, Prime Ticket Cable and NBC, the network of the Olympic Games. The Tim Daggett Gold Medal Gymnastics Club teaches more than 1,300 gymnasts.

15

How Bad Do You Want It?

Tim Daggett

It may not have been the best grammar in the world, but *How Bad Do You Want It?* was what was written on a little sign that had been stuck to the ceiling over my bed from the time I had made the decision to be an Olympic gymnast…somewhere around the grand old milestone of my eleventh birthday. It was that sign that greeted me when I awoke each morning and it was that phrase that drove me to achieve my goals and surpass my ultimate dream—a Perfect 10 at the 1984 Olympic Games in Los Angeles that clinched the first-ever gold medal for the U.S. Men's Gymnastics Team.

It had been nearly three years since that gold-medal performance, and some fourteen years since I'd first stood on my mattress and taped the hand-printed sign to my ceiling. Now, it was February 1987, and although many years had passed, that sign remained. As I lay flat on my bed on a gray Los Angeles morning, I cursed its words because I wasn't sure that what I wanted was even a remote possibility.

Two weeks earlier, while preparing for the 1987 American Cup, I had flown off the high bar performing a release skill, had missed regrasping the bar by mere inches and had fallen fifteen feet, landing directly on my head, rupturing a disc in my neck.

What followed was a trip to the hospital and worried looks from the medical specialists whenever they read my X-rays. Gymnastics is a dangerous enough sport without risking more serious injuries by doing tumbling exercises with a herniated disc. The recommended safe treatment was to "recover and find something else to do with your life."

The most encouraging diagnosis came from Dr. Bert Mandelbaum, the orthopedic surgeon who told me that he *didn't* think my neck would require surgery. Such an operation would fuse the vertebrae together and, among other things, would eliminate my ability to perform gymnastics. He was one of a small minority who thought I might be able to resume my gymnastics career, but the road would not be easy. It would have to be my choice.

Just as it changed my life once before, that hand-drawn sign helped me once again. That sign (*How bad do you want it?*) forced me to choose: Did I want acceptable excuses or did I want greatness? I *did* want to return to my prior level of excellence. I *did* want to be a great gymnast, I *did* want to reach my full potential as an athlete, and *I wanted it bad.* Succumbing to self-pity was not a way to get there.

I've heard that denial is called the "shock absorber" of the soul. If that's true, my shock absorbers were working overtime. It did not matter that I had spent the previous ten days in the hospital in cervical traction, that the restrictive collar I still wore around my neck would remain there for the next few months. It did not matter that many (*most*) gymnasts never come back from an injury of this type. All that mattered was that now I needed to get to the gym.

As badly as I had wanted to win gold in 1984, I now wanted to prove to the world and to myself that I was still, first and foremost, a gymnast. I was not satisfied with being the gold-medal-winning celebrity who had crisscrossed the continent the prior two-and-one-half years doing interviews, television shows and sports specials, telling my story over and over again of how incredible it had felt to win the gold. I was not a movie star. I was a gymnast.

Apart from being part of the team, all I wanted then was to be the best gymnast in the world—me—Tim Daggett. The kid from West Springfield, Massachusetts, one of seven children, the last Olympic gymnast to have "made it" from a public high school gym (not a private gymnastics club, where lessons cost money that a big family with a schoolteacher father could not have afforded).

I had beaten the odds once. I could do it again. I was going to be the best gymnast in the world. And I wanted it *bad.*

Hauling myself from bed, I took one last look at the sign. Yes, I told myself, I want to be great again—not lie idly in bed while the rest of the sport moved forward without me. With that kind of positive attitude, I may not have been ready to deal with reality as the world saw it, but I was comfortable with the decision.

In the meantime, it was important for me to keep the extent of my injury "under wraps," to continue to avoid the media and all but my closest friends.

That morning, as I struggled to dress to go to the gym at UCLA where I had spent most of the past six years, the phone did not stop ringing. I had, however, stopped answering it. Too many people had seen the newspapers. Too many people had seen the account of my injury, which somehow had wound up in the nationwide daily, *USA Today*, and too many people wanted to talk about it. I did not. I kept saying to myself that I had "only" ruptured a disc and it was going to be fine. It was not the first obstacle that I had had to overcome.

Everyone who called seemed to want to hear me acknowledge the end of my career. It was almost as if they were waiting for me to break down in tears and I was afraid if I listened to them, I just might. So I made the conscious decision to ignore them...to put their negative energy someplace where it couldn't touch me. I didn't want to argue with them, I just wanted to train.

I managed to slug my way to the gym. Hindered by the collar that held my neck together and the fact that the injury had left my entire left side incredibly weak, I began by doing basic skills on the apparatus—anything that wasn't too risky, anything I could perform without having to turn my head or look up or look down. It was a gymnast's nightmare.

Everyone in the gym cheered me on in the unspoken, supportive language that passes between athletes who know what it's like to be injured. It's almost as if they don't want to talk about it either. About four o'clock that afternoon I was beginning to feel tired. And sore.

When the phone rang at the far end of the gym, I ignored it.

"Tim," someone shouted, "It's for you. Some doctor."

The last thing I wanted to do was talk on the phone, but maybe it was Dr. Mandelbaum telling me I could take this cumbersome collar off sooner than expected. It was not Dr. Mandelbaum. It was a doctor I'd never heard of, a doctor whose name I cannot remember and could not remember within seconds of hearing his voice.

"I'm a big fan of yours," said Dr. What's-His-Name. "I've followed your career for years and I saw the article in *USA Today*."

Ugh. There was the harsh truth, curling its way through the phone wires, trying to sneak into my brain. I stared at the balance beam where a gymnast from the women's team was doing a skill. I did not respond to the doctor.

"I just wanted you to know I'm sorry," he continued, "but I'm sure with the kind of determination you have, you'll succeed at whatever else you attempt in life. You're a winner, Tim. You'll always come out on top."

I hope I said goodbye. I hope I was at least polite to the man. But when I hung up, a strange, strangling sensation gripped the base of my skull. That was when the cold chill of reality finally slapped me. This doctor, like so many others, believed my career was over.

The activity continued around me.

The women took turns on the beam. Down by the rings, Coach Yefim spotted for another guy. I rubbed the edge of the cervical collar. I wondered if everyone was right. I wanted to cry out, "What's going to happen to me?" I wanted to ask the other athletes if they ever faced such darkness, if they'd ever been...*scared*. I wanted to ask Yefim what I should do. Instead, I simply stood there, too afraid that if I vocalized the words, they would come true: that if I actually said out loud, "I may have to retire," then there would be no choice.

How bad do you want it? returned to my mind. I no longer had an immediate answer. Was "it" worth risking...failure? Until now, that had not been a word in my vocabulary. Perhaps training in this weakened state would be dangerous. I could become paralyzed or worse. This was no longer about missing out on a sports team; this was about life and death.

It's easy to let other people's doubts creep into our minds, but the Olympian within has to be stronger than the negative thoughts that float all around us.

I think it was in that moment, though, that I decided it didn't matter what the outcome would be. What mattered was that I continue to try. Because, for me, once I stopped trying, I knew that would be the greatest defeat of all. It didn't matter that I had already reached the top once already. What mattered was the question, "Who are *you*, Tim Daggett? Against what standards do you measure yourself?"

For some, the standard is an Olympic gold medal. For someone who is injured, merely making the team is enough. For the disabled, just walking across the floor is an accomplishment and, for others, raising a family or starting up a new business counts just as much. Each of us knows what our secret desires include. The trick is to believe in our ability to make the desires happen. Without that fundamental belief, none of the rest is possible.

I had to acknowledge the severity of the injury, but I didn't have to accept it as permanent. Just because I couldn't turn my head sideways that day didn't mean that I would *never* be able to do so.

❖

*Once we set our goals, make our plans and begin our quest,
we have to ask ourselves each and every day, 'How bad do I want it?'*

❖

Years later I was reminded of my determination as I watched Kim Zmeskal before she became America's first World All-Around Champion. At the 1991 American National Championships, Kim found herself unable to perform a significant part of her uneven bars routine, the release move.

As you can imagine, the most dangerous and impressive parts of any bars routine are the release moves, allowing the athlete to move from one bar to the other. The more difficult the trick, the more rewarding the scores from the judges. The release skills are the most critical for timing and, done poorly, can be disastrous. You miss a release, you lose the element, lose $5/10$ths for the fall, and you're out of the competition.

On that day, Kim fell three times in warm-up. Not months before, not days before...but minutes before she attempted to become the best in the country, she could not make the move work. She struggled and worked so hard, and just couldn't do it. But that didn't mandate that she would fall in competition.

A gymnast with less desire would have let the falls, the disappointments, take away her confidence, but not Kim. She just kept doing the same trick until she got it right and then she sat down to patiently wait her turn on the bars.

At the end of the day, Kim Zmeskal was crowned the best performer in the country on that apparatus, earning her first-ever national title. Her difficulty in the warm-up was real, but she refused to see it as permanent.

It was with the same kind of outlook that my own commitment took me back to the gym—at first, gently, but soon after, the collar came off (surgery was not required). I was back to my old tricks, including dozens of routines on each apparatus, new tricks to be learned and refined and, of course, the proving ground of major competition.

I made it back. I finished in fourth place at the 1987 U.S. National Championships. From there, third place in the Pan American Games and, fewer than eight months after the devastating injury, I was on my way to the World Championships. I had made the team; I had come back.

I remember wondering what Dr. What's-His-Name was doing that day.

Photo courtesy of Dave Black

It's now been more than a decade since my neck injury and I've learned a lot. As a sports commentator for NBC, a motivational speaker and the owner of a gymnastics training center, I've learned that even though circumstances don't always turn out the way we expect, it is our decision—and ours alone—whether or not we will give up.

When mothers bring their children to my gym, they often ask how their kids might make it to the Olympics. The first thing I try to do is explain that, yes, all children can aspire to greatness, but not until they decide it is what *they* want and that *they* are willing to pay the price to achieve it.

Once we set our goals, make our plans and begin our quest, we have to ask ourselves each and every day, *How bad do I want it?* If we want it badly enough, we will go out there and give it our all.

Sometimes, that means not listening to the odds.

Actor Christopher Reeve, who was paralyzed as the result of an equestrian accident, believes that it's not what happens to people that matters but, rather, how they cope with what has happened. The remarkable "comeback" of this inspiring man has not—to date—been witnessed in the riding arena, but in his remarkable approach to life as a quadriplegic. In the reshaping of his heart and soul, he is successfully learning the art of rede-fining his dreams, because *life*, apparently, is what he has chosen; it is what he wants *that bad*.

How bad did I want it? Badly enough to eradicate, walk around and leap over the obstacles, which probably has been the most important train-ing—not just for my gymnastics, but for my life. Denial? Maybe. But often we cannot achieve success without risking failure. And if I've learned nothing else, it's that sometimes we must take that risk to reach our high-est dreams, overcome our strongest fears in order to fulfill our greatest potential. And most of all, we must want it badly enough.

CATHY TURNER

Cathy Turner was a promising young skater when she gave up her Olympic dream for nine years to pursue another love, a career as a professional singer and songwriter.

Despite a successful music career, something in her life was missing and she eventually battled severe depression and an identity

Photo provided by Cathy Turner

crisis. Cathy "found" herself when she decided to resume her quest for an Olympic gold medal.

Critics scoffed at the notion that a 26-year-old woman could set out to achieve her Olympic dream after such a tremendous setback. Cathy proved them wrong by winning both gold and silver medals in the 1992 Olympic Winter Games in Albertville, France.

She retired immediately after the 1992 Games, only to make a stunning comeback just seven months prior to the 1994 Winter Olympics in Lillehammer, Norway. Amazingly, she added two more medals to her collection—another gold and a bronze— and a new 500 meter Olympic record. In 1998, as a challenge to herself, Cathy competed in her third Olympics in Nagano, Japan.

Cathy Turner has starred in a touring Ice Capades show as a singer and skater, served as an analyst on ESPN and the Sports Channel, has appeared on numerous talk shows and sports documentaries and has hosted a number of fitness infomercials. She is the president and owner of Cathy Turner's Empire Fitness in Hilton, New York.

16

See It, Believe It, Be It!

Cathy Turner

Sometimes it's an article in the paper or a story on the news that sets into motion a series of events that can confound the world. I know many athletes just like me, who, in their youth watched an Olympian on television and said, "Someday, I want to be just like that!" Dreams are born so easily in the days when we flip-flop from career aspirations such as fireman and astronaut to inventor or movie star. What makes those dreams pop up so easily when we're young, and what keeps them from coming true later in life?

I've learned that dreaming is the easy part. Hanging on to that dream and believing in yourself is what's really important in making any dream come true.

Because the business world and the world of sport have so much in common, whenever I address corporate groups, I like to share my philosophy of achievement: "See it, Believe it, Be it!"

SEE IT

Expecting great things to happen just because things seem to be going great is not a guarantee of success. We need to know exactly where we want to go and have a vision that we can see clearly in our minds to achieve success.

When I was seven, my parents had a large heavy chair in their bedroom that I managed to push in front of the mirror. I climbed up onto that chair, waving my arms way up above my head (in slow motion just like I had seen on TV) pretending I was at the Olympics and crossing the finish line in first place to become the best speed skater in the world! What a rush that was for me! I remember actually feeling the experience. It was so intense I cried with the thrill of it all.

Here I was, a 7-year-old with a vision! So what? All I knew was that I wanted to be an Olympic champion one day. Everyone was calling me "a natural" and saying things like, "Someday, I'm going to watch you win an Olympic gold medal on TV and I'll be able to say to my friends, 'Hey, I know that girl!'"

After years of "going through the motions," I was an athlete waiting for something to happen. I finally realized that dreams like mine, dreams of becoming an Olympian, don't just come true on their own. We have to make them happen.

I could always "see it"...but it would take me more than ten years, watching three Olympic Games on TV for me to finally "believe it."

After having skated most of my life, I quit the sport in 1980 (after having just missed making the 1980 Olympic Team). I had decided to audition, just for fun, for a traveling show as the lead singer and, unexpectedly, I got the part. The decision to hang up my skates for a microphone and a completely different lifestyle was a very difficult one for me. I was pretty certain I would never skate competitively again.

For the next several years, I experienced fun, excitement and serious confusion all at the same time.

I remember watching the 1984 Winter Olympics on TV and becoming so emotional that I cried out loud thinking, "Wow, that could have been me winning a gold medal!"

———❖———

I was pretty certain I would never skate competitively again

———❖———

Another four years passed and it was another season of Olympic Games. While watching one of the events of the 1988 Olympic Winter Games in Calgary, I found myself feeling the same strong emotion I had experienced so many times before. Once again I bawled my eyes out thinking how I had really blown it.

The stress I felt from watching those Games on TV left me each time asking myself, "Who am I? A singer or an athlete? Who am I supposed to be?" This confusion continued to eat at my insides until eventually I found myself feeling very depressed.

In 1986, I went for help and found out that I was, in fact, suffering from what the professionals call an "identity crisis," which had caused severe depression. It was then that I began searching for myself.

I was constantly in the studio, writing music, working out in the gym, even taking up bike racing! I began writing notes to myself, "I am a singer! That's what I am! I am going to write hit songs and get a recording deal!" Then, I would crumple the paper up and start a new one. "I am a world-class athlete! I am going to train my butt off and go to the Olympics! That's what I'm going to do!" Then I would crumple that one up and sit there with that all-too-familiar feeling of frustration.

❖

I went for help, suffering from what the professionals call an 'identity crisis,' which had caused severe depression

❖

My personal struggle continued until one Saturday morning in late August 1988, with the Summer Olympics in Seoul just one month away. I was sitting at the kitchen table reading the newspaper while my mom was cooking bacon at the stove. (I can still smell that bacon!) I read an article about a former teammate, Connie Paraskevin-Young, who was still at it, training for both the Summer and Winter Olympics (cycling and skating). I said to myself, "Boy, if I was like anybody else reading this, I'd probably give anything to be like her."

That's when it hit me—*I am just like her! I am an athlete!*

I remember jumping up from the table and explaining my feelings to my mom. She said, "Well honey, maybe that's what you should do then."

I was 26 and hadn't skated in years, but suddenly I was so overcome with excitement that I immediately called my former coach, Peter Schotting (who was still coaching the United States Team), to find out where the team was training.

Peter, God bless him, said over the phone, "Get your butt out here, *now!*" He still believed in something I had yet to believe in…me! Exactly one week later, I hopped a flight and went off looking for my dream.

When I arrived in Calgary, I hadn't realized all the obstacles I would have to overcome. I had no skates, no money, no prospects. I was so completely out of shape that it was a struggle to make it around the rink more than two times and everyone was calling me "Grandma!" Fortunately, I had enrolled at the University of Calgary, so I didn't have the opportunity to say, "I can't do this," and turn around and go home.

❖

He still believed in something I had yet to believe in…me!

❖

One of the first people I ran into was my old friend from years before, Dan Jansen. Smiling, he did a double-take and said, "Good to see you again, Cathy. What brings you to these parts?"

"I'm here to skate!" I answered.

"So, you're here for the weekend?" he asked, sincerely.

Looking back on it, I guess it must have seemed a bit absurd. I had left the sport almost a decade previously, and only now had I discovered that it was what I really wanted all along. I could still "see" it!

One of the next discoveries was that muscles have memory. Hallelujah! In a few short months, after my legs had recovered from the initial pulls and strains of being so out of shape, I was making amazing progress on the ice. By the time the World University Games Trials came around that December, I was skating faster than I ever had in my life and I won the Trials. I went on to place second in the U. S. World Team Trials the following March, and that's when I knew I had finally become a world-class athlete again.

BELIEVE IT

Imagery is a very important part of any successful accomplishment. It's what gives us the confidence to believe in ourselves and in our mission, by allowing us to provide our own strategies in preparing ourselves for the barriers and obstacles we will face along the way. In my sport there are plenty of barriers!

Short-track speed skating consists of at least four skaters racing at once, around an 111-meter oval track set up on a 100 x 200-meter indoor hockey rink. It's a very athletic sport with lots of jostling for position, inside and outside passes, and dangerous spills into the boards. A 500-meter race is four-and-one-half laps. The owner of the first skate to cross the finish line wins! Overall competition is set up with a series of heats, quarter-finals, semifinals, etc., with the first- and second-place winners of each race (four skaters in each heat) advancing all the way through to the final.

---❖---

It's a very athletic sport with lots of jostling for position,
inside and outside passes and dangerous spills into the boards

---❖---

In October 1991, I met Dr. Brad Olson, a sports psychologist and professor of psychology at Northern Michigan University. At the time, I was in training for the 1992 Olympics at the U.S. Olympic Education Center in Marquette, Michigan. I'll never forget Brad's first words to me: "Hi, I hear you're pretty good. I'm here to get you a gold medal." I thought to myself, "I'm here to get me a gold medal, too!" So, I decided to learn all I could from him. He told me that I had to visualize my race, see myself win it in the Olympics and see myself receive the gold medal—all in my head! How hard could that be?!

That evening when I got in bed, I closed my eyes, relaxed and tried to visualize my 500-meter race: four-and-one-half laps, about forty-five seconds—first lap, second lap, third lap, a lap-and-a-half to go! I was way out in the lead when out of nowhere came two big girls (they were *really* big in my head!) who passed me just before the finish line. I could only see myself getting the bronze medal. This happened over and over again until I realized what was happening. Those competitors were my intimidators, the obstacles to my success.

We all have intimidators. The way to overcome them is to put yourself in the driver's seat through the use of imagery. This puts you in control!

The next time I visualized my race and saw those girls pass me before the line, I would magically make the race longer and pass them back! This control, although only in my mind, gave me such a sense of confidence that I believed I could be the best!

It was this confidence that I took to the starting line with me on February 24, 1992, en route to winning my first Olympic gold medal.

Be It

The final step of my philosophy requires doing the work and winning the race.

The biggest barrier I faced in becoming my own vision was not one that was imposed on me, but one that I had always imposed on myself...*fear!* Mainly, the fear of losing.

My parents were always very supportive of my skating. I grew up winning most of the time, but there came a time when my dad began to thrive on my early success. When I'd win, I'd make my dad proud. When I'd lose, I'd feel like a failure. By the time I was 14, I had such a fear of losing that there were times I wouldn't even compete if I felt there was a chance that I might not win. I was defeating myself! It wasn't until years later that I gave myself a second chance. I learned to address this problem.

When I made my first comeback that September in 1988, I only had a little more than three years to train for the 1992 Olympics. I realized then that I had no time to make mistakes and that I was going to have to deal with my fear of losing once and for all. I began to approach each race, thinking, *I'm going to race anyway, so I can either be afraid of losing and dwell on the negatives or I can learn to look forward to competing and learn from my mistakes.* We always learn more from our mistakes than from our successes, anyway.

Before I knew it, I had conditioned myself to look forward to the challenge of racing again and I loved it! And, of course, when we love what we are doing, we do a better job and by doing a better job, we become more successful at it. That's exactly how it happened for me!

———❖———

I had such a fear of losing that I wouldn't even compete
if I felt there was a chance that I might not win

———❖———

I qualified for the 1992 Winter Olympic Team in December 1991 by winning all of my races at the Olympic Trials. I had been working on my imagery and my confidence was strong. I was ready!

In Albertville, my first event was the 3,000-meter relay (twenty-seven laps). Our team, comprised of Amy Peterson, Nikki Zeigelmeyer, Darcie Dohnal and myself, finished second behind Canada. Wow, an Olympic silver medal! I was so overcome with joy that I slept that night with my medal next to my pillow. I kept waking up to look at it.

The next day, Dr. Brad took the medal away from me and said, "You're not done yet, you have another race. Now, get focused!"

Even though it was hard to believe that I could ever go home with two Olympic medals, let alone one, I did as I was told and began working on that same imagery that had worked so well for me in the past.

Two days after the relay, in the 500-meter heats, I had some interference with another skater off the line and I fell. Fortunately, the officials called a false start and we took to the line once again. My confidence was so high, that on the restart, I decided to allow every other skater to start ahead of me, and I'd pass them one by one...just like the race I had imagined...and I *did!* I advanced to the final where I was to compete against China's top skater, Yan Li, South Korea's Hwang Ok-sil and Monique Veolzeboer from the Netherlands.

Warming up for the race, I found I had a bad left edge and I kept slipping on the turns. I didn't have time to sharpen my blades, so I tried to put it out of my mind so I wouldn't lose my focus. There was a false start and I fell hard on the ice, soaking my uniform and bruising my pelvic bone. Here I was at the Olympics, in the final, and everything seemed to be going wrong! Yet, somehow, I was able to put all negative thoughts aside and remain focused. I returned to the line and said to myself, "Okay, I'm ready, let's fly!"

The next time the gun sounded, I got off the line in second place, feeling strong and comfortable. I thought I'd relax and wait a lap or two before making a move. The South Korean suddenly made a mistake that I took full advantage of by passing her on the outside and moving up into first place. My left skate was not gripping at all and I had to pivot most of my turns on my right. The rest of the race I just tried to hang on and not fall.

❖

I didn't have time to sharpen my blades, so I tried to put it out of my mind

❖

Around the last turn, Yan Li came up on the inside and we clicked skates causing me to lose some ground just before the finish line.

When I saw her begin to lunge for the line, my body just reacted. Though my right foot was behind her trailing foot, my left skate beat hers to the finish by 4/100ths of a second for the gold medal. I didn't see my foot cross the line, so initially I thought I had lost. My dream finally came true when they announced my name as the 1992 Olympic Champion!

From the top of the awards platform, the view was everything I had imagined when I was the little girl standing on my parents' overstuffed chair. At that moment, I had become my own vision. We *can* make it happen. I did it twice!

I came out of retirement seven months before the 1994 Winter Olympics in Lillehammer, Norway, and won two more Olympic medals—another gold in the 500 meter and a bronze medal in the 3,000-meter relay. And, after yet *another* retirement, at the age of 35, I made the 1998 Olympic Team in Nagano, Japan.

Our biggest limitations lie within our own minds and, once we realize this, we can see, believe and be anything! There's no limit if you can see it, believe it, be it!

Photo courtesy of Don Cochran

MATT GHAFFARI

Photo provided by Matt Ghaffari

Iranian-born and an American citizen since 1989, Matt Ghaffari's Olympic and World Championship medals and his seven National titles make him America's most prolific international medal winner in U.S. Greco-Roman wrestling. In one of the most eagerly anticipated matchups in the 1996 Olympics in Atlanta, Ghaffari won the silver medal as he forced the great Russian legend, Alexander Karelin, who had never been defeated, to a grueling 1-0 overtime decision. A close one-two finish at the 1998 World Championships means that the sport is already anticipating an exciting rematch at the 2000 Olympic Games in Sydney.

But it was what Ghaffari did *after* his Olympic competition that made him an enduring symbol of sportsmanship and compassion. He was the first Olympian to visit the victims of the Olympic Centennial Park bombing, sharing his medal with the frightened Fallon Stubbs, whose mother died in the blast. A few days later, he led a throng of thousands as they re–entered the Park after Olympic officials allowed it to reopen. His courage and refusal to bow to terrorism spoke volumes about his commitment to the freedom available in his adopted homeland. His story has been featured on a wide variety of television programs and in publications, including NBC's "Today Show," "The Tonight Show with Jay Leno," CNN's "Talk Back Live," the *New York Times* and *USA Today.*

Matt still competes in wrestling and travels around the country sharing his deep-rooted patriotism and Olympic spirit. In addition, he is a registered financial advisor.

17

Facing the Giant

Matt Ghaffari

The Siberian giant, Alexander Karelin, is raw power and intimidation. With his shaved head, steely eyes and protruding brow, he is a lesser wrestler's nightmare. A 300-pound, 6' 6" bionic behemoth. If he were not real, a Hollywood action-adventure writer would have invented Karelin as the ultimate bad guy. One of his favorite training habits involved twirling a twenty-pound dumbbell, one-handed, strengthening his forearms to better tweak a foe during a vulnerable moment. A devastating combination of strength and technique, he had *never been defeated* in a competition. He was the Olympic champion in the Super-Heavyweight Greco-Roman competition in 1988 and 1992 and was going into the ring in the 1996 Olympics as an undefeated world champion. I had lost in each of my twenty previous matches against him. He was a legend. He was insurmountable…and I knew I had to face him again.

I didn't enjoy being roughed up by the towering Russian. What I really sought in Atlanta was progress. Each of the twenty previous matches were stepping–stones, not setbacks, that I believed would ultimately put me in a position to win against Karelin. That was my ultimate goal and, to me, the only realistic approach to confronting this freak of nature.

To contemplate a challenge as big as Karelin, I needed parallel objectives: An overall "big picture" goal of defeating him to carry me through day-to-day training; and a more refined goal of gaining ground against him, step-by-step, point-by-point.

If we fail to celebrate these small, yet significant, achievements, it is foolish to expect so much as a chance at reaching the overall goal. We have to feel good about the minor victories. They are what propel us along the path we've chosen.

———◆———

The entire Barcelona experience felt like attending a funeral

———◆———

The 1992 Games marked my lowest-of-low point as an athlete. With a torn knee ligament (suffered only two weeks before I arrived in Barcelona), I was unable to march in the Opening Ceremony and was instantly transformed from gold medal hopeful to a long-shot. The entire Barcelona experience felt like attending a funeral. I never made it out of the opening round.

Two years later and after two more knee surgeries, I was looking ahead to the next Summer Games in Atlanta. Erasing my memory of Barcelona was my prime motivation in 1994 when I elected to resign as assistant wrestling coach at Arizona State University. With my wife, Amy, and our newborn daughter, Nicole, we moved to Colorado Springs, Colorado, where I would train full-time at the U.S. Olympic Training Center. We gave up a house in Arizona for a small apartment. I quit a job I enjoyed; my wife quit her job, too. I was in my early thirties and there was no way I was going to be competitive against Karelin or my American super heavyweight challengers unless I signed on for a highly structured training program in a positive environment. But even with a complex program of conditioning, strength development and mental preparation, and despite the financial sacrifices my wife and I made, the timing factor was vital. I could not afford to miss even one day of work on the road to Atlanta.

That was not to be. In April 1995, two weeks before I was to compete in the National Championships, I broke my right leg during a practice match. It was a spiral fracture of the tibia, one of the most severe fractures. I felt as if my ankle was no longer connected to my leg. I would discover during my recovery the importance of those smaller goals...those stepping–stones.

For six of the first eight weeks, I was in a cast and unable to wrestle on the mat. But even as I fell from No. 2 in the world to unranked in the U.S., I continued to prepare and train the parts of my body that were not busy mending. This was a time of tremendous despair, balanced only by the encouragement of my coaches and doctors at the Training Center.

I did not realize until later that, gradually, with all the obstacles and challenges, I was building up a kind of immunity to insurmountable challenges. As I battled in obscurity to rebound from this injury, I decided I would never again be intimidated by any single opponent.

Ten weeks after suffering the type of injury that was more than ample reason to retire, I was ready to compete at the World Team Trials. I defeated most of the ranked American wrestlers and then beat the new national champion, Rulon Gardner, to earn a berth at the 1995 World Championships in Prague. Once there, I continued to wrestle well and made it into the semifinals to face the giant, Karelin. He devoured me, winning by nine points (the wrestling equivalent of being lapped in a running event or losing a soccer match 9-0). Yet I was so thrilled by the many incremental goals I'd achieved by then, it felt great just to be back on the mat with the best wrestler in history. I even carried that positive outlook with me to Russia, where I went at it with Karelin in an exhibition match in his hometown. This time I reduced the margin to 3-0. I looked forward to meeting him again the following year at the Atlanta Games.

—————❖—————

I would never again be intimidated by any single opponent

—————❖—————

Fortunately at the Centennial Games in Atlanta, both Karelin and I advanced to the gold medal match in healthy condition. There would be no excuses. When we met for the Olympic title, NBC had thoroughly hyped the showdown. It was great for Greco-Roman wrestling to have a televised match receive so much attention, but the reality for me was that I was no longer competing against Karelin. To face the giant with the correct state of mind, I had to diminish the giant. I was competing with myself. I raised my personal limits. I visualized Karelin as fat, even lazy. When we walked onto the mat, he seemed weaker and I felt stronger.

We wrestled to a dead heat in regulation, each taking a turn controlling the match. In overtime, the standoff continued. It was left to the referee to award a single point that would essentially declare a winner. The 1-0 decision would go to two-time defending Olympic champion, Alexander Karelin.

So many emotions swept through me on the medal stand that night. But when my emotions subsided, satisfaction overwhelmed me. I had faced my giant with dignity and poise in the biggest match of my life. More important, I had conquered so many other obstacles in the years leading to my Olympic moment that I could harbor no regrets.

Looking back at the history of individuals or corporations, indeed, at the history of man, turning points or milestones always occur whenever a decision is made to defy the insurmountable. What matters is making a deliberate choice not to back down, not to relinquish ambition to fear, not to be discouraged—even if everyone insists that you should be.

I experienced an example of this after my silver medal competition. On a sunny Tuesday morning, thousands of ordinary citizens, athletes and Olympic officials made a choice—to walk through the gates of the downtown Centennial Park in united defiance against the coward who'd shattered the innocence of the Park only days before with a crude but deadly homemade bomb.

If a terrorist's interruption of the world's largest, most revered and most televised sports event is not, at first glance, an insurmountable situation, nothing is.

Although no one hopes for mindless, random violence, the scenario in Atlanta presented the Olympic Class of '96 with a rare opportunity to put the ideals of Olympism into action under a global spotlight. It was a chance to demonstrate that the attributes we associate with an Olympian have substance beyond the playing of games. It was a moment to seize, a time to show the world that when athletes and Olympic leaders talk about courage, determination and will, we are not expressing hollow clichés only relevant for pep talks and scripted sports commentary. It was time to show the world that the terrorist "giant" wasn't going to intimidate us.

In the hours after that bomb detonated, I realized that I was uniquely qualified to respond as a result of having witnessed in my childhood the tangible consequences of political turmoil, chaos and terrorism—insurmountable obstacles.

Photo courtesy of Horace Holmes Studio

In 1977, with his regime beginning to crumble around him, the Shah of Iran was under siege and my native country was on a direct course toward turmoil and, some predicted, a period of dictatorial oppression. Like many other young parents, mine were faced with a huge decision: to stay or to go. Many were inclined to flee but it was a choice with enormous ramifications. For my parents, it meant uprooting three teenage boys and our infant brother, and changing the course of their lives forever. Their decision to come to the

United States (we emigrated to Paramus, New Jersey) required planning, financial sacrifice and timing. I thank my parents for overcoming the odds to come to the greatest country in the world. I was so very proud to become an American citizen twelve years later.

Because I'd survived and met insurmountable odds head on, I can look anyone in the eye and provide encouragement to not give up—and I can say it with conviction and sincerity. This was my message as I visited Atlanta hospitals where those injured by the bomb's force were being treated. If Alexander Karelin, my gigantic opponent in the Olympic gold medal match, seemed an intimidating figure to me, imagine what the future must have looked like to a 12-year-old girl whose mother was suddenly gone, the lone fatality of the Centennial Park tragedy.

Summoning more inner strength than I'd ever needed for a wrestling match, I walked through the door of Fallon Stubb's hospital room to help her face her insurmountable sorrow. It was an Olympic experience I never expected to have, but it strongly reinforced how important it is that those blessed with abilities reach out to others in need. What does it matter how strong, how fast, how smart or how wealthy someone becomes if he cannot inspire others? All I could think was, "What's the point of having an Olympic medal if I couldn't use it to provide some solace to a girl whose mother was killed?" When I walked into the hospital room and placed the medal around Fallon Stubbs' neck, it could not have mattered less that my medal was silver instead of gold. Her smile was my victory.

❖

Imagine what the future must have looked like to a 12-year-old girl whose mother was suddenly gone

❖

The only reason we must be willing to face our career giants, whether in sports or in the workplace, is so that we are ready to face and conquer the obstacles that come along in our family and personal lives. When we conquer the insurmountable to achieve our specific goals, we become incredibly well-equipped to encourage a child, inspire a spouse, comfort an elderly parent or become a community leader. That's the overwhelming dividend of the years that I put into becoming and remaining a world-class athlete. I learned that it's okay to push toward a goal for the sake of achievement, but that the true "success" or fulfillment comes only when I can find a more meaningful way to touch a life and bring about some positive result. I encourage you to face your "giant" and awaken that Olympian within you. After all, that is what the Olympic movement is all about.

ANN MEYERS
DRYSDALE

Ann Meyers was born to a large Catholic family of eleven children and she quickly learned how to compete against the boys. She excelled in sports and broke new ground for all women athletes. The word "first" dominates her resume. She was UCLA's first female full scholarship athlete and the first four-year All-American college basketball player,

Photo provided by Ann Meyers Drysdale

male or female. In 1978, she received the Broderick Cup (the Heisman Trophy for women's sports).

At the 1976 Olympics, in the first women's basketball medal competition, Annie led the U.S. Women's Team to the silver medal. In 1978, she was the Women's Basketball League's (WBL) first draft pick and was voted League MVP. When the Indiana Pacers signed her, she became the first woman to sign an NBA contract. Ann was the first team athlete inducted into the Women's Sports Hall of Fame, the first woman inducted into the UCLA Hall of Fame and, in 1993, she was inducted into the Basketball Hall of Fame.

Ann has worked as a sports broadcaster, covering men's and women's basketball, softball, tennis, volleyball and soccer for ABC, CBS, NBC and ESPN. She will be on NBC's broadcast team for its coverage of the 2000 Olympics in Sydney, Australia.

Ann and her late husband, Los Angeles Dodger pitching great Don Drysdale, have three children.

18

Teamwork on the Field of Play

Ann Meyers Drysdale

I t's been almost twenty years since I became the first woman to try out for the NBA, and now as a broadcaster on the sidelines of women's basketball, I see how far the sport has come and how much of my life I owe to the lessons I learned on that hardwood court.

I grew up the middle child of a family of eleven children, five brothers and five sisters. The loving support of our parents gave us all the confidence to dream, to attempt, to achieve and to excel. As a participant in individual as well as team sports, as a pioneer in the broadcasting field and as a witness to the inner workings of America's favorite pastime (through my late husband, the Dodger Hall-of-Famer Don Drysdale and his relationship with baseball), I have seen and experienced the lessons to be learned from coaches and athletes, lessons that can and do apply to the professional world.

If it's not too presumptuous, allow me to share them with you:

1. Learn our skills well
2. Learn the needs of the other players
3. Adjust your game to complement the team
4. Support the team emotionally
5. Rejoice and suffer together
6. Pick the right people for the right reasons

7. Share authority as well as responsibility
8. Have pride in your team
9. To be the best, we must be measured against the best
10. Sometimes we have to take a chance

LESSON NO. 1:
LEARN OUR SKILLS WELL

Playing basketball requires skills and split-second decision-making based on years of accumulated knowledge. John Wooden, the "Wizard of Westwood," who led the UCLA Bruins to ten National Championships in twelve years, constantly emphasized the fundamentals of ball handling (passing, shooting and dribbling) with his players, because he didn't want them to be worrying about those skills during the heat of a game. He wanted that behavior to prevail quickly and automatically. Practices were a time for studying, learning and making mistakes, to see the results of basic skills when practiced correctly.

My brother, David, was an All-American at UCLA and played for Coach Wooden. David shared with me that even though they would practice the same drills over and over, Coach Wooden's voice never sounded exasperated, never short-tempered. He just articulated his instructions clearly with phrases like:

"Be quick, but don't hurry"

"Don't mistake activity for achievement"

"Failing to prepare is preparing to fail"

"The harder you work, the luckier you'll become"

During my sophomore year at UCLA, I became a member of the U.S. Olympic basketball team that would compete in the 1976 Olympic Games. Billie Moore was the head coach. Billie worked us hard to achieve the team goals to represent our country proudly, get us in shape as players and as a team, and to compete for a medal in the Olympic tournament. Day after day we would do many different drills: "three-man-weaves" and "suicide runs," for example. We honed our skills as individuals while we learned to work together as a team.

LESSON NO. 2:
LEARN THE NEEDS OF THE OTHER PLAYERS

If we were going to play as a team, we needed to learn what each of our teammates was supposed to do and how we could help. We played all positions in practice. We all did dribbling drills, we all did post-up drills because the guards needed to understand what it was like to post-up, and the centers needed to understand what it was like to pass the ball inside to a post.

This also is true in the business world. As an individual, you receive a particular assignment, but still need to understand what your partner, working on some other aspect of the "deal," is going through as well. This doesn't mean you need to do his or her job, but rather that you need to be available to help whenever possible. It's been said that "...Stars play well, but superstars make their teams play well." The main ingredient for super-stardom is the ability to enhance the level of play of the entire team.

LESSON NO. 3:
ADJUST YOUR GAME TO COMPLEMENT THE TEAM

Coach Wooden talked to Lew Alcindor (later known as Kareem Abdul-Jabbar) before he got to UCLA and said, "Lew, you can win all of the college scoring titles your whole career at UCLA or you can be a vital part of the offense and win championships." Lew adapted his game so that the team could be successful. The Bruins won National titles all three years that Alcindor played for UCLA. I guess it's true that there's no limit to what you can accomplish, if you don't care who gets the credit.

LESSON NO. 4:
SUPPORT THE TEAM EMOTIONALLY

My husband, Don Drysdale, would often speak with fondness of the team ethic he experienced with the Dodgers, both in Brooklyn and after the move to Los Angeles. He spoke of Duke Snider, Peewee Reese, Roy Campanella, Sandy Koufax, Gil Hodges and Carl Erskine going out of their way to congratulate the new kid on some smooth pitch or quick fielding move. As competitive as they were on the field, they seemed to genuinely care about each other away from it. They even hosted barbecues at their homes for players of all ages. "You knew you were a part of something bigger than yourself," he would say. Don's batters felt safer when he would announce to the opposing pitcher, "You hit one of my guys, I'm going to take down two of yours." There was never any doubt that he was looking out for his team.

Sometimes belonging to a team might be as simple as how we look or dress. All great teams have at least one or two colorful characters but, by and large, they also share certain standards of acceptable behavior. Wooden's teams had a strict dress code. He knew that his teams would be judged by their appearance and conduct, as well as by their success on the floor. If a first impression is a lasting impression, his players took pride in representing not only themselves, but their team as well. Even when the great Bill Walton told Coach Wooden that he had decided to allow his hair to grow a little longer, which was a violation of the UCLA team dress code, Coach Wooden praised him for his devotion to his principles and then added, "We're going to miss you, Bill." Walton got a haircut that afternoon.

LESSON NO. 5:
REJOICE AND SUFFER TOGETHER

Just as in a strong family, team unity holds us together in good times as well as bad. Good teams instinctively know that a trouble shared is half a trouble and a joy shared is twice a joy. In 1976, immediately prior to the Montreal Games, our team attended a training camp in Warrensberg, Missouri, where we went through a regular routine of two-hour practices three times a day, shooting one hundred shots from each spot on the floor and one hundred free throws. After a couple of weeks of this regimen and the energy required to shoot the balls and chase the rebounds, we all yearned for a little time off. When the coaches declined our request, a few players decided to show up for practice one afternoon wearing pajamas, swim fins and goggles. We thought that the levity would be a good thing for the team, but we were shocked when the coaches told us to take to the floor, pajamas and all, to start the workout. "Lay-ups, everyone," they said, straight faced.

Years later, I found out that the coaches were barely able to contain their laughter, but weren't about to give us the satisfaction of winning the argument, so we did an entire practice dressed as colorful ducklings. To this day, all the players who played along share something special. Because the coaches appreciated our unity there was no punishment involved, unless you count the blisters we got from the flippers.

These ideas should help those who wish to be a part of a winning team, but what about those (such as coaches or managers) who want to *build* a winning team?

LESSON NO. 6:
PICK THE RIGHT PEOPLE FOR THE RIGHT REASONS

Before the 1976 Olympic coaches made the "final cut," we all attended the tryouts. This was a difficult time because we might have twelve guards trying out and the coaching staff had to select the top three, even when one of the guards who was cut might be a better player than one of the forwards who made the team. Here we were being evaluated on the basis of our skills, our positions on the floor and our personality—who was going to be able to get along with the rest of the team.

Even in business, it's not always the best salesperson who gets the job, just as it's sometimes someone underqualified who ends up running the show. Decisions are often made by fallible people or perhaps by smart people choosing among the limited alternatives available at the time. In either case, once the team is selected, we each have a role to play and the good team leader will take the team's chemistry into account and will find a way to get the most out of each player's strengths.

LESSON NO. 7:
SHARE AUTHORITY ALONG WITH THE RESPONSIBILITY

By sharing responsibilities and authority with each of us, Mom and Dad taught us to be proud of each other's accomplishments, which made the family a very supportive place to be and helped develop our personal pride. We were active members of the team, the decisions we made were considered significant and the consequences of our decisions belonged to us.

In business, the successful manager provides room for the "players" to make their decisions under clearly defined company priorities and goals. We have to delegate authority and trust our employees and their decisions. When employees are given some authority, they make decisions as if *their* jobs depend on it, and they follow through to make certain *their* choices prove to be the correct ones. If the boss makes all the decisions, there's little incentive at the staff level to insure that the decisions pan out. In a game where the coach has called for a particular play, an athlete is still responsible for reading the defense, and making a decision to take a particular shot, if the opportunity is too good to miss.

LESSON NO. 8:
HAVE PRIDE IN YOUR TEAM

I can still recall my years as the eager tomboy who kept pushing her way onto the court to play ball with the big boys, no matter what the activity. No one wanted to play with a *girl*, so it was often my older brother David, rather than the other team captain, who picked his little sister. How proud I was for his faith in me. Ever since then, I've tried to make every team I was a part of equally proud to have me on board.

But nothing in my life could have prepared me for the overwhelming sense of pride and joy I would feel when marching into the Opening Ceremony of the 1976 Olympic Games. There is something so honorable and so true about wearing your country's colors, standing amid a large and exclusive group of America's finest young women and men. It remains, to this day, one of the favorite moments of my athletic career.

Even so, there was a part of me that was looking beyond the Parade of Nations. A part of me that was hoping for even more glory.

LESSON NO. 9:
TO BE THE BEST, WE MUST BE MEASURED AGAINST THE BEST

Coming into 1976, the year of the first-ever Olympic tournament for women, the Soviet squad had enjoyed an unbeaten string in international competition dating back to 1958. The Soviet women's basketball team had soundly defeated every country the prior year, with the one exception being a three-point squeaker they pulled out against us in a USA/Soviet touring competition.

Six teams entered the Montreal Olympic Round-Robin Tournament, where every team played every other team. Except for the Soviets, we felt that we were much better than the other teams, both in stature and in quality of play, but somehow, we found ourselves surprised by a small and quick team from Japan. We lost 84-71 in our first game. Although that loss did not *in itself* cost us the gold medal (we would lose that five days later in a 79-56 loss to the Soviets), it made us realize that we had to concentrate and pull together, to be even more determined and focused for the next game.

As a team, we decided to learn from that defeat and we tried to focus on the team goal, which was to win our remaining games. We bounced back to defeat the Bulgarian and Canadian women, before running into that overpowering 7'2" center named Uliana Seminova from the Soviet Union. Because the Japanese also had lost two games, we found that the silver medal could be ours, but only if we could beat the Czechs by a greater margin than the Japanese had.

Photo provided by Ann Meyers Drysdale

As a group, we had a goal and agreed that a silver medal would feel as good as gold, if we could pull it off. With crisp passes and unselfish play, we went from a 37-37 tie at the half to blow past Czechoslovakia for a spectacular 83-67 victory.

Americans often consider anything less than a gold medal to be a sign of failure, but we saw another picture. We saw a team of players devoted to each other, trying against all odds to climb a difficult mountain to regain a spot on the medal awards stand. Today, that silver medal is a symbol not of a tournament lost, but of our team, the women who gave their efforts for a quadrennial, to pursue a common bond and a dream, and of the opportunity to represent our country at the greatest athletic spectacle in the world.

LESSON NO. 10:
SOMETIMES WE HAVE TO TAKE A CHANCE—
SOMETIMES WE HAVE TO CHANGE TEAMS

Following the 1976 Olympic Games, our team began to focus on the Games of 1980. We trained together and looked forward to a rematch with the Soviets. Unbeknownst to us, that meeting would not take place due to President Carter's boycott of the Moscow Olympics, but at the time we were looking forward to it.

It was shortly after the 1979 World Championships that Sam Nassi, owner of the Indiana Pacers, called to offer me an NBA contract with his team and I faced a dilemma. Should I stay with a team just because I had been with them in the past, or should I grab this opportunity to step to the next level? I could remain amateur and play in the 1980 Olympics, earn my degree from UCLA (which I did) and go No. 1 in the WNBA draft, or I could try to play in the NBA, the opportunity of a lifetime.

I looked back at a similar decision I had made years before. In high school, friends had discouraged me from playing on the boys' team for fear that I would be disappointed. They suggested I might not be good enough, I wouldn't get to play much or that I might get hurt. The coaches and parents of the other players weren't sure how to handle the situation. I allowed them to convince me not to try and I had regretted that choice many times over. So when the brass ring of opportunity came around a second time, I was not about to miss this chance to see exactly how good I was.

———❖———

A loss is not what's embarrassing.
What is embarrassing is to play poorly, below our capabilities

———❖———

Winning (the game, the medal or a spot on the roster) is not the *only* way to measure success. I didn't care about being the first woman to play in the NBA, but just about having the opportunity to see what I could accomplish. With this choice, I was going to get the chance to be measured against the best, giving the attempt my every possible effort, to discover how good a basketball player I was capable of becoming.

They gave me a shot and I signed a contract with the Indiana Pacers. I came to tryouts and I had the chance to use my moves and take my shots with some of the very best. Sadly, I never got to play in a game at that level, yet, looking back, I know it was one of the best decisions I ever made.

A loss is not what's embarrassing. What *is* embarrassing is to play poorly, below our capabilities. For that reason I can honestly say that my 1976 Olympic silver medal, just like my brief tryout with an NBA team, does not represent a failure, but rather my success to the highest degree. As Coach Wooden would say, "Who can ask more of a man than giving all within his span? Giving all, it seems to me, is not so far from victory."

I tested myself against the best the sport has to offer and I learned a lot about teamwork—to hone my skills well, to learn the needs of the other players, to adjust my game to complement the team, to support the team emotionally, to rejoice and suffer together, and that the right people are picked for the right reasons, that authority is shared along with responsibility and to have pride in my team. To be the best, I must be measured against the best and, sometimes, I have to take a chance.

I use these lessons every day in my television broadcasting career and in my most important team leadership role, as the mother of Don's three wonderful children—our two sons, Don, Jr. and Darren, and our daughter, Drew. I try to keep the memory of their father alive by teaching them the same principles he learned with the Dodgers, and from what I have learned from my strong family values, and while playing basketball on some of the greatest teams in America.

BRIAN GOODELL

As a high school junior in 1976, Brian Goodell found himself on the strongest Olympic swim team that America has ever assembled. The U.S. Men's Swimming Team that year was so strong that out of thirteen races, the U.S. won twelve gold, twelve silver and five bronze medals. Although that would have been intimidating for anyone, it was particularly so for Brian, who was one of the youngest male Olympic champions of the modern era.

Photo provided by Brian Goodell

At those Games in Montreal, Brian found his greatest competition came from his teammates, but with courage, he stepped onto the blocks and came home with two gold medals in the long-distance races of 400 and 1,500 meters, setting world records in both events. His explosion onto the scene of international swimming began a winning record that includes nine individual NCAA titles at UCLA, ten national titles and would likely have included four more medals at the 1980 Olympics until the boycott shattered that dream. His club coach, Mark Schubert, claimed that Brian's influence at the college level was responsible for UCLA winning the national team title the year *after* his graduation.

Since his retirement from swimming, Brian has been inducted into the International Swimming Hall of Fame, the UCLA Athletic Hall of Fame and the Orange County (California) Sports Hall of Fame. He has served as an on-camera announcer in a variety of sports for ESPN and Prime Ticket. He also has been extensively involved in commercial real estate development of master-planned communities and private correctional facilities.

Fear & Doubt: the Evil Twins

Brian Goodell

I closed my eyes, feeling the weight of the gold medal as it was placed around my neck. From the podium, I could hear the familiar sound of the national anthem in the background, and I felt an enormous swell of support from the crowd when the American flag rose to the ceiling of the stadium.

And then I opened my eyes.

I was just 13 years old. The medal ceremony was only a dream. I wasn't at the Olympic Games at all. The day before, I had watched Mark Spitz on television, winning seven gold medals, setting seven world records at the 1972 Games in Munich. After thrilling at his performances, I could not get the Olympics out of my mind.

Here I was, a kid in junior high, imagining that I was the best swimmer in the world. Had my friends known of my secret dream they would have laughed out loud. I was even afraid of what my parents might think if I told them. It was scary to have such a great ambition because it meant that I could be setting myself up for disappointment and ridicule or that I would have to travel a long path that would include work, pain and a large measure of the unknown.

When I accidentally fell into a swimming pool at age three, I acquired a terrible fear of the water to the point that whenever I was near a pool, my mom strapped a Styrofoam "bubble" around my waist and I often wore it on the walk to and from the pool just in case! I was afraid I'd drown and I doubted that I could learn how to swim. My folks gradually replaced my fear with positive images. They described how much fun I'd have and how wonderful the water would feel, and then they said I had to take swim lessons. They *made* me face it. The instructor worked the opposite side of the coin. He worked on my doubts. Whenever I said I couldn't do something, he just repeated the words, "There's no such thing as can't." While dismissing the negatives, he gave me tools so I could succeed with confidence.

Fear is the worry that something bad *will* happen while doubt is the concern that something good *might not*. The treatment for fear is to confront it, and the treatment for doubt is to ignore its suggestions and to return to the facts as you know them. While my parents emphasized the positive, my instructor taught me how to resist the negative. These skills won't make fear disappear, but that's okay, they said.

Fear in itself is not debilitating, unless it keeps you from action. Courage is not the absence of fear, but rather it is action in the presence of fear.

———◆———

The treatment for fear is to confront it, and the treatment
for doubt is to ignore its suggestions

———◆———

When, at the age of 13, I imagined myself as an Olympic champion, it became clear that to get there I had to face my fears again. They centered on the physical pain of a difficult race and the shame of finishing poorly. To help me face and conquer those fears, I chose to train under the most demanding of circumstances—the distance lane at the Mission Viejo Nadadores Swim Club in Southern California.

Mark Schubert's workouts at Mission were extremely demanding. In the distance (or "animal") lane, we swam more yardage than had ever been attempted on a consistent basis: 20,000 meters or 400 lengths of the fifty-meter pool, the athletic equivalent of running two marathons a day. Sometimes we pushed our bodies to the point of injury and disease, so much so, that Schubert arranged for a nurse to come to the pool at the end of practice to take blood samples from our arms. Those samples were analyzed between workouts to detect any increase in our white blood cell counts, which would indicate we were overtaxing our bodies. Only then would we get an easier workout. I swam twelve workouts per week and came in on Sundays to do extra mileage.

Only as I grew in competence and my workouts grew in yardage, did my familiarity with the pain allow my fear to subside. After training hard enough to throw up for more than 10,000 meters, what could a puny little 1,500-meter race do to me?

Confronting the fear, like turning on the light in a haunted house, forces the fear to justify itself and often it can't. As President Franklin Roosevelt said, "All we have to fear is fear itself."

Knowing the strategy does not mean that you'll *never* have to face the evil twins of fear and doubt. Even after I broke the world record in the 1,500-meter freestyle at the U.S. Olympic Trials, I was still susceptible to the pesky little monsters. I was the best in the world in my event and yet, at the Olympic Games in Montreal, I had an experience that showed the negative power of fear and doubt.

On the day of the 1,500-meter race, I was confident in my training and my ability, but I had never been in an Olympic final before. I was unsure of what to expect. I was used to competing in front of hundreds, not thousands, but suddenly I was facing more than 10,000 spectators in a standing-room-only crowd. The Queen of England was in her royal box, just a few rows in front of my parents.

The 1,500-meter freestyle goes down and back the length of a pool half the size of a football field, fifteen times for a metric mile. Each two-lap 100-meter stretch would take approximately one minute, and my record was 15.06.66. This event is never seen on television in its entirety because it just takes too long!

———❖———

The Queen of England was in her royal box, just a few rows in front of my parents

———❖———

I was practicing pace 100s in the warm-up pool, unable to find the exact speed I would need that afternoon, so I kept repeating the exercise. The Olympic team distance coach, Don Gambril, concerned that I might tire myself out, told me to visit the trainer for a rubdown.

I took a hot shower and about thirty minutes before the scheduled start of my race, I went to lie down on the massage table at the hands of a former Mission Viejo assistant coach and current Olympic team trainer, Selden Fritschner. As he rubbed my arms and legs, Selden began asking me questions about how I felt, what my goals were, what time I thought it would take, how I planned to split the race and he talked about the competition.

His conversation made me painfully aware that my race was, in fact, imminent. In a matter of moments, all I had trained for, my "once-every-four-years" chance would be upon me. I began to wonder if I was ready. What if I didn't do well? I was the man to beat but how embarrassed I'd be if I had a disappointing swim. I doubted that I would be able to swim the race I had trained for. What if I went out too fast? What if I came home without a medal of any color? As my doubts escalated, the fear grew. I felt like the semester final had arrived a week early.

—————❖—————

When my teeth began to chatter he realized something was really wrong

—————❖—————

I caught a chill, started shivering and Selden had me put on my sweats as he continued to rub me down. When my teeth began to chatter he realized something was really wrong. He was standing shirtless in tennis shorts in the humid summer air of the indoor pool in Montreal and I was vibrating like a New York subway car.

He realized that I was scared—*really scared*.

I was shaking so badly that he feared I'd be unable to get up and walk to the blocks. Immediately he changed the subject. He asked about my post-Olympic plans. He got me talking and thinking about an upcoming trip to Hawaii. While he didn't fill my mind with positive images of my race, he at least helped me shake off the spiders of doubt that had begun to creep in. Gradually I relaxed to where the rubdown could take hold.

While Selden helped me keep doubt at bay, Coach Gambril caused me to confront my fear. He came into the room and said it was time for the race.

"I don't feel like I'm ready yet, Coach," I said, "I need more of a rubdown." Like a patient teacher gently separating a kindergartner from his mother, he said, "I'm sorry Brian, but it's time to go."

He escorted me to the athlete ready room, to sit with my competitors immediately before the race. I felt like a condemned man. When our event was announced to the crowd, the people clapped and cheered, a real party atmosphere. They were having a wonderful time.

I walked solemnly toward the starting blocks, staring at my feet. I was so intense, taking deep breaths, that I started to hyperventilate. When I stood on the blocks, I couldn't feel my arms below the elbows and my legs were numb below my thighs.

Had someone asked me if I would be willing to postpone the race, I probably would have jumped at the chance. It's not that I didn't think I'd be *able* to swim well, it's just that I thought I *might not*. Like an actor on opening night, he knows dress rehearsal went well, but he still doesn't know what effect the full-house crowd might have on his performance. The only way to know is to bring up the curtain.

When the gun sounded, I dove into the pool along with the others, but felt like I was moving in slow motion. The water crashed louder in my ears than I'd ever heard it before, like an echo chamber. I noticed each bubble as it lingered on my fingertips with every stroke. Every time I turned my head to breathe, I could hear the roar of the crowd as if from the distant end of a tunnel.

———❖———

It's not that I didn't think I'd be able to swim well, it's just that I thought I might not

———❖———

Almost immediately, Steve Holland from Australia and the other two Americans, Bobby Hackett and Paul Hartloff took off, going out quickly, as was their style. They liked to go out hard and wear down the competition.

My mind returned to the task at hand. I had to consciously hold myself back, resisting the temptation to stay with the leaders, because my training was designed for a faster second half, so I just swam the race I had "rehearsed." I let my training take over and went into my "default mode." I just…did it.

About 400 meters into the race the numbness subsided and I began to feel my arms and legs. That's when the physical pain of such a long race usually begins to make itself known. Believe it or not, the pain became a warm, familiar and calming feeling. It shook the fear that had gripped me. I passed Hartloff and began to creep toward the leaders. The other American, Hackett from Yonkers, New York, was in the lane between me and the Australian.

I was in third place at the 1,100, when I hit "the wall" square on, like the "Heartbreak Hill" of the Boston Marathon. The pain barrier gets its name from the fact that every fiber of your being is screaming in agony. At this point in a race the body has gone into a wholly anaerobic state in which it is impossible to replenish the oxygen that has been burned in the muscles fast enough, and the product of the muscular reaction (lactic acid) is consuming its maker. It's at this point where your stomach feels like it's tied in one big knot and your arms and legs feel like dead logs.

My stamina was wearing out and I began to doubt my ability to keep up the pace.

I took a deliberate look behind me, to see if there was anyone within striking distance. Seeing no one, I thought to myself, "I've got third place wrapped up. Bronze in the Olympics—not too shabby. Most people don't even make it to the Olympics." For one split second, my doubts offered to let me settle for something less than my dream.

------❖------

The pain became a warm, familiar and calming feeling

------❖------

As if watching it on television, the picture showed me in the *third* spot, on one of the lower levels, shaking hands and congratulating somebody else as *he* got the gold.

And then it hit me. That picture didn't jibe with the picture I'd painted a thousand times, and that's when something deep inside me said, *No way!*

I cast the doubts aside like a duck sheds water. I recalled exactly how I had trained for this moment and I willed myself into thinking that I *would* (not *might*) catch and pass the remaining two swimmers.

I started reaching a little farther and kicking a little harder. Fully focused on my dream and relying on my experience, I was no longer afraid.

The race was magically transformed. I seemed to fly across the surface of the water, each pull of my arms propelling me forward a full-body length, the kick strong and powerful. Like a speedboat, I felt myself rise on top of the water, eyes looking forward at my next targets. And I felt no pain at all.

With three laps to go, I moved into second place, passing my teammate at the 1,350. Most distance swimmers sprint the final lap of this event, but all year long I'd been going full-speed on the final *three* lengths. At this point, I knew that I'd have just enough energy in me to last to the finish. I crept past Holland by the 1,400 mark.

After swimming for more than fourteen minutes, it all came down to the final turn. Three pair of feet touched the last wall within $4/10$ths of a second of each other. I guess I was not the only one in this race overcoming fear and doubt. I hit it just right and came off the wall like a rocket.

Accelerating while the others were dropping back, I'd broken through that pain barrier, held form and pulled away over the last twenty meters to stop the clock with a new world record, 15.02.40, four seconds better than my best. The pain had disappeared and all I had to do was catch my breath while Hackett beat out Holland for the silver, just ticks of the clock behind me. The margin of victory in that race was the closest in Olympic

1,500-meter history, with all three of the medal winners finishing within 2.2 seconds of each other. All three of us had times faster than the existing world record, but my time went into the record books. I was the champion.

———❖———

Three pair of feet touched the last wall within $^4/$10ths of a second of each other

———❖———

The rest of the day passed like a blur. For many years I had lived in my secret world where the medal ceremony occurred over and over in my thoughts, often in slow motion. Now it was unfolding in real time, each gesture, each footstep, each smiling face, even the shiny medallion on a chain was exactly as I'd perceived it. I was standing where I belonged, on the top step, and the best swimmers on the planet were congratulating me.

Fear and doubt never held their power over me again. Two days later, I marched around the pool for my second event, the 400-meter freestyle. This time I felt like a performer in command of his stage. I waved to the crowd and looked at the competition and the television cameras as insignificant. This time I had the benefit of my experience with fear and doubt. I had already faced these devils and conquered them, so I wouldn't have to fight them again.

I stepped up to the blocks, but now I was in control of my emotions. I wasn't any better conditioned for that race than I was for the 1,500, but I was more prepared mentally. Like a casual walk in the park, I took the lead from the sound of the starter's pistol, held it to the final wall and again took home the gold with another world record.

I learned a lot from my Olympic experience that I carry with me every day, especially when it comes to fear and doubt. I learned that the way to conquer fear is not to ignore it, but to confront it; to act as if the thing you fear cannot really happen. You won't be fearless, you'll just *act* fearless.

Effort is always required to embrace the positive and shun the negative. To remove all doubt, one has to consciously recognize the negative thoughts for what they are and, by an act of will, ignore them. Hesitation begins when we think, "What if the ball isn't there? What if the customer won't buy? What if it hurts more than last time?" It takes a strong will to shout down the voice of doubt, sometimes disguised as the voice of reason. Doubts are like uninvited guests. Don't entertain them!

Oh, sure, it *sounds* easy, but I'm never going to say that fear and doubt won't return. They always do. I still face them in countless ways in my everyday life. I had the same level of anxiety as I experienced at the Olympics when my wife, Vicki, called to tell me it was time to go to the hospital to deliver our first child.

————❖————

The way to conquer fear is not to ignore it, but to confront it...
Doubts are like uninvited guests. Don't entertain them!

————❖————

Photo courtesy of Steve Ueckert

We all experience similar doubts and fears as we approach new challenges throughout our lives. The fear diminishes and the Olympian within is awakened with the confidence that comes from experience and faith. Sometimes you just have to go for it and see what happens. Jumping into the battle does not guarantee victory, but being afraid to try guarantees defeat.

HENRY MARSH

Photo provided by Henry Marsh

In 1988, Henry Marsh became the second American male runner to make four Olympic teams. He culminated his career with thirteen consecutive years as one of the top ten 3,000-meter steeplechase runners in the world, including thirteen national titles, four American records and three years ranked No. 1 in the world. No other American has ever been so highly ranked. His story was featured in Bud Greenspan's "16 Days of Glory," the official film of the 1984 Olympic Games.

Henry was a five-time All-American in cross-country and track while at Brigham Young University. He received the NCAA's Top Ten Scholar-Athlete Award while graduating with honors in economics, earning him an NCAA post-graduate scholarship. He went on to receive his law degree from the University of Oregon.

Henry has served as a consultant to the President's Council on Physical Fitness and Sports, and as a member of the executive board of the U.S. Olympic Committee. Currently, he is a member of the Board of Trustees for the Salt Lake Olympic Committee for the Games in 2002.

Now a national director at Franklin Covey Co., Marsh directs curriculum development of the "Rethinking Stress" seminar currently being taught throughout corporate America. As author and motivational speaker, he discusses the dynamics of behavioral change, leadership and team building, salesmanship and personal productivity.

The Struggle

Henry Marsh

Baron Pierre de Coubertin, the French nobleman who founded the modern Olympic Games, was reportedly not a very big man. About five-feet tall and barely more than 100 pounds, he certainly had his physical limitations. And yet, his physical stature (or lack thereof) did not deter him. Against incredibly long odds (the Olympic Games, after all, had been dormant for more than 1,500 years when he set about resuscitating the movement in the late 1800s), he embodied resilience and persistence as much or more than any Olympian who would follow in his wake.

To me, it is that spirit of Pierre de Coubertin, of never giving up, of staying the course no matter what, that is the real spirit that drives the Olympic Games. To be sure, it was the spirit that drove me in my role as an Olympic athlete—a drive to always achieve my personal best.

Most of the stories in this book are stories of first-place finishes, of gold medals, of standing on the top platform with hand over heart while the national anthem plays and the country's flag is raised to the top of the pole.

Mine is not such a story.

My story fits more into the category of what the world would call a heartbreak—the kind you turn into a country song. And yet, it is a story that still applies to most Olympic athletes and most people in their varied walks of life.

I choose to think that my Olympic experiences helped shape my life, much for the better. Sometimes, in fact, I wonder what my life would be like if I hadn't had to endure a good dose of what the poets call "character-building experiences." If I had won my gold medal, or gold medals, would the lessons that followed have been as satisfying or as valuable?

I know this: By *not* finishing first and by *not* realizing the fulfillment of all my dreams—when everyone in the world, myself included, fully expected that I would—I was able to gain a much greater appreciation for, and understanding of, the Olympic Creed:

> *The most important thing in the Olympic Games is not to win, but to take part,*
> *just as the most important thing in life is not the triumph, but the struggle.*
> *The essential thing is not to have conquered, but to have fought well*
> —Pierre de Coubertin

Simply speaking, "fighting well" is nothing more than hanging in there, never giving up, never saying "I quit." No matter what.

That's what Coubertin was trying to get across—both by what he said and by what he did. *That* is the Olympic ideal. No quitters. When the going gets tough, the tough don't go home. It's easy to stay the course and fight the fight when you're on top, when you're winning, but what of those times when everywhere you look you see nothing but hurdles and obstacles, blockages and barricades, detours and swamps?

That is when it is hard to continue—when the challenge is to hang on amid defeat, disappointment and despair, far from the adoring crowd— and *that* is when you find out who you are.

I like to think that I was prepared for my Olympic adversity. Before I was even old enough to know better, I was being schooled in the art of never quitting, of never giving up. When I was barely more than one-year-old, I was at my grandfather's house, where my mother was making dinner for Grandpa because he was in bed with a bad case of shingles. While Mom was at the sink preparing the food, I wandered into the backyard and went straight for the fish pond, which was about two feet deep.

For whatever reason, my grandfather was prompted to get out of bed and come into the backyard just as I was settling on the bottom of the pond.

I was unconscious and already turning blue when Grandpa pulled me from the water and performed artificial resuscitation, and got me breathing by the time the ambulance arrived. He saved my life. Later, when doctors took X-rays of my lungs that revealed extensive scar tissue, we would all realize how close I had been to death.

My grandfather, a deeply religious man, gave the credit to God, and so did I, but I also reserved plenty of credit for my grandfather and his doggone determination to save my life in spite of the fact that he was in bad shape that day. He never gave up on me, even when the times were tough—and neither would I.

———❖———

My grandfather was prompted to get out of bed
just as I was settling on the bottom of the pond

———❖———

My father, too, always served as a great example when it came to overcoming obstacles. While growing up, stories of my father's youth were a great source of inspiration. He was a self-made man, working his way through college at Berkeley and later Harvard Law School. All he ever asked of me was to enjoy what I did and to never give up. "Don't quit!" he'd say, and I wouldn't.

As a great runner, Glenn Cunningham said in his book, *Never Quit*, that his father told him "A Cunningham never quits!" and he relied on that family mandate to overcome a severe burn when he was 8 years old that almost cost him the use of his leg. At the 1936 Games in Berlin, Cunningham won the Olympic silver medal in the mile.

All my life, as far back as I can remember, I loved to run. As a young boy I'd use the commercial break during television programs to see how far I could run down the street and back again during the sixty seconds. Something about the feeling of my feet striking the ground and my determination to outlast the pain in my lungs and legs lured me to the sport.

It was the attitude of never quitting that drove me during the tens of thousands of miles of training throughout my career. As early as ninth grade, I would push myself to run ten miles of intervals on the dirt track behind our school. As a tenth grader, I remember running until I couldn't take another step, just to see what my limits were.

I also liked to run because I discovered I was relatively good at it. I met with enough sustained success in my youth to keep going. I was a schoolboy champion in my native Texas, then a state mile champion in Hawaii where I spent my high school years.

Early success and natural ability notwithstanding, one thing that any competitor knows is that the longer you compete, the higher the stakes are going to become, the stiffer the competition is going to become—and the more reasons you're going to have to stop trying.

Time after time after time, as my running career progressed, I found myself looking into the mirror and asking the question, "Have I had enough?"

My first big decision came in college at Brigham Young University, where to my horror, I discovered that I wasn't the only hotshot high school champion on the track team. Everybody was a high school hotshot. Many of them faster than I was. What was I to do? Face the fact and admit defeat?

For a time I did leave the team, my ego bruised, my confidence sinking. But old family traditions die hard and "Marshes don't quit" overruled my ego. I came back, humbled but smarter. I stopped trying to copy everyone else and tailored my training to my own particular strengths. It was in this manner that I "rediscovered success." Within six months I was the runner-up in the 3,000-meter steeplechase at the NCAA championships and a qualifier for the 1976 Olympic Games.

I was stunned by my rapid improvement and even more stunned at my tenth place finish in Montreal where my time was less than a second off the American steeplechase record.

Not quitting had already been very, very good to me. It was a lesson I would learn again and again. Don't quit when it gets hard—simply regroup and try harder.

❖

I stopped trying to copy everyone else and tailored my training to
my own particular strengths

❖

While on the one hand, I developed into one of the top steeplechasers in the world (at various times in the early 1980s I was ranked No. 1), on the other hand I had this "Why me!?" knack of running into problems at the worst possible moments. I got sucker-punched out of two World Championships and one Olympic Games. Like many others, I was a victim of the 1980 Olympic boycott, costing me a trip to Moscow at a time when I was approaching my prime and was considered a good hope for a medal. In 1981, at an event in Rome, I was pushed around the final water jump and got disqualified. In 1983, while charging to the lead on the final straightaway at the World Championships in Helsinki, Finland, I tripped over the final barrier and fell to the ground.

Did I feel like quitting after each of these setbacks? Of course I did. In each case, the disappointment was real and the pain almost debilitating. But I didn't quit.

By the 1984 Games, I was glad I hadn't. I had learned a lot about myself and my ability to rebound from major disappointment because of my various trials. Now, finally, it appeared that my time had finally arrived.

—❖—

I got sucker-punched out of two World Championships and one Olympic Games

—❖—

Not only would these Games be held on American soil and not only was I in my absolute prime as a runner (at 30 years of age), but my three top competitors would be absent from the Olympics due either to injury or the Soviet inspired "counter-boycott."

ABC Sports, that year's rights-holder for the Olympic telecast, picked me as the easiest gold medal "lock" of the Games, ahead of Carl Lewis, Mary Decker Slaney and everyone. It felt great...

Until I got sick.

After winning the U.S. Olympic Trials and qualifying on the team, I caught a severe virus that landed me flat in bed. Here was my dilemma: I needed rest (doctor's orders) and I needed training (Olympian's orders).

To add to the bad news, I couldn't take any prescription medicine because of Olympic rules forbidding many of the ingredients in most of the virus-fighting medications. I compromised as best I could. I lay in bed until it was time to train and then I trained until I had to go back to bed. Not exactly the typical runner's regimen for success. By the night of my Olympic final, I wasn't feeling my best, but at least I was feeling much better than I had the prior two weeks. I decided to go for broke.

The steeplechase covers 3,000 meters, almost two miles. Toward the end of my race, I made my move on the leaders as I usually did, on the final lap (my normal come-from-behind style) and actually came up on the shoulder of the leader, Julius Korir of Kenya, on the back straightaway. This was my split-second of truth. Typically, it was at this moment in the race that I used my strongest attribute, my finishing kick, to surge ahead, first to the tape.

But Korir's shoulder was as far as I got. When I pushed the "surge" button, there was no surge. I watched as the eventual gold medalist pulled away. I wanted to stop running right then, but the Olympian within me couldn't stop.

Bad was soon followed by worse when seconds later, at the final barrier, I was passed by Joseph Mahmoud of France and *a few inches* before the finish line I was passed by my American teammate, Brian Diemer, who wound up beating me by ^{19}/$_{100}$ths of a second.

As I crossed the finish line, I collapsed, spent and unconscious.

———❖———

Perhaps it was a good thing that I blacked out

———❖———

The good news was that it had been the sixth-fastest steeplechase race of all time, a race for the ages, and I had been in the thick of it. The bad news was that I finished fourth, completely out of the medals. Perhaps it was a good thing that I blacked out.

I was delivered by ambulance to the infirmary just outside the Los Angeles Coliseum, and when I came to, the attending doctor announced that I was "over-exerted." Little did he know, but he was redeeming my entire career, by attesting to my adherence to the same Olympic Creed that Coubertin had quoted almost a century before:

> *. . . The most important thing in life is not the triumph but the struggle.*
> *The essential thing is not to have conquered, but to have fought well.*

I had given everything I had to give. No one could argue with that, not the doctor, not my competitors or family, not even me.

Knowing that I had "fought well" made all the difference. Despite what the final results were, in my mind I had won—simply by giving everything I had to give.

I received thousands of cards, letters, telegrams and phone calls, all of them expressing sympathy, as if someone had died. A lot of people thought I would retire for good after that loss. But by now, my penchant for not quitting was so deeply ingrained that I honestly didn't give retirement a passing thought.

By the following summer I was as healthy as I'd ever been and was able to win my seventh U.S. National Championship—and even get a little revenge on my friend, Diemer, in the process. As the 1985 season wore on, I was able to regain my No. 1 world ranking, and toward the end of the season, running in the best shape of my life, I broke my American steeplechase record—a record that still stands fourteen years later.

Energized at the prospect of qualifying for a fourth Olympic team, competing at the 1988 Games in Seoul, South Korea, I continued to compete internationally. I realized my goal of wearing the USA uniform in

Seoul, where at the advanced age of 34, I was able to finish sixth.

After that, I hung up my competitive cleats for the last time. I wasn't quitting, I was moving on. It felt good to retire, to leave the sport I love on my own terms, not surrendering but just saying, "So long."

At the conclusion of my last race, I knelt on the ground and kissed the track in Seoul after that Olympic final, a gesture as much for all the lessons I'd learned as for any of the successes I'd been able to realize.

When all was said and done, I realized the important thing *had* been the struggle, not the triumph. Coubertin was right.

Photo provided by Henry Marsh

---❖---

I knelt on the ground and kissed the track after that Olympic final

---❖---

As I look at people in all their pursuits, in all their dream-chasing, in all their various walks of life, I look at myself with my post-Olympic desires and quests and am reminded of the value of that simple Olympic Creed. Whether in business, athletics, personal relationships or individual pursuits, what is important isn't to have conquered, but to have fought well. To have "fought well" really means that you have conquered yourself in the only competition that really matters.

VALERIE BRISCO-HOOKS

Photo provided by John Naber

Born and raised a mere three miles from the Los Angeles Memorial Coliseum, Valerie Brisco-Hooks had never been inside the venue until the 1984 Olympic Team Trials. By the end of the Olympic Games, Valerie accomplished what no other athlete, male or female, had ever done before. She won both the 200- and 400-meter races at the same Olympics, and she shared a third gold medal with the members of the U.S. 4 x 400 meter relay. What makes her performances even more spectacular is that they occurred fewer than three years after she gave birth to her son, Alvin.

In each race, she set a new American and a new Olympic record. Her mark in the 200 meters lasted four years until it was broken by Florence Griffith Joyner at the Seoul Olympics, and her time in the 400 meters remains the fastest time ever turned in by an American woman.

She currently holds another American record with Denean Howard, Diane Dixon and Florence Griffith Joyner, a result of their 1988 Olympic silver-medal-winning 4 x 400-relay in Seoul, South Korea.

Valerie is a member of the "Xerox Golden 100 Olympians" and currently runs the "Peer to Peer" sports mentoring program in Los Angeles.

21

Kids Don't Have to Slow You Down...

Valerie Brisco-Hooks

In 1974, when I was just barely a teenager, my older brother Robert was a talented 100-meter sprinter turning in times that were fast enough that some were predicting he would become the next city champion. One afternoon while he was training on the track at his high school in Watts, an area in the south central part of Los Angeles, he was shot by a gang member's stray bullet and died from loss of blood at the hospital.

Almost overnight, our lives changed. Prior to Robert's death, Mom had "ruled the roost" with an iron fist to keep her ten kids in line. She didn't have time for lots of hugging and kissing; there was just too much to do. But when Robert died, she began to enjoy us a little bit more.

We had more social time before and after dinner. Family time and relationships became much more valuable, and Mom stopped working so she could be home with us more. That appreciation for the special nature of the family wore off on us. Even today, Mom often has half of her twenty grandkids around the dinner table every night.

By the time I enrolled at Locke High School in 1976, the track carried my brother's name (Brisco-Clarke Field). My P.E. teacher, Miss Cornelius, was also the school's track coach, and when she saw me beat one of the school's track stars in the physical agility sprints, she assigned me to the team. I didn't like having someone assume I wanted to be a runner, so every day when school let out, I skipped the team's workouts and went home to hang out with my friends. Because I missed those workouts, Miss Cornelius gave me an "F" in Physical Education.

When Mom asked, "How can you flunk P.E.?" I felt I had to go back to the workouts. When you run on a track named after a member of your family, it's hard to slack off. I won a race at the first meet of the season, placed fourth at the citywide meet and qualified for the state meet.

The following year, I found myself training with the men's team under coach Don Strametz. His philosophy was that everyone ran distance, regardless of his or her competitive events. He would start me off ten seconds ahead of the guys and, like letting the dogs loose, he set them off after me. None of them wanted to lose to a girl, so they tried very hard to run me down.

---❖---

Mom asked, 'How can you flunk P.E.?'

---❖---

Even with this grueling training, I used to "die" at the end of every 400-meter race in competition. I'd get what we call "booty lock," when lactic acid reaches toxic levels and each muscle in the legs, thighs, hamstrings and buttocks would cramp up after the finish. Teammates and coaches would have to pick me up off the track and massage my legs until I could walk once again. Even so, I began winning races, even at the state level. I had seen myself as a sprinter but now I was doing well at the 400 meters.

It was after high school that I met Bobby Kersee, an assistant coach at Cal State Northridge, who recruited me to run in college along with some of his other runners, such as Florence Griffith and Pam Marshall.

I lived at home for the first semester and every morning at seven, Bobby picked us up in his bright orange Honda and drove us to school, making sure we wouldn't miss practice. After the afternoon workout, he drove each of us home again.

I hated the 400 (think "booty lock!") and tried to focus on my sprints, but Bobby was insistent and he knew how to motivate me. There was a cross-town girl named Yolanda Rich who had beaten me in the past. Bobby got me to think about racing her and beating her. We began to calculate our strategy. He pointed out that she won her races on the curves, so I learned how to pace the race.

Prior to Bobby's guidance, when I ran a race I did it with little or no control—I just ran all-out. I never understood where my body should be, what I should feel like, when I needed to move out. I exhausted myself too early in the race. With his help, I began to understand the sport and my races a lot better. My times dropped remarkably and the "booty lock" became a thing of the past. I beat Yolanda at that year's National Championships and it felt great! It was the first time in my life that I actually set a goal and achieved it. It was at that race that I decided, "This is what I want to do."

That same year, during a badminton class, I met a football player named Alvin Hooks and we began to date.

In April 1981, Alvin received an offer to play wide receiver for the Philadelphia Eagles. He left California in April, and by May I had won the 100 and 200 at the City College Nationals. In June, I experienced bouts of morning sickness. Because of my exhausting training schedule, I didn't suspect anything was amiss, but by July my doctor told me I was three-and-one-half months pregnant.

I had been training and improving steadily. What would this child do to my life? What would the baby's demands do to my running career? Alvin, on the other hand, was thrilled. "Gee, let's get married," he said, "I always wanted to have a baby."

At first, I was reluctant: I didn't think I was ready to get married, but Alvin's persistence won me over. I walked off the track without planning ever to return.

Little Alvin was born in January 1982. I had gained a husband, a child and forty pounds. We moved to Philadelphia and I started working out, trying to lose weight. Big Al was injured returning a punt (he blew out his knee) and was told to recuperate. Because the weather was getting cold, we went back to California to visit family and friends. Everyone wanted to know if I'd start running again. I told them that I wanted to give Little Al my full attention, at least for the first year.

When Bobby Kersee came by, he was more direct. "You can do it," he said, "Just lose the weight."

————❖————

I had gained a husband, a child and forty pounds

————❖————

Then I saw a track meet on television and it dawned on me that I really did miss the sport. I missed the running, the competition, the travel, my pre-pregnancy body and all my friends. I even missed working out. I missed the old Valerie. I decided to give it a try.

That first day was rough. My body had become nothing but water-weight and when I first started jogging, my whole body shook. My body shook so hard it had my flesh itching. There was no way I would ever make it back, I thought.

At the end of the day, Bobby pulled me aside and said, "You know, if you really want to do this, you have to convince yourself that you want it. But first you'll have to lose the weight. If you do everything I ask of you and you lose the weight, I promise that you'll make the Olympic team."

I believed in Bobby and what he said, even though I was overweight with a one-year-old on my hip and had not run a step on the track in almost two years. For the first time in my life I was convinced that I could become an Olympic athlete.

I wouldn't recommend this but, I went home and wrapped myself in plastic wrap, put on a pair of sweats, turned on the hot water in the shower and did my calisthenics in the bathroom. Sit-ups, push-ups, jumping jacks, running in place, you name it. And I ate rice and shrimp every day.

Inside of six weeks, I was back to my original fighting weight.

By December 1983, I returned to the track, smiling and said, "Kersee, I took care of my part of the bargain, you take care of the rest."

But before I could resume my training, I had to resolve the challenge of being a responsible mother. Little Al made the transition easy for me. He came along to practice and to all the meets, peaceful as you please. Big Al was often at the track, helping with the baby, except when it came time to breast feed. Alvin was potty trained and weaned on the track, watching his mommy gradually become slender and faster.

Bobby didn't like the idea of my bringing my son to workouts, but frankly he didn't have a choice. That item was nonnegotiable.

Right away, it was as if I was back in high school. Bobby would send me off a few seconds ahead of the rest of the team and they'd try to run me down. "Go get her!" he'd yell and I'd pump my arms as fast as I could, huffing and puffing my way around the track. They'd come tearing around the turn, blowing past me long before the finish.

The others were doing a sprinter's workout and I was doing mileage. I cried every day, I cussed every day, we argued every day, but I finished the workout. And Little Alvin sat contentedly where he was told, never ran away, never crossed the track—a perfect young man.

At first it seemed like the others were miles ahead of me, then just one mile, and then a quarter-mile, and eventually, by around March or April 1984, I was even with them.

One day, with the Olympics only three months away, I arrived late to practice with my arms filled with little Alvin, a gym bag, a diaper bag and other stuff. Bobby called the other runners over and read me the riot act.

"I can get here on time and these folks can get here on time. If you can't make it to practice on time then maybe you don't belong here!" he yelled. "My time is precious, and if you're not serious, perhaps you'd better find some other place to train." Oh, I cussed him out something fierce and he kicked me off the team. He wouldn't let me leave, though, until *after* I finished the workout.

———❖———

I cried every day, I cussed every day, we argued every day, but I finished the workout

———❖———

I went home so angry, it took me three days to cool off enough to write him a foul-tempered letter protesting his unfairness. We spoke on the phone right after that and, although neither of us wanted to back down, he "reluctantly" took me back.

Interestingly, once I rejoined the team, every time he gave me a workout I did it with such ferocity, anger bubbling inside, that I had perhaps the most fruitful three months of training in my life. He had awakened the Olympian within, pushed all my buttons and played me like a musical instrument.

At the National Championships in San Jose before the Olympics, Bobby challenged me to name the exact time I would run the 400. I said I wanted to be the first American woman to break 50 seconds. He made me visualize every part of the race, and said that, as a result of my workouts, his pre-meet prediction was a 49.87. I won the event with a new American record, covering the distance in 49.89 seconds.

Some thought my devotion to my child might take something away from my running, but I didn't see it that way. I had always made Little Alvin a part of my running, because I didn't want to miss the first time he crawled, his first step, his first word. I wanted him to get used to me and the schedule I would be required to keep, and I honestly think his joining me in this effort allowed me to concentrate more on what I was doing, because I wasn't worrying about him. He was always just a few steps away. In everything I did, Alvin was always a part of it.

I think I tried harder, too, because I wanted him to be proud of his mother.

Before every race, I had a private word with God: "Glory to God, please protect me when I go to my race and protect Alvin so that nothing happens in between. Thank you for Alvin and thank you for allowing me to come back."

The Olympic Trials were held a little less than two months before the Games on the new track inside the Los Angeles Coliseum. The stadium is just three miles from my high school, but I'd never been inside. I was excited and confident.

————◆————

The madman had jumped a security fence at the turn and ran the entire length of the final straight with security guards, guns drawn, in hot pursuit

————◆————

In my best event, the 400, I finished second, behind Chandra Cheeseborough, and lost my record in the process. But I won the 200.

Seven weeks later I was back in the Coliseum, set to race in the 1984 Olympic Games. My first event was the 400. During the final, I came out of the last turn to hear Bobby's voice as I had so many times before, "Move, move, move! Arms, arms, arms!" He always stood at that turn. In past races, he had seen me fading as I entered the last turn and when he'd see me "catchin' rig" (ormortis), he'd yell for me to keep going. I wasn't allowed to stop until he gave me permission.

At the critical place where Chandra passed me in the Trials, his voice rang out and I kept up the pressure, all the way to the tape, where I regained the American record and set a new Olympic mark of 48.83.

I began my victory lap. When my time was announced, I wanted to share that moment with my men. Immediately, I ran back to where I knew they'd be, and within seconds I was hugging my two Alvins in the finish area.

My husband looked over my shoulder and said, "Here comes Bobby."

The madman had jumped a security fence at the turn and ran the entire length of the final straight with security guards, guns drawn, in hot pursuit. Bobby tackled me and we fell, rolling to the ground. The man almost threw my back out with all his excitement.

With more than 100,000 spectators in the arena, yelling and screaming, it was Bobby who was the most excited at my victory.

Two days later, I was set to race again, this time, the 200. After my great time in the 400, I knew I was in shape and I had a lot of confidence. I set my second Olympic record, beating teammate Florence Griffith for my second gold medal. Once again, my first stop was with my family. When it was announced that Florence won the silver, together we paraded around the track.

Each day, each race, my family was there, for me and with me. In the post-400 race press conference, Little Alvin had been on my lap during the interviews, until way past his bedtime. As a result, after the 200 race, we avoided the press and went straight home...as a family.

The U.S. 4 x 400 relay team qualified easily and the four of us—Lillie Leatherwood, Sherri Howard, Chandra Cheeseborough and myself—won by almost three seconds, giving me my third gold medal and third Olympic record.

Looking back on my athletic career, I realize that being a mother forced me to wear different hats, kept me stable and structured my time and energy around both my child and my career. My love for my son kept me driven and ambitious, not just for myself, but for him, too. I had to work to the best of my ability and yet have "mother ears" to hear if Alvin needed me at any time. I had to give him what he needed to get what I needed, which was to maintain the feeling that I could win at the Olympics.

If it weren't for Alvin, I'm sure I would not have been able to win at all.

In fact, toward the end of my career, Little Alvin took care of me. "Do you *really* need to go out tonight?" he'd ask. I was happy to sacrifice the entire European season just so we could be together. Now, however, not-so-little-anymore Alvin is the responsible one. He gets up early, sometimes cooks a meal, helps me stay on schedule and looks after his mom.

———❖———

Being a mother forced me to wear different hats, kept me stable

———❖———

With all of the working mothers out there, I'm sure many of them wonder whether the effort required to be a good mother detracts from their professional careers, but I know that in my case each job helped the

©1984 Allsport USA/D. Johnson

other. When I knew my baby was safe, I could focus on running, and when I ran well, I was better able to provide for my Alvin.

By the time I was awarded my gold medal, I had forgotten the pain of "booty lock" and the inconvenience of carrying the diaper bag to workout. All of that seems insignificant when compared to the rewards of my gold medal performances on the track *and* at home.

I'm as proud of my son as he is of his mother.

You can do both: be a great parent and a great professional. It takes more effort, but trust me, it's worth it.

Karch Kiraly

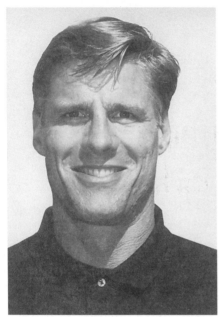

Karch Kiraly has one of the biggest names in the sport of volleyball and has the trophies and prizes to support it. Three Olympic gold medals and almost $3 million in career prize money just begins to cover his success on both the hardwood floor of the indoor game as well as the outdoor sand court. The sport chose him as "Best Player in the World" on two occasions.

Photo courtesy of Allsport USA

A member of the U.S. National Team from 1981 through 1989, he was selected the Team's MVP four times. He helped lead the Americans to gold at the 1984 Olympic Games and, as captain, Karch and his teammates found gold again in the 1988 Seoul Olympics and he was voted the Tournament MVP.

His dominance in the sport continued when he resumed two-man beach volleyball on the Association of Volleyball Professionals (AVP) Tour, winning nearly eighty tournaments in his first five years back. Seven times voted the AVP Most Valuable Player, he recently became the all–time leader in beach volleyball with 141 career victories.

His crossover to the beach game coincided with an explosion of television coverage and international popularity that eventually led to the sport's inclusion in the 1996 Olympic Games, where he won his third Olympic title alongside his long-time partner, Kent Steffes.

Still competing, Karch has set his sights on an unprecedented fourth gold medal at the 2000 Olympics in Sydney, at what will be the grand old age of 39.

22

Making Winners Out of Nobodies

Karch Kiraly

I n the history of men's indoor volleyball at the Olympics, our teams had good athletes, but the results proved miserable. Beginning in 1964, the year indoor volleyball became an official Olympic sport, the U.S. Men finished ninth and seventh, and then failed to qualify for the next three Olympics. We had a whole generation of players who couldn't even tell you what an Olympic village looked like, let alone how to compete for a medal. When a group of new players, which included me, joined the team in 1981, our team was ranked a lowly nineteenth in the world.

The main obstacle to our men's success was the program's lack of year-round support and training—we wasted all the talent of the '60s and '70s by throwing all-star teams together at the last minute, unpaid teams with two to six weeks of preparation, which we hoped could compete with professional teams from the Eastern bloc, teams that had been together for *four to ten years*. It was an impossible task. Things had to be done in a new way.

With no experience, no history of success, no talent development and little or no support, we had no business shocking the volleyball world by clawing our way to the top of the rankings and staying there for five years. Yet we did it—we won Olympic gold medals, the first medals of any kind for our program, in both 1984 and 1988. How? Everyone involved with our program had to help perform a total corporate turnaround. We accomplished those changes by starting back at the foundation with a simple formula: We needed to *Believe* in ourselves and our program, lay out our goals in a comprehensive *Plan, Commit* to the plan and *Attack* the work set out in our plan. As a metaphor, I use aspects of the game of volleyball to illustrate.

THE SERVE/BELIEF IN YOURSELF

No volleyball play can begin without a serve. And the serve is the only technique that is totally under your control, since no player can touch the ball before you. In other endeavors you cannot succeed without believing in yourself, and that belief is completely under your control—nobody else can generate it for you.

Although I began playing volleyball when I was 6 years old, I didn't start believing I could become an Olympian until 1976. I was so fanatical about volleyball that I couldn't wait for the Montreal Olympics to begin, since it was going to be my first chance to watch the world's best compete, albeit on television. These were the players I had only read about or seen in pictures. Until then, I could only imagine how high those players could jump, how hard they might hit a volleyball, how quick their reflexes were. I spent day after day glued to the TV waiting to see the masters at work.

Seemingly every sport *but* volleyball was televised, and the announcers didn't even mention my sport for most of the Games. Finally, fifteen days into the competition, on the next-to-last day, ABC showed the last twenty minutes of the gold medal match.

I learned two things from those brief moments. Lesson No. 1: The best volleyball players in the world were not jumping as high, hitting as hard or reacting as quickly as I imagined they could. I could learn to do those things, too. And after I calmed down from my anger at ABC for showing so little of my beloved sport, I thought about what had been on TV—only the sports with medal-winning American athletes. So I learned Lesson No. 2: If I wanted to see volleyball on television at the Olympics, our team would have to improve enough to qualify for the Games, and then would have to improve even more. We had to contend for a medal.

I decided at that moment that I could make a difference. I could learn to play at a world-class level to help our men's team play world-class volleyball. The belief in myself began right then.

Not only did each athlete need to build faith in himself, but USA Volleyball also demonstrated its belief in our potential, as any good employer or manager should. A new, full-time training center was established in San Diego, California that would allow us to train and compete together year-round, something no previous volleyball team had had at its disposal. USA Volleyball also hired two of the best coaches in the country to lead us to Los Angeles.

————❖————

You cannot succeed without believing in yourself, and that belief is completely under your control—nobody else can generate it for you

————❖————

What can you do to believe in yourself? Keep a weekly log of your successes and celebrate the most significant ones. Keep improving your skills and your confidence by reading business publications and talking to colleagues to find role models in your vocation (or avocation) who, by example, can: a) teach you how to do things a little better every day; or b) show you that their level of success is, in fact, attainable.

PLAY-CALLING/PLANNING

If you had watched any given play during one of our matches, you would have seen specific and decisive planning at work: If our team was serving, the blockers all gave signals behind their backs showing which part of the court they would defend. If we were on offense, the setter told each of our hitters exactly what to do and where to go. In that sense, each play was a microcosm of the second key to our success: *Planning*.

Once the core of our team was assembled, we spent time with our coaches and facilitators looking at our three-year schedule, assigning goals and priorities to the five most important competitions of each year, which we'd use as checkpoints. In essence, we wanted to become one of the top five teams in the world by the end of 1982, one of the top four the next year and among the top three by the 1984 Olympic Games in Los Angeles. By training together for those first several months we were already beating teams ranked in the top ten, so winning a medal seemed within reach. To make it easier to track our progress and win that medal, we broke things down into smaller increments, aiming to move up the rankings just one position in each of the last two years.

If you believe that you're capable of accomplishing a special goal, then, of course, you need to lay out the road map—how you intend to get there. If it's your personal career or business plan, project out three-to-five years, including your top priorities for each year.

We also had to analyze our competition, just like you. We tried to incorporate the best traits of our strongest opponents. The Japanese were known for their great defense and their never-give-up attitude; the Soviets had the strongest blocking; and the Brazilians ran a wide-open daring offense. We tried to copy all of those qualities, and added several innovations of our own, which evolved into our American style of play. Even though we had laid it all out in our plan, it still surprised us to see the legion of scouts and coaches showing up at our events to learn, copy and dissect our game. It was a real compliment—that's when we knew we had arrived.

Maybe there's a new market you want to enter or a new goal to set. This is where planning is doubly crucial. Set a reasonable timeline and check your progress often.

DEFENSE/COMMITMENT

As I mentioned before, the Japanese were known for their outstanding defense. We tried to emulate their techniques, but even more important, their attitude—an all-out commitment to playing the ball. No ball was impossible to get, no matter where it went. If our coach threw a ball that was going to hit the wall fifty feet up, we were expected to try to run up the wall to play it. And if we didn't make that attempt, there were severe consequences. It didn't take long for that attempt to become an involuntary reaction. In the same way, every great team I've been on has made *Commitment* the third element of success.

Pat Riley, the NBA coach, has a simple quote about commitment: "There are only two options...you're either *in* or your *out*; there's no such thing as in between." Each of us, when pondering a strong commitment to something or someone, must ask, "Is this a worthwhile pursuit?" For me, the answer was a resounding "Yes."

It started in high school at Santa Barbara, California, where my friends and I loved to play volleyball so much that we'd sit around pretending to be international superstars, taunting each other until we got so fired up that we'd sneak into the gym at our high school, set up the net and play until the janitor kicked us out. Every summer day, we'd try to be the first ones on the beach courts in the morning and the last ones to leave.

By the time the tryouts for the U.S. team were held in 1981, all of us knew that if we could make the final twelve-man roster, we'd become Olympians by virtue of the automatic host-country berth, since the Olympics were to be held in Los Angeles three years later. The answer became even louder, "Yes, this is absolutely a pursuit worth committing myself to." After the tryouts, the coach, Doug Beal, made it clear what kind of commitment each one of us would have to make. He said we'd need to train at least five (but more often six to eight) hours per day on most of the 160 days we'd average at home and we'd have to devote most of our waking hours to the team when we were traveling, often more than 200 days per year.

Twenty years later, I'm still playing and still loving it. I have what I believe is the greatest job in the world—I get to play a kid's game, volleyball, and earn a living doing it. That's why it's so easy for me to commit to paying the price for success. That's why it's so easy to practice for three hours, to lift weights for another two hours, and to do all the other things I have to do, every day, to be a part of the best team in the world, to be the best player I can be, and to try to improve each year that I compete.

———❖———

We had Bulgaria on the ropes, but choked away the game suffering our most painful defeat of the year

———❖———

That's the trick—finding something you so enjoy doing that most of the time it doesn't seem like work. Are there facets of your profession that you would enjoy doing even if you did them as a hobby? Maybe it's servicing a particularly appreciative customer. Or bringing the negotiation to a conclusion and finally closing the deal. Or it could be solving that nagging problem with an entirely new and creative approach. Try to focus on the fun parts of your job when your commitment seems to wane.

There was another facet of commitment that we faced, maybe the most important—when we failed at a major checkpoint. That is exactly what happened in 1982, when our goal was to finish in the top five at the World Championships.

We had Bulgaria…the defending Olympic silver medalists, on the ropes (12-4) in the fifth and deciding game, but choked away the game and lost (16-14) suffering our most painful defeat. We ended up taking thirteenth place, far short of our potential, but we learned a lot:

❖ We needed to add specific tactics to our arsenal for specific opponents

❖ We needed to use our personnel more efficiently and give greater responsibility to players in their areas of expertise

❖ We would never let the opponent off the hook again

❖ We would respond decisively in the face of adversity

These were great lessons that translate perfectly into the business world. We adjusted, adding tactics, delegating authority and increasing our tenacity. We never lost to Bulgaria again but, rather, beat them more than thirty times in a row until I retired from the indoor team in 1989.

I choose the players who respond best after failure

We learned another great lesson: The times when we were most motivated and wanted to strengthen our commitment to the goal of an Olympic medal were the times after our *worst failures*. We felt a great sense of urgency after failure that we never felt after strong success.

The coach of the Soviet team, which dominated the world rankings for seven years until we reached the top, said something I'll never forget. He was asked, "With so many great players to choose from, how do you decide on your lineup?" He responded, "I don't choose the players who handle success most easily, I choose the players who respond best after failure."

Each of us will have failures—if we are reaching high enough. At the same time, we shouldn't make the same mistake twice. Use your failures to their fullest, for learning important lessons, for future motivation and for strengthening your commitment.

THE SPIKE/FINISH AGGRESSIVELY

A big spike is the most spectacular, the most aggressive play I can make on a volleyball court. It is an all-out attack on the competition. On the one hand, a huge spike never displays the tremendous amount of work that went into setting up the play and making it succeed—work that can, if you let it, become monotonous and dull. On the other hand, the spike signifies how we should never just complete our tasks, we should attack them.

We spent five hours a day, five or six days a week, about fifty weeks a year, for three years, preparing for Los Angeles. More than 200 days each year were spent traveling to seek out the best competition. We spent about 10,000 waking hours doing what had to be done to become the best, which averages about ten hours a day. In any given practice we would do about

about 300 maximum jumps, which, at three feet per jump, meant 900 feet of jumps. After practice we did, on average, four stations of six sets of twenty "max-jumps" of three feet each, which added up to another 1,440 feet of jump-training drills. We were jumping the equivalent of almost twice the height of the Empire State Building during *each workout*, five days a week.

There were times when a player just didn't want to or couldn't go on. That's when the advantage of having co-workers or teammates became apparent. We could always rely on another player to push us, usually with, "Yeah, well I'm the Soviet team and I'm loving watching you quit trying right now because it means you'll probably wilt when the gold is on the line." It wasn't cheerful, but it was effective.

————❖————

We were jumping the equivalent of almost twice the height of the Empire State Building during each workout

————❖————

Another trick I learned when the hard work started to get me down was visualization. Every day after practice and jump-training, we would measure our jump. One day I was having trouble even touching eleven feet, which should have been easy since my maximum was 11'2". My UCLA teammate, Peter Ehrman, pretended he was the play-by-play announcer saying,

The Americans and the Soviets have been going back and forth for more than three hours. It all comes down to this. With a sellout crowd of 15,000, the score tied 14-14, and the gold medal on the line, the set goes to Kiraly. He's lined up against 6'7" Alexander Savin, the greatest blocker in history, and he...

After setting the scene in my mind, I went to leap and hit a new high of 11'3". My teammate continued,

Kiraly puts it down, and now it's the gold medal point. The crowd is going nuts, the Americans serve, they play it up and the set goes back to Kiraly and he...

I took another jump and hit another personal record, 11'4". On the Olympic Team, we continued using that technique to coax extra effort from each other whenever exhaustion set in.

Whenever you find yourself hitting the "wall," envision every detail you can summon about the goal you're trying to attain—don't let your hard work become a grind...attack it!

It takes extra effort to create a legacy of success where there had been none before, but with belief in yourself, long-term planning, a commitment to the goal and the plan, and by attacking the workload, anyone can enjoy the tremendous inner reward of accomplishing special career goals.

The U.S. Team walked into the Opening Ceremony of the 1984 Olympic Games in Los Angeles with a twenty-four match winning streak including four victories over the world champion Soviets. We were upset by Brazil in a meaningless preliminary match but when we met them again in the finals, we won the gold medal in three straight sets.

Later, I was elected captain of the indoor team for the four years leading up to the 1988 Olympics, which made me responsible for galvanizing the team—helping everyone *believe* in himself, helping build our *plan*, showing by example a total *commitment* to our goals, and *attacking* the workload with relish every single day.

We were undefeated heading into the Olympic finals in Seoul. The thirteenth point of the final game of the gold-medal match epitomized our whole strategy: I believed in my ability, planned on the Soviet player crushing the ball at me, committed to making the play, and attacked it. Then Steve Timmons (the big guy with the red flat-top—you couldn't miss him) spiked it back even harder to put us in position to win. We beat the Soviets for the gold 3 games to 1.

It works. Good luck!

Photo courtesy of Peter Brouillet

TERRY SCHROEDER

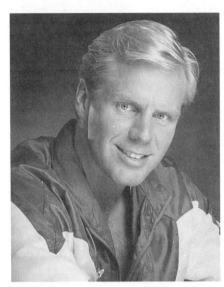

Photo provided by Terry Schroeder

Terry Schroeder is the most recognized water polo player in the United States and one of the premier players the sport has ever seen.

For Terry, water polo combined his love of water with the excitement of a basketball game and the toughness of football. He made his first national team in 1978. His leadership skills are evident, as he was chosen to captain the U.S. National team each year from 1983 through 1992 and was placed on four Olympic teams (1980, 1984, 1988 and 1992). Terry was selected by his peers to carry the American flag into the Closing Ceremony of the 1988 Olympic Games, was twice voted "Water Polo Player of the World" by *Swimming World* magazine and named MVP of five different all-world tournaments.

Because he was considered to be the perfect athletic specimen in 1984, sculptor Robert Graham used Terry as the model for the male bronze figure that stands atop the gateway entrance to the Los Angeles Memorial Coliseum.

He has worked as a television analyst for his sport on Turner Broadcasting and conducts a popular water polo summer camp, while also finding time to give back to his alma mater as the head water polo coach at Pepperdine University in Malibu, where he orchestrated the team's National Championship in 1997. In private life, Dr. Terry Schroeder is a chiropractor.

23

Never Lose Sight of the Ball

Terry Schroeder

T he shot clock had more time on it than did the game clock. If the U.S. Water Polo Team was to advance to the medal round in the 1988 Olympic tournament, we would need to score a goal on Hungary within the next fifteen seconds. I was the "hole man," setting two meters, and my teammates controlled the ball. The long pass floated in my direction.

I've been a "hole man" throughout my entire water polo career. Not unlike a center in basketball, the two-meter man goes down the length of the pool and sets up deep near the opponents' goal (just two meters from the goalie). Usually, half the job is playing the role of punching bag. Teammates try to pass the ball into the two-meter man for a quick, close shot on goal, and part of the strategy for the defenders is to foul the two-meter man to prevent him from shooting. Unlike basketball, however, there is no limit to the number of fouls that players are allowed to commit. Consequently, in the course of a match, the two-meter man takes one heck of a lot of abuse. Some two-meter men have been known to get fouled more than 100 times in a game (imagine getting hacked by Shaquille O'Neal 100 times in a game). If a two-meter man is good, he stays focused on the game and never shows negative reactions—physically or otherwise, either to the officials or to the defender.

A sportswriter once wrote that "The ideal two-meter man has to be able to get hit on the head with a two-by-four and not show any emotion. Instead, he must keep his energy focused on the game." In other words, never lose sight of the ball.

Grabbing, pulling and punching are not allowed in our sport, yet, because they are effective and the official can't call what he can't see, many players use those tools in the heat of battle. In fact, every game begins with a fingernail inspection by the officials, just to be certain that no one gets scratched.

Numerous times I've been hit, kicked or grabbed by defenders, sometimes accidentally, usually on purpose, and to be candid, it wasn't always possible to let go of the anger. After taking a punch or kick to the face (I managed to collect more than 100 stitches in my face during my career), I'd be angry. Who wouldn't? Sure, I felt the urge to go after the defender and get even, but I never did. I went back to work and focused on my job. I always told myself that the best way to get even was to score a goal or make a good assist. If I'm lured out of my position to return a punch or a knee in the groin, the other guy wins because then I'm not in position to do what I'm supposed to do.

———❖———

The ideal two-meter man has to be able to get hit on the head with a two-by-four and not show any emotion

———❖———

Staying focused is something I think about all the time and it is applicable beyond sports. It applies to the way I go about my everyday life. It applies to the way I approach my occupation, the way I relate to my family, friends and co-workers. That's one of the reasons that Olympic sports are such a fine metaphor for living. Staying focused and in control of our emotions can make all the difference in the world between success and failure...the difference between mediocrity and fulfillment.

I joined the U.S. Water Polo Team in 1978. Still in college and playing for Pepperdine University, being a member of the national squad was a tremendous step toward fulfilling a dream I had had since the age of 7: to compete in the Olympic Games.

For almost two years, my teammates and I worked, sacrificed and generally made Olympic water polo competition our lives. We ate, slept, swam and did everything with one goal in mind: to eventually stand as a team on the top podium during the awards ceremony at the 1980 Moscow Olympics.

But it was not to be.

In late 1979, the Soviet Union invaded Afghanistan. Shortly thereafter, President Jimmy Carter called for the entire U.S. Olympic Committee to boycott the 1980 Games. The news of his action came as a crushing blow to my teammates and me. Yet, I knew I had more to offer, because unlike a handful of my teammates who chose to retire, I felt that I had more Olympics in me.

———❖———

The best way to get even was to score a goal or make a good assist

———❖———

I do have to say it was a tremendous learning experience, though. It made me take stock of what was really important. It made me sit back and reflect on the truly valuable aspects of the sport, how much I loved being around my teammates, striving for a common goal, encouraging each other in every aspect of the sport. I appreciated playing the sport and I enjoyed leading the team from my two-meter position.

Returning to the priorities I had learned as a child, I felt better equipped to lead the team. With the retirement of a few members of the 1980 squad, I was elected captain of the 1984 U.S. team. It is one of the great honors in my life. I knew what the honor meant and that it also brought with it a great responsibility. I felt it was up to me to provide leadership from the water and to keep the team together. I am reminded of the final words uttered by Leonard Nimoy as Doctor Spock in an early "Star Trek" movie: "The needs of the many outweigh the needs of the few." The Olympian within understands that the good of the team comes first and this principle is vital to being a successful leader.

Denied the opportunity to play in Moscow, we approached the Los Angeles Olympics focused and united. We trained and competed with enthusiasm.

The 1984 Olympics in Los Angeles went well with a partisan American crowd and the advantage of a familiar home court. We were firing on all cylinders, unbeaten going into the gold medal game.

That year, the international rules had no provision for overtime or a shoot-out, and because the Yugoslavians had a "goal-differential" advantage, a tie would mean the U.S. would receive the silver medal. We had to win the game to win the gold.

Despite holding the lead until the middle of the third quarter, we couldn't stave off their attack. After four years (and four hard-fought quarters), we tied, 5-5, and were declared second best.

It hurt more than an elbow to the nose. As great as it was to play in my home pool, it was also more devastating to not win the gold medal.

But when I looked at the loss as a blow from a defender, I realized that the gold medal (while certainly important) was not the only reason I had played. The camaraderie, the teamwork, the common goal, the genuine affection we had for each other, these were the things that kept me involved. These were the things that would keep me involved for another four years.

The team's focus was "well-played water polo" and we *had* played well.

Two years later, in the midst of training for the 1988 Games, I was forced to learn that lesson again.

During a particularly serious workout, I broke a finger on my right hand, my shooting hand. For nearly two months, because of the waterproof cast, I could not catch or throw the ball with my right hand. I could still swim and participate in all the conditioning drills, but for my position on the team as the hole man in front of the net (a water polo team's quarterback) it was vital that I be able to pass and shoot. I no longer knew what my role on the team was.

Then it hit me: Why not use my other hand? Somehow I managed to persuade the coaches that I should work on throwing the ball with my left hand. Over the next eight weeks, I took 200 left-handed shots in every workout. Practicing twice a day, six days each week, I took about 20,000 shots with my left hand. It made an amazing difference in my game. I could once again focus on what was important—contributing to the team.

------❖------

Then it hit me: Why not use my other hand?

------❖------

The end result of this potentially debilitating injury was, in fact, very positive. From that point forward, I scored more goals left-handed than I did off my "natural" right side. There was no doubt about it; the injury opened the door for me to make myself a better player. I became much tougher to defend because I could go either way on a shot—right or left. And in a game where most players shoot with only one hand, my newly developed talent made me much more valuable to my team.

Even an automobile accident that tore my rotator cuff and gave me whiplash didn't seem like the end, but it did force me again to refocus my efforts on the ways I could contribute. Rehabilitation was extensive and the comeback slow. For the first time in a decade, I missed the opportunity to join the U.S. Team on a European tour, the all-important warm-up for the 1988 Games. On a subsequent tour I joined the team, but was unable to play much. While I knew I would recover in time to play in Seoul, I also knew I wouldn't be in "top" form. I thought it was important that my teammates not know that I was in pain and unable to throw the ball as hard as I used to.

My first two years as captain of the U.S. Team were a crucial period in my development as a leader. I learned that the best kind of leadership comes from "the quiet man," the one who leads by example. I always tried to be the first one in the water at practice. I always tried to work harder than anyone else. I realized that in the heat of the battle it was better for me to sometimes take responsibility for a bad pass or shot (even when it was not necessarily my fault) in order to defuse the situation as quickly as possible. It helped keep the team together and focused.

I also found it was important to be a good listener, whether I was speaking with a coach or one of my fellow players. It's important to be "big enough" to weigh the advice from anyone willing to offer it.

————❖————

The best kind of leadership comes from 'the quiet man,' the one who leads by example

————❖————

In part because of that leadership, the team played well in the Seoul Olympics, and I was able to contribute. Once again, I found myself in the pool, with fifteen seconds on the clock, and in a position to deliver the necessary goal to allow the U.S. to advance over Hungary to the medal round.

With the clock running down, our chances were bleak.

Between me and the Hungarian goaltender were two meters of water and a 6'4", 230-pound defender named Imre Toth. Hungary had earned medals in twelve consecutive Olympics prior to 1984 and this particular defender had been on the World All-Star team for six years. The Hungarians have always had dynamite polo teams, large and aggressive, because their big athletes in high school don't have football or rugby as an option. The scene at two meters often resembled two sharks fighting over a piece of meat, with whitewater obstructing the officials' view of what was happening below the surface.

I positioned myself in the usual place in front of the net and when the ball came to me I felt the defender grab and tear at my suit, shoving me aside to get to the ball. I tried to ignore his brutality and gathered every shred of training and discipline to get the shot off before the end of the game.

With a short backward flick of my left shoulder, I pushed myself forward, grabbing the ball with my right hand. Ignoring the pain of the torn rotator cuff in my shoulder, I swept the ball across my body and threw it with all my might toward the goal. It sailed past the Hungarian goalkeeper for the winning score.

The cheering in the pool was wild! When a news reporter asked me later how it felt to score the winning goal, I replied, "It felt like every man on the team was helping me to throw the ball into the goal," and every man was sharing in the celebration. It truly was a team effort. My devotion to the team made it easy to bury the pain and it made it possible for the team to advance.

We then defeated Russia by a couple of goals and met the defending champions, Yugoslavia, in the gold medal game. Ironically, that game, like the one in Los Angeles, ended in a tie, but the rules had since changed. Had the old rule been in effect, we would have won the gold, as the U.S. owned the better goal differential, but in 1988 we played two three-minute overtime periods. Yugoslavia found the goal twice to our once, and won in overtime. We were silver medalists once again. We had played even with the best in the world, but to our chagrin, we were sent home with the silver.

During one of my more poignant post-Olympic moments, a couple of children asked to see my medal. After handling it and studying it carefully, one of them remarked how nice it was. "Yeah, but it's not gold," the other said. I had to remind myself once again about the real meaning behind my participation. The team again had played well and I had overcome so much to even be in the pool. I had to overlook the pain of the boy's comment and focus on the bigger picture.

I really felt my playing days were over. I had delivered on my promise to play well and contribute. All of the other lifelong priorities that had been "on hold" since first joining the U.S. Team ten years earlier had to take their rightful place in my life.

❖

We would be victorious at the Games in Spain. What actually happened was even better

❖

I was a practicing chiropractor and, along with my wife, Lori (also a chiropractor), we were growing a healthy and successful business. We also planned to start a family. There was no time, as far as I could see, for the intensity and dedication needed to play Olympic water polo.

In fact, when the governing body pleaded with me to rejoin the team at the last minute to play in Barcelona, Lori and I thought about it long and hard. We came back to the coaches with the following offer: "Water polo is third place when it comes to my priorities now. My family and our practice come first. If you can live with that, I'll play again."

In 1991, we won the FINA World Cup in Barcelona, beating every top team in the world, including our old nemesis, Yugoslavia, in overtime play. I felt we had moved out from under the dark shadow that had been hanging over us for years. We were the best in the world. We were on our way to the Olympic title.

Barcelona was to be the crowning achievement of my career. Adversity and circumstances aside, we would be victorious at the Games in Spain. What actually happened was even better.

We didn't win the gold. Or the silver. Or the bronze. We were fourth. The U.S. Team made it to the semifinals, only to lose to the Spanish home team (the eventual silver medalists).

Afterward, as Lori and I walked back to the Olympic Village, I felt exhausted and depressed. I was 33 years old and I didn't have another Summer Games ahead of me. I knew it, Lori knew it and the international water polo community knew it. But, still, I was having a hard time living with the reality that I would never play on an Olympic champion team.

Then on the way back to the Olympic Village after the bronze medal match, I crossed paths with an old friend.

Kirk Kilgour wasn't really all that well-known until the 1984 Olympics in Los Angeles, when he began a new career as a television sports announcer. Prior to that, volleyball players everywhere knew his name. He had, after all, earned recognition and respect as a collegiate standout and a former member of the USA Volleyball Team. My relationship with Kirk, though, began during my days as a student-athlete at Pepperdine University, where he was the men's volleyball coach. I remember those days, seeing Kirk buzz around our gym, directing practices, coaching matches. He was your prototypical Southern California volleyball guy, always upbeat and energetic; always smiling with a good word for whomever he met.

Those qualities were hard to miss. So, too, was his wheelchair.

You see, Kirk is a quadriplegic—permanently paralyzed in a volley-ball training accident during a time when he was on the ascending side of a brilliant career as a player.

Seeing Kirk there, confined to the chair that he steered with just his tongue, made me put my situation into perspective.

————◈————

Always upbeat and energetic. . .those qualities were hard to miss.
So, too, was his wheelchair

————◈————

Kirk asked how things had gone. I started to reel off all the supposed reasons for my bitter disappointment, while he just looked and listened. As I recounted each and every "questionable" call by the officials, the fouls not called and the opportunities missed, a realization sank deeper and deeper into me. Here was Kirk, nearly cut down in the prime of his life (certainly in terms of his athletic career) sitting in that wheelchair listening to me gripe, complain and bellyache about *a game*. Kirk has never asked for pity and it's not something that even enters my mind when I think of him. He's enthusiastic, vital and successful. He's got a great mind and an even better personality.

He never said anything outright and yet it was as if he were reaching out to me in his own way, telling me, "Get on with it, Terry. Get on with life. This chair doesn't keep me down, so don't let your 'setback' keep you down."

It was a sobering moment and a humbling wake-up call. And it was one of the most defining moments for me in terms of keeping things in perspective. What had I been thinking? I had been blessed with abilities and enjoyed more opportunities than most people ever dream of. Then and there, I began thinking differently. Instead of concentrating on the officials and the losses, I remembered how much I enjoyed the competition and the boisterous crowds.

I thought of making four Olympic teams in sixteen years, and of playing in three Olympic tournaments. I recalled the many close friends, exciting road trips and thrilling competitions. And the great honor of carrying the American flag in the Closing Ceremony in Seoul. The sadness, the disappointment and the bitterness that so filled my life moments before, drained out of me.

I went to the 1996 Games in Atlanta as a spectator. Shortly before those Games, Lori had given me a beautiful and healthy daughter, and our practice grew more successful than ever before. In December 1997, I got the chance to "go for the gold" once again. Not as a player, but as coach of Pepperdine's water polo team. Moments after the horn sounded at the end of the 1997 NCAA National Championships, I was one of the first to celebrate our victory by jumping into the pool fully clothed.

As happy as the team's win made me feel, the perspective I gained from Kirk Kilgour in Barcelona helped me put it in its correct place. I was thrilled, to be sure, but I also knew that the championship was just a game.

Now, when I tell my players at Pepperdine to "never lose sight of the ball," that it's their focus that's really important, I hope they learn something from these experiences. My dad, the college football player who explained, "You gotta' take the hit and keep on playing the game," also said, "When you've done the best you can do, you should be happy."

If my players approach the game and the competition the right way, they will enjoy a sense of growth and they will realize that the day after each and every match, all of the most important things still remain.

To have a great life, I really do not need an Olympic gold medal, especially when I have my health, a rewarding career, a relationship with God, the love of my family, my friends and teammates.

Compared to that, nothing else comes close.

Photo provided by Terry Schroeder

PETER VIDMAR

Photo provided by Peter Vidmar

Peter Vidmar became the premier male gymnast for the United States at the 1984 Olympic Games in Los Angeles. As USA team captain, he led his teammates to their stunning gold medal victory over the People's Republic of China. Peter went on to win the silver medal in the All-Around competition, making him the only American male ever to do so. With a perfect score of 10.0, he also captured the gold medal on the pommel horse. A member of the U.S. Olympic Hall of Fame, Peter is the highest-scoring American male gymnast in Olympic history.

Since his Olympic triumphs, Peter has worked as the gymnastics announcer for CBS Sports, served on the Boards of USA Gymnastics and the U.S. Olympic Committee, and has been appointed to the President's Council on Physical Fitness and Sports, as well as the California Governor's Council on Physical Fitness and Sports. He has become well-known as a motivator of America's top corporations and associations by blending his thoughts, humor and anecdotes with a live performance on the pommel horse.

His high energy and sense of drama produce standing ovations time and time again. Perhaps that's why *Successful Meetings* magazine has listed him as one of the top ten speakers in the country.

24

How to Take Risks with Confidence

Peter Vidmar

I fell nine feet and that wasn't even close to the worst of it. The year was 1983, the country was Hungary, the city was Budapest, and the guy who was walking miles from his hotel and *not* hailing a cab was me. Teammate Bart Conner could have driven up in his Porsche and tossed me the keys and I'd have tossed them back. Sometimes you have to walk. I had to walk.

Just moments before I'd been in the Budapest Sports Arena, going through a routine on the high bar that I thought was going to turn me into a world champion. I was 22 years old at the time and competing in my third World Championships. These weren't just any World Championships. With the Los Angeles Olympic Games coming up in fewer than eight months, these Worlds were serving as a tune-up, a final preview of the upcoming Olympic medalists.

I was in second place going into the high-bar finals; close enough to the lead that my winning the title wasn't out of the question. I wasn't the only one thinking along those lines. Between the preliminaries and the finals, word had spread to the broadcasting team from ABC's "Wide World of Sports," which was primed to tape the finals. When the Japanese gymnast, who was leading the competition, fell during his routine, their cameras focused on me, Peter Vidmar, United States of America, all set to chronicle my ascent to the top. I thought I was ready. All I had to do was nail my routine and I would be the new world high-bar champion.

The value of the TV coverage was not lost on me. I knew that it was "Wide World of Sports" that had made Kurt Thomas the most famous American gymnast ever. I knew it was Kurt Thomas in the early '70s who forged a reputation as the best "gamer" in the history of gymnastics. He always saved his best for whenever they turned on the red light. When it counted, in other words. By using television, Kurt Thomas had easily done more for U.S. Gymnastics than any American gymnast in history. He hadn't done too badly for Kurt Thomas, either.

Now it was my chance to be the next Kurt Thomas and I knew it. (And so, I suspect, did Kurt Thomas, who, along with Al Michaels, was handling the broadcast that night for ABC).

There was one slight problem.

I was suddenly having difficulty with a particular skill in my high-bar routine—a tricky maneuver that I'd managed to pull off without a hitch in the preliminaries, but which was now giving me problems. This was a skill that had gotten me into world championship contention in the first place. Indeed, this was the skill I needed to perform if I wanted to get my bonus two-tenths of a point for risk.

But, as I said, it was tricky. It called for me to swing around the bar, then let go, fly straight up over the bar into a half-turn, straddle my legs, come back down, catch the bar, swing and immediately let go again, do a back flip with a half-turn in the pike position, come back down and catch the bar. Trust me, it's hard.

As I warmed up before the finals, I kept messing it up and, as a result, kept getting more and more frustrated. This was no time for things to go bad.

Of course, worry soon gave way to panic. Not good. I remember I looked at my coach, Makoto Sakamoto, and said, "Mako, you've gotta' help me. I've got fifteen minutes until the competition starts and I can't do this right! It's my only risky skill! What's wrong?"

Mako watched me.

"Oh, just pike more on your swing," he said.

"Uh, arch more at the bottom."

"Try letting go of the bar a little later."

All these insightful tips, followed by the ultimate coaching wisdom that we've all heard before:

"Just do it right!"

But I wasn't doing it right and, for a fleeting moment, I decided I'd just bag it. I'd leave it out. Why not? I'd lose the two-tenths of a point for risk, but I could still score as high as a 9.8. That would put me on the winner's rostrum for sure. That would mean a medal, maybe even a silver.

❖

I kept messing it up and this was no time for things to go bad

❖

But it wouldn't earn me the World Championship and I knew it. I knew others would take a risk and someone else would make it count and that person would become the World Champion, not me. Someone else would get the gold medal. I also instinctively knew that it wasn't every day that I got a chance to be a world champion—in anything. Now that I had that chance, was I going to play it safe? Was I going to throw out the risk when I was so close?

No! I wasn't. That was my answer. I decided to stick to the game plan. I'd leave that risky skill in. With it, I would ride to the top of the world—or else.

When my name was called I signaled the superior judge and jumped up and grabbed the bar. The risky skill came right at the beginning of the routine, so I swung around the bar, let go, came straight up over the bar, did a half-turn, straddled my legs, came back down, caught the bar, immediately let go again, did that back flip with the half turn in the pike position, (so far so good) came back down to catch the bar...and the bar...

...was...

...not...

...there.

That's when gravity, the supreme justice of gymnastics, prevailed.

After dropping nine feet, I hit the mat, face first on a foam pad four inches thick.

Now, the rules in gymnastics are adamant about one thing: You're only allowed one dismount in a performance.

I did the only thing I could do. I jumped up off the floor, grabbed the bar again, and finished my routine. But I was already out of the running. I landed my "second" dismount perfectly (big deal), saluted the judges, jumped off the platform, grabbed my bags and left the arena. I was devastated. Destroyed. Inconsolable. I'd blown it, I'd choked and I'd failed. I knew it, and I'd managed to do it on ABC's "Wide World of Sports"! My teammates told me that when Kurt Thomas in the broadcast booth saw this "wannabe" crash and burn, he just flipped his pencil in the air in disappointment.

I finished eighth. And if you're thinking, *Hmm, eighth place in the world is not that bad,* I thank you. But there were only eight people in the competition.

Not being the world champion wasn't what bothered me most. It was that I'd had the opportunity and I hadn't come through. I hadn't done a Kurt Thomas. And the thing is, I really thought I would. That's what got to me, that's what I kept thinking about over and over again as I walked back to my hotel. I thought I would come through and I hadn't! Doubts suddenly came creeping in from all corners. Deep down I wondered if I would *ever* be able to rise to the occasion under pressure. Did I have what it takes to deliver the goods when it came time for real world-class competition or would I crack under the strain?

That's what consumed my thoughts as I walked head down through the dark Budapest night. A light snow began to fall. How appropriate, I thought.

———❖———

Deep down I wondered if I would ever be able to rise to the occasion under pressure

———❖———

It wasn't until I got to the hotel and was halfway through the front door that Mako caught up with me. I didn't much feel like talking to him but we were in the space between the hotel's double entry doors, the area that keeps the heat from getting out and, in this case, was keeping me from getting in. He had me cornered.

He said a lot of things. But this is what I remember:

"This is not the end."

"Everything is a learning experience," said Mako, "even competition. What you did tonight can be a valuable learning experience. You can benefit from this."

Mako didn't know it at the time—because I didn't tell him—but what he said struck a chord with me. This *had* been a valuable learning experience. I didn't want to hear it but I knew he was right. That fall taught me something that I somehow hadn't completely learned until that night:

Never, *ever* take anything for granted.

Especially don't take risks for granted.

I realized that I had made the decision to take the risk, but I had forgotten to *really* prepare myself for taking it! Knowing how important that particular skill was…that I couldn't leave out that trick and still win the title, I should have been better prepared. I was certain to have to take the same risk at the Olympics and no matter how the skill might feel in warm-up, I had to commit *now* to taking it there as well.

I promised myself that from that day forward, if I were going to take a risk, I was going to be ready.

❖

I had made the decision to take the risk, but I had forgotten
to really prepare myself for taking it!

❖

This time, there would be no more fooling around. I had known that the double release move on the high bar was extremely difficult. I was the only person in the world doing it at the time, so that should have been my first clue. I received maximum risk points for it precisely *because* of its difficulty. It was a move that needed extra attention. It wasn't something I could take for granted. But every day in the gym I had treated it just like the 200 or so other tricks I had to work on. I'd given it no extra care. And now I knew it needed that.

The Olympics were fewer than eight months away. I resolved that from that moment on, I'd go back to the high bar at the end of my workouts and I'd work overtime on that risky double release move. I was determined to learn my lesson. The next time the pressure was on, I would not fail.

So that's what I did. For the next eight months, there wasn't a workout between Budapest and Los Angeles that didn't include an extra session or two, working on that high-bar double release. I practiced it twice as much as any other skill. Twenty times as much as some. I worked on it and I worked on it, and then I worked on it some more. To be honest, I never really liked doing it because I frequently missed the bar and crashed to the floor. But I did it anyway—always with the memory of a missed world title.

By the time the Olympics came around, I was a lot more comfortable with that double release. Not quite eight months after the fall in Budapest, I jumped up and grabbed the bar in the All-Around finals at the Olympic Games. About one minute later I came back down—when I was supposed to. I scored a Perfect 10 on the high bar.

Photo provided by Peter Vidmar

Looking back (it's always easier looking back), I can say I'm glad I failed in Budapest. And you know what? I really am. Sometimes it's necessary to fail. That's how we learn. It wasn't fun when it happened, but it taught me how important it is to focus on what we need to focus on, not what we would like to focus on. Respecting a risk is every bit as important as taking one. Maybe more important.

If I hadn't fallen off that high bar in the World Championships I might have fallen off when the pressure was even greater. And you sure wouldn't be reading my book, *How I Blew It At the Olympic Games.*

———❖———

I practiced it twice as much as any other skill. Twenty times as much as some

———❖———

When I talk to corporate audiences about risk, I like to begin with that story about my fall in Budapest because it combines so many of the important elements of taking risks—and because it has a happy ending.

The point is that I needed that risk. I never could have realized my potential without it. But I also needed to respect it. We all need risks. The challenge is to know how to control them, instead of letting them control us.

———❖———

Respecting a risk is every bit as important as taking one

———❖———

Risk-taking goes beyond just a necessary step, beyond just a requirement to reach the Perfect 10. Risks—sensible, calculated, prudent, rational risks—are the obstacles that make reaching the destination worthwhile. Without them there would be no struggle and no satisfaction.

I'm not saying *all* risks are good and I don't recommend that we take a flyer on every outlandish gamble that comes our way, but progress in business or sports occurs only when we risk going someplace we've never been before. A new product or a new territory or even new packaging can be risky but it's also more rewarding when the risk pays off. To awaken the Olympian within, we should look for those hidden risky opportunities, places to go and ways to stretch our abilities. These daily challenges and events outside our comfort zone can be a valuable part of our journey through life and we should resolve *in advance*, to prepare for them and to meet and beat them.

Triumphs that are truly meaningful are triumphs that require effort. If there weren't a "rough" on the golf course, could we appreciate driving a golf ball dead in the middle of the fairway nearly as much? If the marlin just jumped in our boat, would catching it be as satisfying? If not for risks, rewards would lose much of their value.

I currently ride a mountain bike both for the exercise and the thrill of careening down a mountainside. The risk of danger is real (and I've crashed more than I care to admit), but I have done my homework there as well. I train hard for the uphill climbs and I keep my bike's brakes and shocks prepared for the dangerous downhill descents. As a result, I feel better physically and I can't begin to describe the personal satisfaction I get from being on the mountaintop, the thrill of dodging the trees and boulders, and the adrenaline rush I get from racing to the finish line.

Risks give life its zip. Why else would people bungee jump, climb mountains, jump out of airplanes or run with the bulls? Approached sensibly, risks can bring excitement. They bring exhilaration, they bring zest and fun, they bring inspiration and, when one prepares for them, they can bring deep satisfaction and impressive results.

———❖———

If not for risks, rewards would lose much of their value

———❖———

My fall in Budapest taught me the lesson well. It didn't teach me to avoid risks, but rather it taught me that a life without risk, a life of safe mediocrity, hurts more than a "face plant" from nine feet.

AL JOYNER

Photo provided by Final Kick Marketing

Al Joyner and Florence Griffith met while competing for spots on the ill-fated 1980 Olympic Track and Field Team. Four years later, in the city where they trained together, they each qualified for the Games in Los Angeles, where Al won the gold medal in the triple jump and Florence won the silver medal in the 200 meters.

Al, the "Rodney Dangerfield" of track, was forever known as Jackie Joyner's older brother, running in her shadow, performing the hurdles and triple jump. Often overlooked but never overwhelmed, Al kept focused on his potential, perpetually improving and surprising the better-credentialed athletes.

With his gold medal jump in the 1984 Olympics, Al became the first of the Joyner family to win an Olympic title, beginning a dynasty as both his sister and his wife would go on to become the two greatest female track-and-field athletes in history. His wife, Florence, would become the fastest woman on the planet, and his sister, Jackie, the greatest all-around athlete, earning eleven Olympic medals between them.

Al continues his involvement with the sport through his coaching and marketing company, Final Kick Marketing, which emphasizes relationships instead of paychecks.

FLORENCE GRIFFITH JOYNER

Photo provided by Final Kick Marketing

Florence was born the seventh of eleven children, raised in the housing projects of South Central Los Angeles. Watts is a difficult place to grow up, but Florence learned the values of independence and individualism. She began running at age 7, under the auspices of the Sugar Ray Robinson Youth Foundation, quickly establishing herself as a sprinter, often defeating boys her age. A straight-A student studying business at Cal State Northridge, she transferred to UCLA on scholarship.

At the Games in Seoul, she was dubbed the "Fastest Woman on Earth," setting records in the 100 and 200 meters that still stand. Honors rolled in, including the James E. Sullivan Award, the USOC Sportswoman of the Year award and the Associated Press and United Press International Sportswoman of the Year awards. Along with her gold medals, her style and flair made her an instant celebrity on and off the track.

She designed her running clothes, which later led to apparel lines, including the NBA's Indiana Pacer uniforms. She was a licensed cosmetologist, published children's books, produced an exercise video program and was chairwoman of the President's Council on Physical Fitness.

Florence died tragically on September 21, 1998, at the age of 38, the week after she passed along the following stories.

25

It Doesn't Matter What Others Think

Al Joyner & Florence Griffith Joyner

Long before I met Florence, my favorite sport was swimming. It was better to be in the cool water during the summer months in East St. Louis, Illinois, than running like a fool in the hot sun. As a teenager, I wanted to work near the water and I lied about my age so I could become a junior lifeguard. That was until my sister, Jackie, got me involved on the track with her sport.

The problem was that I just didn't like to work out. Even so, the high school coach saw something in me and, as a result, got permission from my parents to discipline me to make sure I attended practice every day. On more than one occasion, he pulled me in front of the school assembly and gave me a public paddling before the whole auditorium. He kept saying, "You're going to come to workout." I hated him, but eventually I did start coming to practice.

By my senior year, I had a cocky attitude, so I thought I'd impress the team by attempting the challenging and technical field event: the triple jump. The takeoff board was thirty-eight feet in front of the sand pit, but could be moved closer for the younger or less-experienced jumpers. I left it where it was because I wanted to show off. Running down the runway, I hit the board perfectly, and began the hop, skip and, finally, the jump into the air.

I didn't even make it into the pit.

It was the most embarrassing moment in my life. The whole team roared with laughter. While they were pointing and laughing, I was thinking, "I'm better than that. I'll show them. It's in me somewhere." Along came Coach Earl McDowell, who wanted to improve my strength by making me do "finger push-ups." When I wasn't able to complete the set, he kicked me off the team—just like that.

I went back to the swimming pool, where my boss, the head lifeguard, "Pop" Myles said, "Sweetwater, right now, you're not physically able to do them, but if you keep trying, it'll come." He told me forcefully: "Don't ever say you can't do something. You just can't do it *now*. Keep trying."

I went home and practiced my push-ups until once again the track coach welcomed me back to the team. That very afternoon, I beat their No. 1 hurdler.

My breakthough happened in my last year of high school. I was running the hurdles in a county-wide meet. Since eighth grade I'd been running against tough-talking Anthony Hopkins (we called him "Weed Hopper") who, like Muhammad Ali, would predict the hurdle at which he'd run past me, and doggone-it, he always did it just as he said. At our last head-to-head meeting I wanted revenge. Side-by-side, we dropped into the blocks...and I jumped the gun. Disqualified. I was out.

————❖————

Don't ever say you can't do something. You just can't do it now. Keep trying

————❖————

Walking away from the track, I was so upset that I took my anger and frustration over to the triple-jump pit and promptly set a new meet record. Wow! I looked back and realized that I liked performing in front of a crowd and that my earlier laziness had deprived me of this experience. I decided right then to work harder to see how far I could climb.

Up to that point, I had never heard my name at the meets, either. Instead, the announcer would say things like Albert Joyner, Alfred Joyner, Alan Joyner...or they'd spell it wrong on the scoreboard, (Joiner, Jointer, Joynur, Joener, etc.). It was pretty depressing.

The following year, I jumped a 50' 4-3/4" on my first attempt, breaking the old mark by almost three feet and for the first time I imagined what it might feel like at the Olympic Games when the announcer said my name correctly over the loudspeaker. "Ladies and Gentlemen, the 1978 Junior Olympic gold medalist, Alfredrick Joyner."

Shortly after that meet, I got a call from the coach at Tennessee State, David "Spiderman" Boyd. Spiderman claimed that with the right coach-

234 **Awaken the Olympian Within**

ing, I could jump fifty-five feet. I thought he was offering me a scholarship. I never believed I'd get to college because we couldn't afford it, so I headed off to Tennessee and became the first member of my family to study beyond high school.

When I arrived, I discovered that they were just building a program and didn't actually have any scholarships to offer. I had to work part-time around the practice schedule. I look back at this disappointment as a blessing in disguise because it forced me to "learn the ropes." I spoke with the president of the University, I learned my way around the financial aid office, I registered for my classes. I grew up real fast.

Because we were rebuilding, the coach kept reminding us that we'd have to work harder than the other established schools like UCLA and USC. He said it didn't matter what those programs had accomplished in the past, "They have to do it again, *today*," he said. With those words, he planted the seeds of confidence in the underdog.

I moved to Arkansas State for a scholarship and the chance to work with Coach Guy Kochel, who was known as a great pole vault coach. I told my mom I was moving there, having only seen the campus in a recruiting brochure. On the wall in the coach's office was a picture of three of his former athletes and they were all wearing USA sweats. Earl Bell (1976 pole vault), Thomas Hill (bronze, 1972 hurdles) and Ed Preston (1976 relay alternate) had made the country's Olympic team.

I told him, "I can't be your first Olympian, but I'm going to be your first gold medalist and then you'll be known as a great triple jump coach as well."

In a dual meet against Kansas State, I met the national record-holding triple jumper, Sonya Owallabee. His record was more than 55', but on that day he jumped 53'2". Just like Spiderman Boyd said at Tennessee, "They have to do it again *today*." I jumped 53'5" to beat him.

Watching Owallabee, I was in awe of his amazing hamstrings. I thought, I gotta' get me some hamstrings like that. At the big meets, even though I'd led after the qualifying rounds, often I wasn't strong enough to come back and repeat that effort in the finals. In high school, whenever I'd complain of soreness in my legs, the coach would joke, "You don't even have any leg muscles to pull." My natural ability had taken me as far as it could. Now I needed to do more work.

I learned about the world's best performer in my event—at the time it was the three-time Olympic champion from Russia, Viktor Saneyev. I decided to train just as he did. I learned what he had done and I did like-wise. I carried weights, did bounding drills, leg curls, jumped off boxes, all in an effort to get my legs strong.

By my junior year at the 1983 NCAAs, I finished second behind the great British triple-jumper Keith Connor, who was competing for SMU, but ahead of Mike Conley. That year's National Championships selected the World Championships team and Mike, Willie Banks and I made the team. We went to Helsinki and, coming out of the entry tunnel during the Opening Ceremony, I saw 100,000 spectators and said to myself, "This is it! This is what it's going to be like in the Olympics."

I tried too hard in my attempts and finished dead last. The others thought I just wasn't very good. They continued to discount my ability and overlooked my potential. The eventual winner was a Polish jumper named Zdislaw Hoffman, who came out of nowhere. I'd never seen a "fifty-seven foot lie" before, but he came off that board and *Whoom!*, dropped into the sand like a bird. His performance shocked the field and reminded me to never count *anybody* out of the contest, including myself. After the Worlds, I was on the flight home when I got chills thinking about the 1984 Olympic Games, now less than a year away.

I like to say that Jackie put me on the Olympic Team. At the Trials, it was her toss of the javelin that inspired me. I was on the runway getting ready to jump when I noticed Jackie had just thrown a new personal best. I got so excited, I sprinted down the runway and jumped 56' 4-1/2" earning my spot. So many people had doubted me all along and I might even have surprised her.

In Los Angeles on the day of my Olympic event, an announcer on the television set in the lobby of the athletes' village dormitory promoted my event later in the broadcast: "Coming up, three Americans competing for gold in the triple jump." The voice went on, "The battle will be between Willie Banks and Mike Conley."

"Dang!" I thought. "That's the last straw." Now, I not only had to jump well, I had to win. I couldn't let the guy on television be right. The lobby was across the street from the swimming venue, where it seemed the American anthem was being played at least twice a day. Stepping outside, I thought to myself, "Today, this song is going to play for me!"

Walking to the stadium I prayed, "God give me strength to hold on to what I have." I didn't ask to win, I asked to jump to the best of my ability, *today.* If I did that, inside I knew I was going to win. When someone asked me how I knew, I answered, "Because nobody else thinks I can." I was going to pull a "Zdislaw Hoffman."

My first jump traditionally had been my best one and I wanted this opener to be good, too. I took off my sweats and let the wind feel my face. By watching the stadium closely, I had noticed a swirling breeze and felt sure that wind in my face at one end of the runway would be wind at my back by the time I reached the board.

I took a breath and took off running.

As I ran, I quickly shifted gears like a drag racer and told myself, "You're an airplane." I felt the nose come up just as I hit the board and was airborne. *Boom!* I hit the second step. *Boom!* I went flying through the air, landing in the pit by the Olympic and World record markers. The officials measured the mark in the sand at 17.26 meters or 56′ 7-$\frac{1}{2}$″, my lifetime best by more than three inches, though slightly wind-aided. I was the leader.

There were five jumpers in the final who, on any other day, could manage to clear 57′. Just the day before, Mike Conley leapt 56′11″, but as Spider said, "It doesn't matter what they've done before. They've got to do it again, *today.*"

In the following round, Conley landed 56′4″—which was good, but not good enough.

Preparing for my fifth jump, I noticed Jackie was about to start her last event in the heptathlon (the 800-meter run), so I took a pass (and sacrificed my fifth attempt) to cheer for her as she ran by the pit. I was on the sidelines yelling, "Come on, Jackie, just pump your arms, stay relaxed, pump your arms, you can do it, you can do it!" The press expected her to win and I wanted to be a part of her success as well.

Conley's final jump must have traveled at least 58′, a foot-and-a-half farther than mine, but sadly for him he fouled and the jump wouldn't count. All the jumpers were done when I stood up for my final attempt. The announcer's voice echoed across the Coliseum, "Ladies and gentlemen, for his sixth and final jump, here's our 1984 Olympic Champion, Al Joyner." Conley took the silver and Keith Connor from Britain, the bronze.

The awards ceremonies in track take place in immediate succession at the end of the day. Jackie received her silver medal for the heptathlon,

Photo provided by Final Kick Marketing

stepped off the podium and immediately I stepped forward to receive my award. When the gold was placed over my shoulders, I raised my arm to salute the crowd and I noticed that Jackie was crying. I came over and said, "Oh, come on, Jackie, you'll win the gold next time."

She wiped away the tears and said, "I'm not crying because I lost. I'm crying because you won. You fooled them all...again."

WHEN AL MET FLORENCE...

At the 1980 U.S. trials in Eugene, Oregon, I met Florence Griffith in the hallway. I thought she was a trainer because she was far too beautiful to be an athlete. I caught her eye, talked a while and moved on. I heard later she was headed to UCLA where my sister, Jackie, was enrolled. When I asked Jackie to set us up, she said, "It won't help. She's not going to like you, because I don't like you, so I'm not even going to talk to her for you." We both laughed.

In 1983, I decided to move to California to train. I wanted to become acclimated to the Los Angeles environment, feel the weather, listen to the sounds, adjust to the air quality, get the lay of the land. I wanted no surprises in 1984. That year, Jackie had chosen to sit out her eligibility at UCLA in order to focus on her training. I needed a place to stay and she gave me permission to sleep on the floor of her apartment. I got to know Florence better while we trained together under Bobby Kersee's watchful eye.

Man, that woman could train. I don't think I've ever met a woman (other than Jackie) who worked out as hard with such complete devotion and focus. Florence impressed me with her work ethic and impressed everyone with her flashy style, and, ohhhh, how I tried to get her attention.

FLORENCE: I earned a silver medal in the 200 meters in Los Angeles and remembered being proud for Jackie's brother's triple jump. We had trained together and I admired his work ethic. We were the only two Olympians on Bobby Kersee's team to actually stay in the athletes' village that year. We wanted to enjoy the experience and remember the flavor. When it was time to go, Al came over to say goodbye and said, "I came out to Los Angeles to win the gold medal, not to sightsee. But if I ever come back, will you show me around?" A lame excuse for a date if I ever heard one, but I said okay.

With my 1984 Olympic silver medal finish and my share of other first runner-up results, I earned the nickname "The Silver Queen." I could relate to Al's feelings of being overlooked, but I knew there was gold in me somewhere.

In October 1986, Al returned to California to train with Bobby, and we ran into each other as I was leaving a bank in a Halloween costume (which happened to be a wedding dress). The first words out of his mouth were, "So, are you ready to marry me?" I said, "Sure, let's go," and he stammered out that he didn't have the ring and we walked our separate ways. We began dating shortly afterward.

Unbeknownst to me, Al had planned a very fancy, very romantic evening for July 17, 1987, but after a long workout, I was so tired that I asked if we couldn't go out for fast food instead. Crestfallen, he agreed, but met me with a limousine anyway. On the drive out of town, he dropped a pillow on the floor of the car, knelt on one knee and presented me with a ring. I cried for forty-five minutes.

We were married on October 17, 1987. He became my husband and my full-time coach. He was the one who pointed out that I might have won the gold medal in 1984, but I had tried too hard. He noticed I ran with my hands in a fist, tense and tight for much of the race. "As long as you hold your hands tight," he said, "You're just going to 'rig-up'—tie up and decelerate toward the back end of the race." He taught me to relax, to ease up to go faster.

Al is very analytical and liked to study his sport. I just loved to train. Sit-ups, long runs, sprint sets, weight-lifting sets, it didn't matter. I loved feeling the ground move beneath my feet and feeling strong and in control. In my case, someone had to tell me when to *stop* training.

I had always had a fast-top gear, but Al taught me how to reach that gear sooner in the race.

Al was with me at the 1988 Olympic Trials, almost one year to the day after he popped the question, when I ran a 10.49 in an early round of the 100 meters, shattering the world record by almost three-tenths of a second. I finished four heats of the event, beating the old mark four consecutive times.

I had prepared myself to break the world record in the 200 meters two days later, but perhaps I wanted it too much. My running, while fast, was a bit forced. I settled for an American record. After those trials, I had become the odds-on favorite for three gold medals (the 100, the 200 and the 4 x 100 relay) in Seoul. In contrast to Al being overlooked in Los Angeles, the world *expected* me to win. It would have been a major disappointment if I had lost the Olympic gold in Korea.

THE 1988 OLYMPICS IN SEOUL, KOREA

The media attention in Seoul was remarkable. Everybody wanted to ask about my one-legged racing outfits, the six-inch nails, the flashing head of hair, the sparkling jewelry. "What was I trying to say?" they asked. I pointed out that I had always looked like this but they had never noticed me because I had never been the favorite before. The media couldn't see me as an athlete *and* as a fashion designer at the same time.

It reminded me of one of my schoolteachers. My mother raised her kids to think that they could do and be anything they wanted. As a child in school, I had a teacher who asked the whole class to write out their dreams on a sheet of paper. Reading my paper out loud, I said, "I want to be an actor, a designer and I want to go to the Olympics...."

The teacher interrupted saying, "Whoa, you've got to pick just one thing." Crying to my mother, I said, "You lied to me. You said I could be *anything*, but the teacher says I've got to pick one thing." My momma confronted the teacher and told her she couldn't put limits on my life.

------❖------

My mother raised her kids to think that they could do and be anything they wanted

------❖------

While cameras zeroed in on my painted nails as I placed my hands on the starting line of the 100 meters in Seoul, the athlete in me was focused on my desire to better my time once again. Al reminded me that I could set a record in any meet. The Olympics only come along once every four years. He said don't try doing better than I'd ever done before, but rather just do what I had trained myself to do, what I knew I was capable of...and remember to enjoy the experience.

On the first day of the Olympics, I broke the Olympic record twice in the 100, and that helped set up the final. Evelyn Ashford, the defending champion, was two lanes to my right, the great East German runner, Heike Drechsler, between us.

A fair start and we were off. I thought, "Drive, drive, drive, drive, okay, relax, relax, relax," as I shifted through the gears. The field thinned out and I was ahead of them at the 80-meter mark when, two lanes to my left, the Belorussian Anelia Vechernikova, pulled up lame. I didn't even notice her because I was running with a smile on my face, thinking, "Ain't nobody goin' to catch me now." I was almost too relaxed, if you ask my husband. My hands were open, almost karate chopping the air when I raised my arms before the tape. It felt like I was flying.

It was a wind-aided 10.54 and a new Olympic record. Evelyn won the silver and Heike took the bronze.

My next challenge was the 200. In the semifinal, I broke the world mark running 21.56 and, ninety minutes later, I was toeing the line for the final. I was in lane four, with Jamaica's Grace Jackson two lanes to my right. On the outside lane was the German woman I had faced in the 100-meter final two days earlier, Heike Drechsler, who also was the former 200-meter world record holder.

In prior years, the field had always beaten me through the curve and I had to make up the distance on the straight. As I stepped to the blocks, some stranger yelled out, "Hey Flo-Jo, you got it...21.3." A new record by two-tenths of a second? Minutes after my last race? Ridiculous, I thought.

Even so, I knew I had to get out on the curve.

When the gun sounded, I looked at the runners who were staggered ahead of me. I picked them off in the first 20 meters. Entering the straight, I was three-to-five meters ahead of the pack and I began to "let it go." I relaxed my hands and pulled away. Again, at the tape, my arms were raised to the skies and the electronic timer clocked me at 21.34, almost four-tenths of a second faster than my wildest expectations. I had been clocked at 23.2 miles per hour.

The following day I earned my third gold medal on the 4 x 100-meter relay and, less than an hour later, the U.S. coaches asked if I was up to one more run. Though I hadn't qualified on the Olympic Team in the 400 meters, I had run that event in the past and, because I was having a great meet, the coaches invited me to race on America's 4 x 400 relay team.

©1988 Allsport USA/Mike Powell

Without any international experience in the mile relay, I still had the fastest split on the U.S. Team, anchoring the squad to a silver medal. To this day, that medal means more to me than any of the golds, because the team and the coaches believed in me, sight unseen.

I retired immediately after the Olympics. Some wondered why I would stop at the peak of my career and I told them of an experience I had had when I was a kid. We used to travel to the Mojave Desert and, being without toys, one of my brothers dared me to catch a jackrabbit. When I brought back the prize, they dared me to do it again and I refused, saying "Why? Why should I try to prove something to you if I already know I can do it?" That's one of the reasons I could leave the sport of track without a backward glance.

In a way, Al and I handled the expectations that others placed on us in the same way—even though going into the Games each of us experienced different expectations. In Al's case, he was the underdog and he used that to motivate him to his gold medal performance. But what was important was that he stuck to his training plan and trusted the results to be there at the right time. That's what he taught me to do as well. I tried hard to ignore the opinions of the television announcers and sports writers, and instead focused on the mechanics of moving the way I had been taught; relaxed and confident, running for the sheer pleasure of it. Al and I both had resolved not to allow other people's opinions to matter at all!

NIKKI STONE

Photo courtesy of Rip Black

At the Olympic Winter Games in Nagano, Nikki Stone became America's first ever Olympic Champion in the inverted aerials. What made this performance so unbelievable, was the fact that less than two years earlier, a chronic injury prevented her from standing, much less walking or skiing down a slope at almost 40 miles per hour.

Her tenacity and refusal to step down from a challenge found a perfect home in the newly adopted sport of inverted aerial skiing, where she earned 35 World Cup podiums (top three finishes), eleven World Cup titles, four national titles and two Overall World Grand Prix titles.

After failing to reach the Olympic finals in 1994, she found herself commentating along with Paula Zahn on the CBS television coverage. The following year she became the Aerial World Champion on her way to winning the 1995 World Cup Aerial Grand Prix. In 1998, she was crowned the World Cup Aerial Grand Prix Champion and became the first pure aerialist ever (male or female) to become the Overall Freestyle World Cup Grand Prix Champion.

A Magna Cum Laude graduate from Union College in Schenectady, NY, her senior thesis was entitled *"Elite Female Athletes' Retirement from Sports."* Nikki's retirement is less than restful, as she still promotes her sport through television appearances, public speaking and sponsor promotions for major international companies. She was also featured on a variety of television news programs, has appeared in a national advertising campaign and on *The Late Show with David Letterman*.

She was recently named the Marketing and Development Manager for Wasoo.com.

26

You Don't Have to Look Before You Leap

Nikki Stone

At age five, I was so inspired by the perfect routines of Nadia Comaneci on the uneven parallel bars at the Olympic Games in Montreal, that I made my own gold medal platform out of the living room furniture. I had caught Olympic fever and began training zealously at Nadia's sport, but at fourteen years of age, realized that gymnastics would not take me to the Olympics. I happened to chance upon a television news-magazine that showed "aerial" skiers jumping off a tall plastic ramp, doing flips and somersaults in the air, landing in a swimming pool, and once again, I was captivated.

I had skied since I was three, so I quickly enrolled in the Waterville Valley summer camp where I was taught acro-skiing (formerly ballet-skiing) and "upright" aerials (twists but no somersaults).

Believe it or not, I have always been afraid of heights, so flying through the air, looking at the world beneath my feet was scary. When flipping however, I could relax because I was using my gymnastics background. I was more concerned with body position than the altitude, which was now my friend instead of foe. After just two years of freestyle, I qualified for "water ramping" (somersaults into water).

At a training camp outside Lake Placid, the water ramp was ten feet wide, built on a hill and featured a forty- and a sixty-foot descent (or "in-run") at approximately 45 degrees. Its surface was covered with circles of plastic whiskers like those on a very firm brush. These bristles reduced the surface tension on the skis, allowing them to slide down the ramp at speeds approaching 40 miles per hour, but were very unforgiving on skiers who fell, acting like cheese-graters on bare skin.

A short, flat "pre- jump" area led to a curved surface of the actual jump (called the "kicker") that (depending on whether you're attempting a single, double or triple) was anywhere from six to ten feet high and almost vertical in its appearance. As soon as the skiers reached the flat area at the bottom of the in-run, they locked their legs and back into a firm position so they wouldn't collapse under the "G-forces" of the kicker that launched them skyward.

————❖————

Now he was asking the "rookie greenhorn" to attempt
something I had not even imagined before

————❖————

Of the twenty athletes on the ramp that week, I had the least experience by far, but after only two days, was successfully completing my single flips, landing on both skis almost all the time. The U.S. national team coach, Wayne Hilterbrandt, came to me at the end of a particularly long day of training and said, "Nikki, I think you're ready to try a double." I thought he was kidding. This was my third day of water ramping, and now he was asking the "rookie greenhorn" to attempt something I had not even *imagined* before. Terrified, with skis over my shoulder, I began the slow march up the steps.

"Higher," he yelled, "You'll need more speed and height, if you want to get two flips in."

My pulse was racing. I was feeling capable yet unprepared at the same time. I knew that I had learned how to jump, flip and land, but I had never tried doing two flips in one sudden burst of activity.

The ramp dropped away, narrowing in perspective, and the kicker at the end of the flat looked like a wall, interfering with my ability to see the water. Jumpers on the ramp must commit to the jump before they can see the landing area, so you might call it a leap of faith.

Knowing that once I turned my skis down the ramp, I wouldn't be able to turn back, I made a conscious decision. I decided not to worry about the second flip, until *after* completing the first one. I trusted that my skills and my judgment would still be with me after the first layout, so I just decided to take that leap and tackle the challenge.

———❖———

I was beyond the point of no return, my tips pointing down the fall line. My stomach dropped and I began to accelerate

———❖———

Just as the engineer doesn't wait for ALL the lights to turn green, before pulling the train out of the station, we, too, have to move forward, one light at a time. Any risky endeavor gives people reason to pause or delay. Whether it's launching a new product, entering a new territory or undertaking a new career, we all have doubts or second thoughts. But if we've done our homework, we really shouldn't wait until the task seems easy or success is guaranteed. Waiting for all the lights to turn green at the same time is futile. That moment never comes. Inevitably we'll need to take that leap of faith.

With a little hop-turn, I was beyond the point of no return, my tips pointing down the fall line. My stomach dropped and I began to accelerate as the wind whipped around my face. I was already committed, so any change of heart would have been both useless and counter-productive... even dangerous.

I was soon airborne and upside-down. I watched the swimming pool water come into view overhead, and gradually, as the world oriented itself around me, I found myself almost 30 feet above the water. I had plenty of time to add another somersault, so I held position, but bent at the hips and knees just a little, and began the second rotation. I got a peek at the pool as it swung into view again, and spotted my landing point. I pulled my tips around and landed skis first. SPLASH!

What a thrill! I was overcome with a sense of joy, a personal satisfaction at facing up to a worthy adversary, and just doing it! I was happy, not just for the satisfaction of survival, but rather the triumph over my fears.

Thanks to my gymnastics background, and the hard work of training, I placed third in my first-ever World Cup appearance, and by 1993, was ranked third in the world and qualified onto the 1994 U.S. Olympic Team.

Thirty women entered the Olympic aerials in Lillehammer, Norway. We perform two different jumps in the semis, and the top twelve cumulative scores advance to the finals the following day. By chance, I was the last to go.

Beginning my Olympic career with a layout somersault followed by a full twisting somersault, I was eager to "Go for it" in front of the cameras. I shot down the mountain, hit the flat and then the kicker... *fly over once, now flip and twist, open up for the great landing. Yes!*

———❖———

*I felt I was going to be number one.
And then I let something bad happen*

———❖———

After the first round, I was leading. A CBS television camera captured me grinning, with my index finger pointing to the sky. The symbolism was obvious. I felt I was going to be number one.

And then I let something bad happen.

I began thinking about how great the gold medal would feel. I was looking ahead at a moment I hadn't even reached yet, and took my eyes off the one directly in front of me, the one most important at that time.

I was so "amped" by my first jump, that I started thinking about winning in the finals. I pushed the rotation too hard on the second qualifying jump, over-rotated, missed my feet, hit my back and came back up, but the damage was done. The low scores on that jump dropped me to 13th place, .57 points out of the finals. I had squandered my chance to win an Olympic medal.

The woman who qualified 12th (and just edged me out of the finals) was the defending World Champion and the only woman attempting a triple somersault in the Olympics. She was Lina Tcherjazova from Uzbekistan, and she went on to win the gold medal the following day.

Sometimes it's possible to be too focused on the final goal, that we take necessary attention off the intermediate steps. If we're looking too far down the tracks, we may stumble when we otherwise wouldn't.

———❖———

The crash pulled muscles away from my ribs and I coughed blood for two days

———❖———

That summer, I was attempting a "Lay-Tuck-Full" (a triple with a twist, and that's *not* a cocktail order), when I caught an edge on the in-ramp, throwing off my timing. I did the triple without the twist, and hit the water *flat on my back.* My whole body stung, right through the "dry suit." The crash pulled muscles away from my ribs and I coughed blood for two days. That crash may have been the beginning of a long and protracted problem with my back.

In September 1995, I was competing on snow in Germany when my back began hurting. At first, I thought it was just a muscle spasm, but the twinges of pain persisted. I tried an easy "Lay-Full" in practice, and collapsed on the landing. For fifteen minutes, I tried to get up again, but couldn't. Eventually, someone lifted me off the snow and slid me towards the ski lift for my next jump. I thought I'd "power my way" through the contest, so I ignored that first red light.

The next time down the ramp, the pain was so intense that my eyes were watering. I don't know how I completed the first somersault, but by then I was in such pain that I couldn't even *attempt* a smooth landing. I just crashed to the ground and slid down the hill to a stop.

After an MRI and a bone scan, the diagnosis came back, "Internal Disc Disruption." I had put such stress on the discs, that they were badly misshapen and in serious risk of bursting.

The recommended treatment would require surgery to fuse my lower spine together. That would relieve the pain, but would prevent my ever doing somersaults again. The lesser option was cortisone shots and bed rest while I waited for my back to heal itself. All the doctors agreed that it would be at least two years before I'd jump again. Frankly, with the Olympics just 18 months away, neither option was acceptable. I didn't want to quit the sport, but didn't have time to recover naturally, either.

———❖———

I didn't want to die, but I didn't want to live very much, either

———❖———

I saw no way out. I felt defeated, and it seemed like *I was going to feel this way for the rest of my life.* At home, I sat around the house, doing nothing, feeling sorry for myself. I was losing weight, muscle tone and flexibility. I slipped into a deep depression. I didn't want to die, but I didn't want to live very much, either. I cried every day, for months.

In June 1996, a sports psychologist for the ski team, Dr. Keith Henschen, pointed out that it's hard to be optimistic when you're depressed. I had to get back on track, so he prescribed some anti-depressants, and I renewed my search for a way out of my predicament.

If we spend our time looking at the red lights farther down the track, or if we forget to switch the first (or next) light to green, it's easy to get discouraged. Sometimes a short journey in reverse is necessary.

Luckily, I discovered Dr. J. Rainville, a specialist out of Boston, who treated a man with whom I could really relate. This patient was a skydiver, who tried to see how close to the ground he could open his chute. (I'm not kidding!) I smiled when I discovered a sport that was crazier than aerials! Naturally, his back was worse than mine. If that jumper could recover, so could I!

Dr. Rainville convinced me that I would have to develop the muscles that supported my back in order to compensate for the degenerated condition of my lower spine. It would require some serious weight training, and in my current condition it would be extremely painful. I knew it was going to hurt, but if I didn't try, I'd miss the Olympic Team, and I'd regret it for the rest of my days. My life-long dream was at stake.

Under strict supervision, I began lifting weights twice every day. Yes it hurt, but I was cautious at first and then slowly added more weight. While I'd never be the same as I was, gradually, I returned to the point where I was able to jump again. I was no longer a victim waiting for a rescue, now I had awakened the Olympian within and was once again making progress towards my goal. Within a month I was back on the ramp landing single somersaults. The smile had found its way back to my face.

The 1997 season saw me in events across Europe and Japan. I entered the World Championships on the future Olympic hill of Iizuna Kogan outside Nagano. All the best aerialists were there, like me, trying to rehearse for the Olympics one year away. I finished twelfth. Even though I wasn't fully recovered, I was shocked to realize that I would not have been able to win the event, *even jumping at my best!*

Aerials are scored by adding the judges' scores and multiplying the total by the degree of the jump's difficulty ("d.d."). It dawned on me that I would have to increase my difficulty as well as my proficiency, if I was going to get scores high enough to win gold.

I returned to Park City and began training with a renewed sense of urgency. I accelerated my workout schedule, adding more strength training, running and biking, more water ramping (more than 30 jumps per day), added flips and twists, honing my skills and enhancing my precision. During bad weather, when the rest of the team decided to take a day or two off, or do easier tricks, I trained my toughest jumps in swirling wind and falling snow, thinking, *the Olympic contest might occur on a day like this. I should be ready, just in case.*

By the time the Olympic Winter Games began in Nagano, I had added a triple somersault and a "Full-Double Full" to my repertoire (raising my total degree of difficulty from 6.05 to 7.05), and overheard someone say that, "Nikki Stone is going to win this one." I recalled the lesson I learned in Lillehammer.

My first jump in the semis was the layout full twisting somersault followed by a double twisting somersault. Sadly, that jump was less than stellar. My hands touched down on the landing (a big deduction), and I finished the first rotation in twelfth place. Eric Bergoust (America's other aerial champion) refuses to wear gloves in competition as an added incentive to never touch the snow.

My second jump (the triple) was much better, and this time I landed well and my score moved me into fourth place. I had qualified to compete for the medal!

On the morning of the finals, the winds became strong and unpredictable. I was fourth-to-last in the order, followed by the favorites, including the top qualifier, Xu Nannan from China. Her jumps were as difficult as mine, and she always did them well.

In my sport, skiers have the option to "ski out" (refuse the jump) at the bottom of the in-run, if they feel their speed isn't right for whatever reason. The two skiers in line before me both "skied out" on their way to the jump. *They wanted to wait for better conditions.*

My turn. By breathing quickly to calm my nerves, I relaxed a bit and looked down the ramp to the kicker at the midpoint of the hill and the capacity crowd just beyond. I couldn't see the landing area, but I'd worry about the landing *after* executing the jump. The winds were howling, but I was focused on Coach Wayne, standing alongside the jump sending me the "all clear" signal.

By taking each challenge one at a time, I was ready. With the wind swirling all around, I was confident in my ability under these conditions, rewarded for my decision to train hard in inclement weather.

—❖—

I felt no pain, heard no sound, aware only of my form. I wrapped my arms around my body, twisting like the gymnast I had once been

—❖—

I decided to take a small side-step *down* the mountain. Remember, this was the jump I missed in the semis with too much rotation. I felt it would be easier to pull my knees into a tuck if needed, than to slow the rotation more than my second somersault might allow. Once again I took that leap of faith.

Gathering speed down the in-run, I hit the flat going 39 m.p.h. and quickly locked my body into position, barreling toward the wall. I hit the kicker and was catapulted into the air. I felt no pain, heard no sound, aware only of my form and motion. My legs went up and over, and at the top of the arc, I wrapped my arms around my body, twisting like the gymnast I had once been.

I heard Wayne's voice, "You're good... Reach... now!" and I opened up, spotting the landing area as I came out of the flip. My skis touched down lightly, more like hopping off a curb than jumping off a building, and the scores were wonderful, 98.15 points on the jump, and suddenly *I* was the one to beat.

Photo courtesy of Allsport USA

By 11:30 that morning, I was standing at the top of the hill, awaiting my last jump, the final green light. I side-stepped *up* the hill a couple of paces for good measure, checked and re-checked my footing just to make sure I was standing in the right place. Once more, I rehearsed the trick in my mind.

While it's important to leap into each challenge, it's also important to be prepared for every eventuality.

With one last deep breath, I attempted to hop-turn my way into history. Flying down the hill, I thought to myself, *lock-out on the take-off.* Moving faster than ever before, I snapped my body into position and took to the air.

The layout and tuck part of the "Lay-Tuck-Full" went exactly according to plan. By the time I entered the twisting third somersault (somewhere around forty feet in the air) I thought, *I've got it. I'm going to stick this trick.*

On "re-entry," I heard Wayne yell, "Reach!!" and I pulled out of the twist.

From that height, I landed with such force that my legs fully compressed to where I was almost sitting on the back of my skis, but I didn't touch the snow. It was as good a jump as I could have done.

The scores came up, 94.85 on the jump for a total of 193.00. The board also showed the number "1" in the bottom right-hand corner, indicating my place in the rankings. I was the leader with three skiers remaining. The next two women made great attempts, but my total score was just too high.

———❖———

*She executed a beautiful "Full-Double Full," the same
jump as my first... and she did it better than I had!*

———❖———

When the Chinese athlete, Nannan, came down the hill, she executed a beautiful "Full-Double Full," the same jump as my first... and she did it better than I had!

When she landed, I just stared at the scoreboard, afraid to see the number "1" but too focused to look away. After what seemed an eternity, her score flashed up and the number "2" appeared in the corner. She earned the silver, and I won my country's first-ever Olympic gold medal in aerial skiing.

The greatest journeys begin with a single step, taken with confidence and ambition. If our dreams are guaranteed, all the fun goes out of the pursuit. It is the daunting risk that provides the greatest satisfaction, and the pearl of great price that is treasured over time. Those are the lessons I've learned on the hill, their value, greater than gold.

Moments after landing that final jump, the defending champion from the Games in Lillehammer, Lina Tcherjazova, came over and presented me with a bouquet of flowers, smiling through her tears. She, better than anyone, understood exactly how I was feeling.

MIKE ERUZIONE

Elected as captain of the 1980 Lake Placid Olympic hockey team, he scored the winning goal in the "Miracle on Ice" game against the heavily favored team from the Soviet Union. After the gold medal victory against Finland, the boys from Lake Placid became a sensation across the country. *Sports Illustrated* called their performance one of the top ten athletic achievements in history.

Photo provided by Mike Eruzione

On his way to the Olympics, Mike ended a stellar career at Boston University as the third leading scorer in B.U. history as well as being cited as the Best Defensive Forward in the East, earning Eastern Collegiate team titles in each of his four years. While playing amateur hockey in the International Hockey League (IHL), he received the McKenzie Award, usually presented to the outstanding American-born hockey player in the league.

After Lake Placid, Mike was quickly drafted by the television networks (including ABC, CBS and MSG) as an expert analyst and field reporter, covering stories from both Olympic Summer and Winter Games from 1984 through 1994.

Today, Mike travels around the country on behalf of major corporations as a motivational speaker and spokesperson, thrilling his audiences with the magical stories that surround America's team. He is also the Director of Development for Athletics and Assistant Hockey Coach at Boston University.

27

It Wasn't a Miracle on Ice

Mike Eruzione

"You're too small."
"You're too short."
"You're not fast enough."
"You're not strong enough."
"You don't weigh enough."
"You weigh too much."
"You don't have the experience."
Looking back on the 1980 Olympic Winter Games in Lake Placid, and that young U.S. Olympic Hockey Team, I clearly remember how many people told us that we *could not* win, we weren't experienced enough, we weren't good enough and that we would be defeated by many other countries.

How could so many people be so wrong?

We tend to forget that sometimes more than ability is required. We also need the intangibles! There are tests to see how smart we are, how fast we can run, how well we can see and how much we can hear. But no one can ever measure our desire, pride, courage or heart. These are the qualities that enable good teams to become great teams and enable individuals to achieve great success.

At the 1980 Olympic Winter Games, ABC's television broadcast showed the end result. People saw a hockey team that for two weeks in Lake Placid achieved victories that few in the world thought possible. Looking back, it was the things that television *couldn't* show, the intangibles that made the end result, that wonderful gold medal, somewhat less surprising.

DESIRE, PASSION, COMMITMENT...

I come from a very close-knit working-class Italian family in Winthrop, Massachusetts, just outside of Boston, where we had relatives living in the apartments above and below us. My dad worked various jobs simultaneously, as a maintenance mechanic during the day, bartender/waiter at night and welder on weekends. My mother got up early in the morning to feed her six kids and would drive us to our respective activities. As a family, we were close and competitive in many areas, but because there were so many of us, my folks had to limit their efforts on our behalf until they were sure we knew what we wanted. They wanted to see a measure of the foremost of the intangibles: *Desire.*

As a young boy, I wanted to play hockey badly... and that's exactly how I played it...badly. Although I had grown up dreaming about ice hockey, my parents did not have enough money to automatically buy me a pair of skates. I had to prove to them that hockey was something I really *wanted* to do.

———❖———

They took that year's supply of S&H trading stamps and redeemed them for a pair of hockey skates in my size

———❖———

Every day after school, I used to take my sister's small, lightweight figure skates and go down to the public tennis courts. That's right, during the winters in Boston, the Parks and Recreation Department flooded the tennis courts and allowed the water to freeze, creating a temporary ice rink.

I would skate with my friends for an hour or two, before my sister returned home from school and came down to the tennis courts to retrieve her skates. After this went on for a few months, my parents realized that hockey really was something that I was serious about, so they took that year's supply of S&H trading stamps and redeemed them for a pair of hockey skates in my size.

My teammates' stories are the same. We all came from similar backgrounds and made similar sacrifices. We all got up early to go to the rink, spent our allowances on sticks and pucks, experienced hard practices and sacrificed other areas of our lives to play a sport that we loved. As a result, we each had the unqualified support of our families, friends, coaches and peers to succeed.

FAITH, CONFIDENCE...

Another of the great intangibles is an undying belief in the *achievability* of our desire. Wanting to win and knowing we can win are two different things. Without confidence in the *possibility*, any substantial effort might seem like a poor investment.

During the Olympic Games, immediately before the game against the highly touted team from the Soviet Union, Coach Herb Brooks called us together and said, "Gentlemen, each of you was born to be a player. You were meant to be here. This moment is yours."

I thought long and hard about what those words meant, "...born to be a player."

Maybe I *was* born to be a player. Not only did I have the desire, but I also thought of myself entirely in terms of my hockey. I had played hockey during study hall in high school, and before and after class as well. I was meant to be there because of the time I had spent making myself a better player. Both my high school and college coaches taught me the right way to play the game, including the skills and the tactics I would need. They taught me about winning and losing, where even the defeats became valuable lessons and helped me to better appreciate the victories. Each skill or practice contributed to my confidence.

———❖———

Brooks didn't want any superstars, he wanted a unified team

———❖———

Confidence does not negate the need to work, rather, it often highlights it.

Our Olympic coach, Herb Brooks, understood the need for hard work, and he was willing to pay a personal price for our team's success. Brooks didn't want any superstars, he wanted a unified team.

In the past, there had been rivalries between America's players from the East (primarily Boston and New England) and those from the West (Wisconsin and Minnesota), undermining the team's unity. Coach Brooks decided to eliminate that from the beginning, by fostering an "us against him" attitude. His philosophy was that he was going to be the bad guy and that would allow the rest of us to unite against him and grow closer together. The teasing behind his back and his unavoidable loneliness were the burdens he carried to keep us together.

If Mark Johnson was caught discussing Wisconsin football, we'd all yell, "Shut up and don't get regional." And when I'd begin to brag about the Beanpot or some other Eastern tournament, they'd all jump on my case as well.

A few months before the Olympic tournament, we played the Norwegian National Team. While we had much more talent and should have won handily, we were not focused or prepared to play. We played lackluster hockey, finishing in a tie.

——❖——

The teasing behind his back and his unavoidable loneliness were the burdens he carried to keep us together

——❖——

As soon as the game was over, Coach Brooks came out on the ice wearing his skates and promptly put us through an extra hour of grueling practice. We did a series of skating drills (we called them "Herbies") that made us skate at full speed back and forth between the lines until we were exhausted. When the team doctor finally persuaded the coach that we'd had enough, Coach brought us into the locker room and said, "Gentlemen, if you play the same way again tomorrow, you're going to do more 'Herbies' again."

The next day we won, 8-0.

He had made his point. We didn't have enough talent to win on talent alone and we had to go out and work hard to achieve our goals. We had to play with fire in the belly. We had to play with passion, desire, heart, pride, courage and commitment. We couldn't go out there for the sake of it, just like one can't go to work every day merely for the sake of collecting a paycheck.

By putting in the effort and mastering the skills, we were also strengthening our confidence.

That intangible of confidence affected how I saw myself, how I saw my teammates and how I saw our chances of success. Working hard made us feel better about each other and, magically, the hard work didn't seem to hurt as much. If desire makes others want to help you, then confidence makes you want to help yourself. That same optimism can also lead to the third great intangible...courage.

PERSISTENCE, COURAGE, HEART...

Some say that courage is not the absence of fear, but rather action in the presence of fear. Likewise, persistence is ongoing sacrifice, without a guarantee or even the likelihood of a reward. One of the ways to increase persistence in the face of insurmountable odds is to lean on another who shares our faith and desire.

We were ranked in seventh place going into the Olympic Games and there weren't too many people outside the team who thought we were capable of winning the gold. But *we* knew. Twenty members of that team, two coaches, two trainers and the doctor *all* believed we were capable of winning. Our locker room conversations were filled with positive statements and we were always mutually supportive.

During the prior year, the U.S. Hockey Team traveled extensively, taking on the European teams as part of our training, but other than the Norwegians, all of our opponents sent only their "B" teams, which we easily beat. While this helped our confidence, we weren't blind to the fact that the Olympics would feature a much better field.

At the beginning of the Games in Lake Placid, we were all a bit nervous, not certain what to expect. Our primary goal was to win enough games to finish in the top two of our bracket and qualify into the "final four" for medal play.

Our first game was against the eventual bronze medalists from Sweden, where Bill Baker scored on a dramatic goal to tie them at two, with twenty-seven seconds left on the clock. We didn't play all that well, and that helped us realize that if we played up to our potential in the future, we might really impress some folks. The Czech team was the only team that anybody felt had a chance to beat the Soviets, and we dominated them, 7-3. Now we really knew we were on to something.

Our first two games had been against what we felt were the toughest teams, so our third game against Norway (who tied us before the "Herbie practice") was a bit of a letdown. Perhaps we were overconfident, but after the first period, we were tied again. Coach Brooks lit into us, saying we weren't doing the little things, we were playing as individuals, not a team. He must have struck a chord, because we returned to the ice, scored four more goals, winning 5-1.

We walked over Romania, 7-2, and faced West Germany to close out the bracket. As was the case in almost every game, we trailed going into the final period but eked out a 4-2 victory. Those late rallies were a tribute to our training, work ethic and the coaching staff that got us ready for what was to come—the Red Army team from the Soviet Union.

——— ❖ ———

We weren't blind to the fact that the Olympics would feature a much better field

——— ❖ ———

Three days before the Opening Ceremony, we had played the Soviets in an exhibition game in New York's Madison Square Garden, where we spent most of the time standing around staring in awe at the great list of famous players such as Vladislav Tretiak, Valery Kharlamov and Slava Fetisov. Earlier, they defeated the NHL All-Stars as well as a few NHL teams. On that day they beat us like a drum, 10-3.

When we took to the ice against the Soviets, we were understandably nervous because we had so much respect for them, but we were still excited to play. We knew we'd done our homework and (unlike our last meeting) we were ready to give them our best game. Coach Brooks would remind us, "Play *your* game, use *your* strengths."

Perhaps they took us a little lightly. I think the Russians were a bit surprised by our skill, speed and stamina. No longer in awe, we played up to our strengths; short on experience, but long on enthusiasm and conditioning.

Usually, the Soviets clinched their wins in the third period when their opponents were running out of energy. This time the Russians led much of the game but every time they scored, we countered with another goal, and when the third period arrived, our youthful energy was still going strong, thanks to all the "Herbies" weeks before.

The score was 3-3 with ten minutes left to play when I received a pass. As the puck came to me, I saw a defenseman between me and the goal, and my options were few. If he stayed, I'd use him as a screen and shoot; if he came at me, I'd pass it by him to John Harrington, Davey Christian or Bill Baker. He stayed and I shot.

My body was moving left to right, and I decided to shoot it back to the right side. I had an opening, a perfect angle and I used a little wrist shot, exactly where I wanted. I pulled it a little as the puck left the stick, but I got enough of the shot that the goalie didn't see it and it went under his arm. We took the lead for the first time in the game.

After a loud celebration, I came back to earth quickly when I realized the Soviets were so desperate and powerful that they'd be capable of scoring multiple goals in the time remaining. The shots seemed to be coming from all over the ice, but all of a sudden, plays were being made by every member of the U.S. squad. The guys on the team were all over; Ken Morrow would block a shot, Billy would block a shot, Davey dove out, Mike Ramsey dove for a loose puck, each shift playing the best hockey we'd ever played. Our goalie, Jim Craig, played so well that we never said a word to him. He was in "the zone," so we just let him play.

We were so focused that while we were on the ice playing the game, I couldn't hear a sound other than a teammate calling for the puck or Coach Brooks yelling to change the line. But when I sat on the bench, the crowd was *all* I could hear.

———❖———

All of a sudden, plays were being made by every member of the U.S. squad

———❖———

Those last ten minutes seemed to crawl by. Every time I looked at the clock, it seemed to have moved just a couple of seconds. When the clock finally ticked off the final moments, I could feel the weight of the world lift off my shoulders, as Al Michaels was saying, "Do you believe in miracles? Yes!"

Perhaps nobody outside our little group expected our team to win, but almost everybody wanted us to. Under these circumstances, we exceeded people's expectations and we captured the imagination of the American public. We embraced the spirit of what makes the Olympic Games so special—the undeniable truth that on any given day, *anything* can happen.

The parents of the U.S. Team had rented a large lodge in Lake Placid (we called it the "Hostage House" after the Americans who were held hostage in Iran that year). Each family was responsible for preparing a meal. On one day somebody's mom would fix breakfast and somebody else's father would fix dinner. In that way, all our parents joined their kids in becoming one family. My mom slept in a bunk; Davey's father was in the bunk above her and John's mother was below her.

The following morning, while we were all smiles, signing autographs at the practice rink, Coach Brooks flipped out on us. We had all been so caught up with beating the Soviets that we were overlooking our next and final game. He wanted us to regroup and prepare for the gold medal game. We had watched Finland play, but we had never actually played against them.

I guess we were a little cocky going onto the ice against the Finns. We played well, throwing everything we had at their cage, but their goal tender "stood on his head" and we trailed 2-1 after the first period. Goalies have been known to steal games (witness the dominating play by the Czech Republic's goalie at the 1998 Nagano Olympics) and we were beginning to wonder if this guy might be having the game of his life.

Once we'd gathered in the locker room at the break, Coach Brooks walked in and said simply, "Gentlemen, if you lose this game, you'll take it to your %#*?!&$ grave," and then he walked right out of the room. My adrenaline climbed to record levels. We all jumped up and couldn't wait to take to the ice.

◈

We had all been so caught up with beating the Soviets that we were overlooking our next and final game

◈

After hearing those words, we went out and played great second and third periods, holding Finland scoreless while we scored three times, including a short-handed "back-breaker" goal, and won 4-2.

We won the gold.

The coach was right. Our desire extended beyond a victory against the Soviets, all the way to the awards platform. The temptation to be satisfied with the silver was great, but we had worked so hard to accomplish so much that the pain of letting it slip away would've stayed with us forever.

Prior to the Olympics, I was elected captain, which I took as an honor. As each guy on the team had been a leader at his own school or club, I saw myself as a "captain among captains." This group didn't need my directions and I wasn't the best player on the team, so I tried to set an example by working hard and organizing the occasional party.

At the awards ceremony, space on the medal stand was limited. Each player was introduced and received his gold medal, returning to where the group was standing on the red line, about twenty feet behind the podium. As captain, I was the last man privileged to receive the medal, and I was left to stand alone on the podium during the playing of the "Star Spangled Banner," but I felt very uncomfortable being the only one up there.

When the final note sounded, I turned around and raised my fist in the air toward my uncle who was sitting in the stands, and then I turned and saw my teammates. They were looking at me, feeling what I was feeling, and I just called out, "Get up here, come on guys, come on!"

In no time at all, the guys were all over, jostling for position like worker bees. One guy would fall off and he'd jump back up, grabbing on to someone's arm, until another guy got squeezed off. Eventually, all our arms were interlocked and all twenty of us occupied the same gold medal platform as one body. Just as we'd supported each other during the season, we were now holding each other up during the final chapter.

———❖———

I felt very uncomfortable being the only one up there

———❖———

After the crowds dispersed, we headed back to Hostage House to celebrate. It wasn't until later, when we saw the replay of the game, that we heard Al Michaels declare, "This impossible dream comes true!" That's also the first time we understood how many people in the United States and around the world had been following our progress.

I think the viewers were so involved with the team because they related to us. They saw in us what Coach Brooks would call, "a lunch-pail, hard-hat group of athletes" who came to the rink every day with a purpose of working hard, doing their best. People cared about our performance, mainly because we were ordinary guys and big underdogs.

Some time after we won the gold in Lake Placid, *Sports Illustrated* published an article about the 1980 team titled, "The Lesson and Message of What We Can Be." In it, E.M. Swift didn't talk about the plays that Jim Craig made or about the goals that I scored or the goals that Mark Johnson scored. He talked about the players themselves, about a group of athletes who had the ability to overcome whatever challenges were put in front of us. We *were* the boys next door; the kids that you see rollerblading in front of your house with hockey sticks in their hands. The article talked about the work ethic of the team, its closeness, and about how if we surround ourselves with people who believe in the same things that we believe in, we *can* achieve great things.

It wasn't a miracle on ice. It was an accomplishment by a group of athletes who believed in themselves and who believed in each other. It

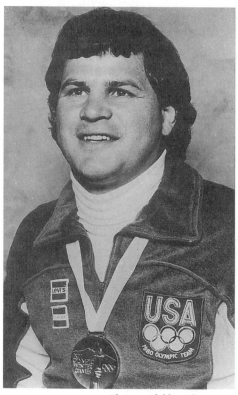

Photo provided by Mike Eruzione

was an achievement by a group of "lunch-pail hard hats," who ignored the beliefs of the majority and continued to train with courage and heart.

The ones who said we weren't good enough—that we were too small, we didn't have the experience, we weren't strong enough, our team wasn't fast enough, we couldn't learn the European style of play in such a short period of time—were proved wrong. But the reason they were wrong wasn't because they misjudged our abilities. Our abilities probably deserved seventh place. They were wrong because of the "intangibles." How can you measure desire, commitment, faith, passion and courage? They weren't able to measure those. They weren't able to see how much heart we had, how much pride we had, how close we were as a team. And, in the end, those *intangibles* were the qualities that enabled us to win.

————◈————

The reason they were wrong wasn't because they misjudged our abilities

————◈————

The night of the gold medal game, as we returned to the athletes' village, signs and banners were visible everywhere, printed in the various languages of the countries represented in the Games, congratulating the 1980 U.S. Hockey Team.

I still keep the gold medal in a safe place and take it out every now and then. But when I want to recall what the Olympics really meant to me, I think of the puck striking the net, the feel of a group of guys hanging on to each other while waving to the world, the arena echoing with the shouts of patriotism and delight, the banners of congratulations...these are the memories that will stay with me until the day I die, more precious than gold.

The Gold Medal Experience

The Gold Medal Presentation Ceremony is perhaps the most glorious of my Olympic memories from 1976. The three medal winners marched in a single-file parade, finally stopping at the turning end of the Olympic swimming pool. Before me was the three-tiered awards platform with a fiberglass podium four-feet wide and two-feet deep, the surface covered with a sandpaper texture. Those eight-square feet symbolized the final rung of a ladder I had chosen to climb years before.

In front of me was the water's surface, smooth as glass, with floating lane lines disappearing in perspective at the far end of the pool. The announcer called my name and I stood on the top step, bending down on one knee to have the chain of my medal draped over my shoulders, its substantial weight tugging on the collar of my sweat jacket. When the three of us had received our medals, the crowd grew silent and over the public address system came the strains of the "Star Spangled Banner."

On either side of the pool, a standing-room-only crowd of 12,000 people, representing every nation, language and political philosophy in the world, rose to honor me and my country for what I had done in the lane in front of me moments before. Looking down the length of the pool, I noticed, on the water's surface, the mirrored reflection of my flag, the Stars and Stripes, silently gliding toward me, almost embracing me with its symbolism.

I have often described the feeling of winning my last Olympic gold medal as similar to the feeling one gets while turning the last page of a really good book. The journey was so rewarding that I didn't want it to end. The sport had taken me to faraway places and introduced me to a variety of interesting people. I had experienced sorrow and joy, struggle and strife, challenge and triumph—and now it was coming to a close. The satisfaction of a dream fulfilled, all those memories and more came together during the presentation of that final golden medallion.

The experience was sad and sweet and, at that moment, I wished time would stand still so I could enjoy the feeling forever. It was with some reluctance that I stepped off the podium and began the rest of my life.

Now, as you turn the last page of this book, I hope that you've experienced a feeling of what it's like to compete at the Olympic Games. It's my desire that you remember what you've read and use what you've learned to win in the game of life.

Each Olympian author has a story to tell and can almost always be called upon to tell it well. Perhaps that's why we speak to corporate and civic groups with such frequency. While editing the chapters of this book, I came home each evening filled with the same positive energy and optimistic ideas. I can't think of anything I've ever done that has kept me so earnestly involved over such a long period of time (other than the long years of training for the Olympics) because I became the benefactor of each of their thoughts. And now you have, too.

While reading these stories does not guarantee that you'll swim faster or jump higher or skate, luge, wrestle or play ball any better, I hope that they gave you a better perspective on what Olympians go through to reach their goals. Perhaps this awareness will help you to see your path to personal success more clearly. The examples taken from sports apply to the real world. Specific instances in an Olympian's life can be used as parables for personal growth and can be easily translated into useful applications in any personal or professional endeavor.

The best tools in sport are useless unless they are put to work. Just as weight machines, the training table, a coach's experience or slow-motion video technology are more helpful when used consistently, so too are the traits described by these Olympian authors. The reading of this book should be more than a pleasant diversion; it should offer a blueprint to significant changes that you'll make in the way you think and behave in the future—or at least in the way you perceive the world.

It does Olympians no good to share their experiences if those experiences fail to provide you with better results in your chosen field. Set your sights on your own gold medal performance, believe in yourself, dare to dream a wonderful dream, set a definite path through regular checkpoints, play according to the established rules of the game, be willing to invest a fair price to reap a fair reward, have the resolve to overcome each and every obstacle that will inevitably come your way, take advice from the people you admire, join with other like-minded individuals, share the intangibles that come with teamwork, make time to enjoy the process, show compassion for those you meet along the way, give back to your community and, at the same time, help others reach their goals.

Great achievers in sport enjoy great recognition because what they do is so easily captured on videotape, but the goals and aspirations of the rest of the population are no less important. Swimming quickly while on my back provided no significant value to my community (it's not as if I towed a boat to safety or anything). Yet it is through the personal growth developed through the rigors of sport that we can achieve what the founder of the Modern Olympic Movement wanted: a better class of individual, better able to take his or her place in society; a more mature adult who practices the nobler virtues, such as dedication and sacrifice, goal setting and teamwork; and one who is willing to apply these values in his or her life on a regular basis. By doing so, they can pursue their personal gold medal experience.

Baron Pierre de Coubertin would not want his Games to stand for gold medals and commercial endorsements for the few, but rather as a means to awaken the Olympian that resides within us all.

John Naber

CONTACT INFORMATION

GREG BARTON
Epic Paddles, Inc.
6657 58th Avenue N.E.
Seattle, WA 98115
Telephone: (206) 523-6306
Fax: (206) 524-4888
E-Mail: greg@epicpaddles.com

JEFF BLATNICK
P.O. Box 4249
Halfmoon, NY 12065
Telephone: (518) 399-8147
Fax: (518) 384-4042
Website: www.blatnick.com
E-mail: Blatnick@aol.com

VALERIE BRISCO-HOOKS
Voice Mail: (213) 827-4481

MILT CAMPBELL
Attn: Terri Campbell
1132 St. Mark's Place
Plainfield, NJ 07062-1410
Telephone: (908) 754-2164
Fax: (908) 754-0538
E-Mail:
    milt.campbell@mcione.com

**NADIA COMANECI &
BART CONNER**
Paul Ziert and Associates
Attn: Paul Ziert
3214 Bart Conner Drive
Norman, OK 73072
Telephone: (405) 364-5344
Fax: (405) 321-7229

TIM DAGGETT
172 High Meadow Drive
West Springfield, MA 01089
Telephone: (413) 733-3609
Fax: (413) 781-4184
E-Mail: Itzaten@aol.com

MIKE ERUZIONE
Murray & Murray
Attn: Bob Murray
2 Center Plaza
Boston, MA 02108
Telephone: (617) 720-4411
Fax: (617) 723-5370

ERIC FLAIM
P.O. Box 727
Killington, VT 05751
E-Mail: eflaim2@aol.com

PAM FLETCHER
Woolf Associates
Attn: Kristen Kuliga
101 Huntington Avenue, Suite 2575
Boston, MA 02199
Telephone: (617) 587-3106
Fax: (617) 587-3181
E-Mail: pfletch101@aol.com

DICK FOSBURY
Post Office Box 1791
Ketchum, ID 83340
Telephone: (208) 726-9936
Fax: (208) 726-4783

ROWDY GAINES
4948 Caldwell Mill Road
Birmingham, AL 35242
Telephone: (205) 980-4645
Fax: (205) 252-2212
E-Mail: ashof@bellsouth.net

MATT GHAFFARI
Ghaffari Silver Lining, Inc.
32834 Fox Chappel Lane
Avon Lake, OH 44012
Telephone & Fax (440) 930-4666
E-Mail:
   Matt.speaks@worldnet.att.net
Pager: (800) 946-4646 pin # 2003067

PAUL GONZALES
Post Office Box 1966
Montebello, CA 90640
Telephone: (323) 881-6570
Fax: (323) 264-1619
E-Mail: ghettogold@aol.com

BRIAN GOODELL
Gold Medal Speakers Bureau
13 Via Honesto
Rancho Santa Margarita, CA 92688
Telephone: (949) 713-5748
E-Mail: goldspeaker@home.com

NANCY HOGSHEAD
Holland & Knight LLP
50 North Laura Street, Suite 3900
Jacksonville, FL 32202
Telephone: (904) 798-5452
Fax: (904) 358-1872
              (include a cover sheet)
E-Mail:
   Nhogshea@HKLaw.com

DAN JANSEN
Integrated Sports International/SFX
Sports
Attn: Peter Raskin
5335 Wisconsin Avenue,
   Suite 850
Washington, DC 20015
Telephone: (202) 686-2000
Fax: (202) 686-5050

AL JOYNER
Final Kick Marketing Group
P.O. Box 3810
Mission Viejo, CA 92691
Telephone: (949) 859-4802
Fax: (949) 859-4042

KARCH KIRALY
International Management Group
   (IMG)
Attn: Steve Lindecke
22 East 71st Street
New York, NY 10021-4911
Telephone: (212) 772-8900
Fax: (212) 772-2617
E-Mail:
   slindecke@imgworld.com

HENRY MARSH
Marsh Productions
1664 South Stone Ridge Drive
Bountiful, UT 84010
Website: www.HenryMarsh.com

ANN MEYERS DRYSDALE

Lampros & Roberts Management
Attn: Nick Lampros
16615 Lark Avenue, Suite 101
Los Gatos, CA 95032
Telephone: (800) 841-7767
Fax: (408) 358-2487

JOHN NABER

Post Office Box 50107
Pasadena, CA 91115
Telephone: (626) 795-7675
Fax: (626) 568-0446
E-Mail: John@JohnNaber.com
Website: www.JohnNaber.com

TERRY SCHROEDER, D.C.

794 Ravensbury Street
Thousand Oaks, CA 91361
Telephone: (818) 889-5572
Fax: (818) 889-7368
E-Mail: TASDC@pacbell.net

SINJIN SMITH

International Creative
    Management, Inc. (ICM)
Attn: Jill Smoller
8942 Wilshire Boulevard
Beverly Hills, CA 90211
Telephone: (310) 550-4000
Fax: (310) 550-4100

NIKKI STONE

Post Office Box 680332
Park City, UT 84068
Telephone: (508) 366-5213
E-mail:
    nikkistone@compuserve.com

CATHY TURNER

Edge Sports
Attn: Keith Kreiter
3649 West Chase Avenue, Suite 100
Skokie, IL 60076
Telephone: (847) 675-6549
Fax: (847) 675-1230
Website:
    www.Edgesportsintl.com

PETER VIDMAR

Telephone: (949) 766-0110
Fax: (949) 766-0198
Website: www.vidmar.com

BONNY WARNER

Bonny Warner, Inc.
5612 Drakes Drive
Byron, CA 94514
Telephone & Fax: (925) 634-9269
E-Mail:
    bonnys@compuserve.com